Lecture Notes in Computer Science 7163

Commenced Publication in 1973
Founding and Former Series Editors:
Gerhard Goos, Juris Hartmanis, and Jan van Leeuwen

T0213458

Svetla Petkova-Nikova   Andreas Pashalidis
Günther Pernul (Eds.)

Public Key Infrastructures, Services, and Applications

8th European Workshop, EuroPKI 2011
Leuven, Belgium, September 15-16, 2011
Revised Selected Papers

 Springer

Volume Editors

Svetla Petkova-Nikova
University of Twente, the Netherlands
and Katholieke Universiteit Leuven ESAT-COSIC
Kasteelpark Arenberg 10
3001 Leuven-Heverlee, Belgium
E-mail: svetla.nikova@esat.kuleuven.be

Andreas Pashalidis
Katholieke Universiteit Leuven ESAT/SCD (COSIC)
Kasteelpark Arenberg 10
3001 Leuven-Heverlee, Belgium
andreas.pashalidis@esat.kuleuven.be

Günther Pernul
University of Regensburg
Department of Information Systems
Universitätsstraße 31
93053 Regensburg, Germany
E-mail: guenther.pernul@wiwi.uni-regensburg.de

ISSN 0302-9743   e-ISSN 1611-3349
ISBN 978-3-642-29803-5   e-ISBN 978-3-642-29804-2
DOI 10.1007/978-3-642-29804-2
Springer Heidelberg Dordrecht London New York

Library of Congress Control Number: 2012937469

CR Subject Classification (1998): K.6.5, C.2, E.3, D.4.6, J.1, K.4.4

LNCS Sublibrary: SL 4 – Security and Cryptology

Typesetting: Camera-ready by author, data conversion by Scientific Publishing Services, Chennai, India

Printed on acid-free paper

Springer is part of Springer Science+Business Media (www.springer.com)

Preface

This book contains the proceedings of the 8th European Workshop on Public Key Infrastructures, Services, and Applications (EuroPKI 2011), held in Leuven, Belgium, during September 15–16, 2011.

The aim of the EuroPKI workshop series is to stimulate and promote international research and collaboration on all aspects of public key services, applications and infrastructures, including innovative applications of public key cryptography. The workshop is intended for security researchers and practitioners as well as for participants from industry that are active in the field of public key services, applications, infrastructures and, in general, information security. This year's workshop was co-located with the 16th European Symposium on Research in Computer Security (ESORICS) and took place at the Katholieke Universiteit Leuven. Previous events were held in Samos (EuroPKI 2004), Kent (EuroPKI 2005), Turin (EuroPKI 2006), Mallorca (EuroPKI 2007), Trondheim (EuroPKI 2008), Pisa (EuroPKI 2009), and Athens (EuroPKI 2010).

This volume holds ten refereed papers and the presentation papers by the invited speakers, Chris J. Mitchell, Peter Gutmann, and Olivier Pereira. In response to the EuroPKI 2011 call for papers, 27 submissions were received. Each submission was subjected to a thorough review by at least three Program Committee members and external reviewers, resulting in a stringent selection and careful revision of the accepted papers. After the workshop, authors revised their papers again and provided improved versions for inclusion in this volume.

We wish to thank everyone who contributed toward the success of the workshop: the authors of submitted contributions, the Program Chairs and the Program Committee for their efforts in reviewing and discussing the submission under tight time constraints. Many thanks also to Christian Broser for his publicity work and to Michael Weber for collecting the papers and his help editing this book. We are grateful to our sponsor LSEC, and to Ulrich Seldeslachts for organizing a special session with speakers from the security industry during the event, as well as for moderating the lively discussions between workshop attendees and speakers. Special thanks go to the local organizers including, among many others, Saartje Verheyen for dealing with a host of administrative and bookkeeping issues; Sebastiaan Indesteege for his help with the EuroPKI 2011 website; Roel Peeters for managing electronic workshop registrations and payments; and Bart Preneel for his general support.

September 2011

Svetla Nikova
Andreas Pashalidis
Günther Pernul

Organization

General Chair

Andreas Pashalidis   Katholieke Universiteit Leuven, Belgium

Program Committee Chairs

Svetla Nikova   Katholieke Universiteit Leuven, Belgium and
University of Twente, The Netherlands

Günther Pernul   University of Regensburg, Germany

Publicity Chair

Christian Broser   University of Regensburg, Germany

International Program Committee

F. Bao	Institute for Infocomm Research, Singapore
L. Batina	Radboud University Nijmegen, Katholieke Universiteit Leuven, The Netherlands, Belgium
D. Chadwick	Kent University, UK
S. Chow	University of Waterloo, Canada
M. Cremonini	University of Milan, Italy
P. D'Arco	University of Salerno, Italy
S. De Capitani di Vimercati	University of Milan, Italy
A.W. Dent	Royal Holloway, University of London, UK
R. Di Pietro	University of Rome III, Italy
S. Furnell	University of Plymouth, UK
J. Gonzalez-Nieto	Queensland University of Technology, Australia
P. Gutmann	University of Auckland, New Zealand
S. Katsikas	University of Piraeus, Greece
S. Kent	BBN Technologies, USA
D. Kesdogan	University Siegen, Germany
E. Konstantinou	University of the Aegean, Greece
K. Kursawe	Radboud University Nijmegen, The Netherlands

C. Lambrinoudakis	University of Piraeus, Greece
H. Leitold	TU Graz, Austria
J. Lopez	University of Malaga, Spain
F. Martinelli	National Research Council, Italy
C. Meadows	NRL, USA
S. Mjølsnes	Norwegian University of Science and Technology, Norway
Y. Mu	University of Wollongong, Australia
R. Oppliger	eSECURITY Technologies, Switzerland
M. Pala	Dartmouth College, USA
O. Pereira	Universite Catholique de Louvain, Belgium
B. Preneel	Katholieke Universiteit Leuven, Belgium
S. Radomirovic	University of Luxembourg, Luxembourg
P. Samarati	Università degli Studi di Milano, Italy
S. Seys	Katholieke Universiteit Leuven, Belgium
S. Smith	Dartmouth College, USA

Subreviewers

Au, Man Ho	Fuchs, Ludwig	Lazouski, Aliaksandr
Chen, Xihui	Gmelch, Oliver	Netter, Michael
Chu, Cheng-Kang	Han, Jinguang	Pham, Vinh
Dietrich, Kurt	Ibraimi, Luan	Zefferer, Thomas
Fritsch, Christoph	Krautsevich, Leanid	

Table of Contents

PKI Applications

Secure Applications

Secret Handshake Scheme
with Request-Based-Revealing

Yutaka Kawai* and Noboru Kunihiro

University of Tokyo 5-1-5 Kashiwanoha, Kashiwa-shi, Chiba 277-8561, Japan
kawai@it.k.u-tokyo.ac.jp, kunihiro@k.u-tokyo.ac.jp

Abstract. Secret handshake (SH) schemes enable two members who belong to the same group to authenticate each other in a way that hides their affiliation to that group from all others. In previous works, the group authority (GA) has the ability to reveal the identity (ID) of a handshake player who belongs to his group. In this paper, we focus first on the classification of traceability of GA. We classify this feature as follows: (i) GA of G is able to reveal IDs of members belonging to G by using a transcript of a handshake protocol; (ii) GA of G is able to confirm whether handshake players belong to G or not by using a transcript of a handshake protocol. In some situations, only the latter capability is needed. So, we consider a SH that GA has only an ability to confirm whether a handshake player belongs to his own group without revealing his ID. Thus, we introduce a *SH scheme with request-based-revealing* (SHRBR). In SHRBR, GA can check whether handshake players belong to the own group without revealing a member ID. After a handshake player *A* executes a handshake protocol with *B*, if *A* wants to reveal a handshake partner (in this case *B*), *A* requests GA to reveal a handshake partner's ID by bringing forth his own ID and secret information. We define the security requirements for SHRBR and propose a concrete SHRBR in the random oracle model.

Keywords: secret handshake, anonymity, traceability, privacy.

1 Introduction

Background. Secret handshake (SH) schemes are very useful authentication protocols when a user belonging to a group G wants to communicate secretly with another user of G which is generated by a group authority (GA). The SH scheme enables two members who belong to G to authenticate each other in a way that hides their affiliation from all others. The SH scheme was introduced by Balfanz et al. [2]. They constructed a two party SH by adapting the key agreement protocol of Sakai et al. [11]. Subsequently, Castelluccia et al. [3] developed a more efficient 2-party SH through the use of a so-called CA-oblivious encryption. In their schemes, since the member sends his ID in a handshake protocol, their SH schemes do not satisfy unlinkability. [14] presented the first construction of a SH

---

* Supported by JSPS Research Fellowships for Young Scientists.

S. Petkova-Kikova, A. Pashalidis, G. Pernul (Eds.): EuroPKI 2011, LNCS 7163, pp. 1–16, 2012.

scheme with unlinkability using a reusable certificate. Ateniese et al. present the first SH scheme that allows for matching of properties different from the user's own. Property credentials are issued by a certificate authority in the standard model. In this scheme, no one can reveal a member's ID. In [8], the authors considered situations in which the group authority's ability is too powerful in cases in which SH is applied to a whistle-blowing system. For this purpose, [8] introduced new security requirements, viz. co-traceability and strong detector resistance.

In all previous SH schemes, a GA cannot confirm whether players belong to his group or not without revealing the member's ID. This fact is troublesome if SH is applied to some situation. We give an example that this fact is troublesome. Consider a community supported by a social network service. A member of this community might want to know if his friend belongs to the same community, and wants to communicate with the member secretly by initiating a SH. In this scenario, the GA need not known to the member's ID. However, GA may want to know the number of executing handshake protocols and time when handshake protocols were initiated for each community to improve some service in this service. In this situation, the number of executing handshake protocol should be known to GA and a member's ID should not be known to GA.

Motivation. In SH systems, one of the capabilities of GAs is to reveal a handshake player's ID. In this paper, we call a member's ID revealing algorithm IDReveal. Previous work can be classified according to anonymity from GA in respect to "revealing the ID of a player by GA." This ability to reveal handshake players is important in the event of disputes. Previously, the following three types of anonymity against GA exist: (1) No one (even GA) can reveal IDs of handshake players [1]. (2) GA can reveal IDs of handshake players [3]. (3) GA can reveal the ID of a handshake player by cooperating with another player [8]. In all of the above cases, GA cannot check on whether handshake players belong to his own group without revealing the member's ID.

In this paper, we consider anonymity against GA that cannot be covered in previous researches. We discuss new anonymity from the view point of "confirming the player's group by GA". In previous SHs with IDReveal, GA has the list of ID. If the GA of the group G reveals the ID using IDReveal, GA can confirm whether handshake players belong to G or is not using ID and ID list. In contrast, if neither the ID list nor ID is used, GA cannot confirm whether handshake players belong to his own group. Therefore, previous SH schemes cannot be applied to situations where GA can confirm whether players belong to his own group or not, but GA cannot reveal the member's ID. If a member's ID does not exist, no one is able to reveal the handshake player's ID in the event of disputes. Here, we consider the following scenario: Handshake player A executes a handshake protocol with B. GA cannot reveal either ID of A or B. If A wants to reveal a handshake partner (in this case B is a handshake partner), A requests GA to reveal a handshake partner's ID by bringing forth A's ID and secret information. In this paper, to achieve the above scenario, we propose *Secret Handshake with Request-Based-Revealing* (SHRBR).

Contributions. In this paper, we propose a SH scheme that satisfies the following properties. (1) GA can know whether handshake players belong to the own group by observing a transcript of a handshake protocol; (2) GA cannot reveal alone IDs of handshake players; (3) In the case that A executes a handshake protocol, GA can reveal a handshake partner of A by receiving from A himself his ID and secret information of A. First, we introduce a new algorithm Group-Trace, which is executed by TA. Given TA's secret key and a transcript of the handshake protocol, GroupTrace outputs yes/no. Second, we introduce a new algorithm RequestReveal, which is executed by handshake player A and TA. Given TA's secret key, a transcript of the handshake protocol and A's secret key and ID, RequestReveal outputs a handshake partner ID for A. Security requirements of SHRBR should be satisfied as follows. (1) When an honest member $A \in G$ executes the handshake protocol with $B \in G$, GA of the group G can confirm whether A belongs to G by executing GroupTrace. (2) An honest member cannot reveal a handshake partner ID without executing RequestReveal with GA. (3) GA cannot reveal handshake players ID by observing a transcript of the handshake protocol. We define formally these security requirements. We introduce the new security requirements *group traceability*, *member anonymity* and *trace authority traceability*. Intuitively, group traceability means that a member A cannot forge a transcript of a handshake protocol so that GroupTrace outputs no when A outputs acc in this handshake protocol. Also, member anonymity and trace authority traceability means that a member ID is revealed only by executing RequestReveal with GA and an honest handshake player.

Related Works. SH scheme was introduced by Balfanz et al. [2] firstly. They proposed concrete two party secret handshake protocols which are secure under decisional bilinear Diffie-Hellman assumption. Castelluccia et al. [3] proposed a more efficient two party SH under some specific requirements. They construct the SH scheme from PKI-enabled encryption schemes. Their scheme is secure under the computational Diffie Hellman assumption. In [14], Cu et. al proposed the first construction of a SH scheme with unlinkability using a reusable certificate. Unlinkability means that nobody can link two occurrences of handshaking by the same party with each other. Their scheme is secure in the meaning of unlinkability until that a handshake player executes a handshake protocol k times for him. Ateniese et al. present the first SH scheme that allows for matching of properties different from the user's own. Property credentials are issued by a certificate authority. In [1], SH is extended with roles, so that a group member U can specify the role which a group member V must have in order to complete a handshake protocol successfully. In this extension, a member who belongs to a group has the role. And members can require that group members' group are revealed only to members who hold specific roles in the group. In [8], Kawai et.al introduced new security requirements, viz. co-traceability and strong detector resistance in order to apply to a whistle-blowing system. Also, in [15], Yamin et al. extended Kawais' SH scheme in [8] from the view point of revocation for users. Their scheme has the backward unlinkability property. In [12], Sorniotti et al. presented new revocation mechanism "RevocationMatching." A natural next step is multi-party settings with similar security requirements[6,13,7]. The work of Tsudik and Xu [13] extended the SH to the *multi party* setting They combines three building blocks, a group signature scheme, a group key distribution scheme and distributed group key agreement to construct a framework for multi-party SH. Jarecki et al. [6] also constructed an efficient multi-party SH by combining the scheme of [3] and a group key agreement protocol.

2   Preliminaries

In this section, we review bilinear maps and complexity assumptions. Let $\mathbb{G}_1,\mathbb{G}_2$ be two cyclic groups of prime order p and G_1 and G_2 be generators of $\mathbb{G}_1$ and $\mathbb{G}_2$ respectively. Let ψ be a computable isomorphism from $\mathbb{G}_2$ to $\mathbb{G}_1$, with $\psi(G_2) = G_1$. Let e be a non-degenerate bilinear map $e : \mathbb{G}_1 \times \mathbb{G}_2 \to \mathbb{G}_T$. Let $\mathbb{Z}_p$ be the ring of integers modulo p.

Definition 1 (Discrete Logarithm Assumption). The discrete logarithm (DL) problem in $\mathbb{G}_1$ is defined as follows. We say that a PPT algorithm A has an advantage $\mathsf{Adv}_{\mathcal{A}}^{\mathsf{DL}}(l)$ in solving the DL problem in if $\mathsf{Adv}_{\mathcal{A}}^{\mathsf{DL}}(l) = \Pr[\mathcal{A}(xP, P) = x : x \in \mathbb{Z}_p, P \in \mathbb{G}_1]$. We say that the DL assumption holds in $\mathbb{G}_1$ if no PPT algorithm has non-negligible $\mathsf{Adv}_{\mathcal{A}}^{\mathsf{DL}}(l)$ in l in solving the DL problem in $\mathbb{G}_1$.

Definition 2 (Decisional Linear Diffie-Hellman Assumption). The decisional linear Diffie-Hellman (DLDH) problem in $\mathbb{G}_1$ is defined as follows. We say that a PPT algorithm A has an advantage $\mathsf{Adv}_{\mathcal{A}}^{\mathsf{DLDH}}(l)$ in solving the DLDH problem in $\mathbb{G}_1$ if $\mathsf{Adv}_{\mathcal{A}}^{\mathsf{DLDH}}(l) = |\Pr[(\mathcal{A}(U, V, H, aU, bV, (a + b)H) = \mathsf{yes} : U, V, H \leftarrow_R \mathbb{G}_1, a, b \leftarrow \mathbb{Z}_p] - \Pr[(\mathcal{A}(U, V, H, aU, bV, Q)) = \mathsf{yes} : U, V, H, Q \leftarrow_R \mathbb{G}_1, a, b \leftarrow \mathbb{Z}_p]|$. We say that the DLDH assumption holds in $\mathbb{G}_1$ if no PPT algorithm has non-negligible $\mathsf{Adv}_{\mathcal{A}}^{\mathsf{DLDH}}(l)$ in l in solving the DLDH problem in $\mathbb{G}_1$.

Definition 3 (q-strong Diffie-Hellman (q-SDH) assumption). The q-strong Diffie-Hellman (q-SDH) problem in $(\mathbb{G}_1, \mathbb{G}_2)$ is defined as follows. We say that a PPT algorithm A has an advantage $\mathsf{Adv}_{\mathcal{A}}^{q\mathsf{SDH}}(l)$ in solving the q-SDH problem in $(\mathbb{G}_1, \mathbb{G}_2)$ if $\mathsf{Adv}_{\mathcal{A}}^{q\mathsf{SDH}}(l) = |\Pr[(\mathcal{A}(param, G_1, G_2, \gamma G_2, \ldots, \gamma^q G_2) = (\frac{1}{x+\gamma}G_1, x) : \gamma, x \leftarrow_R \mathbb{Z}_p]|$. We say that the q-SDH assumption holds in $(\mathbb{G}_1, \mathbb{G}_2)$ if no PPT algorithm has non-negligible $\mathsf{Adv}_{\mathcal{A}}^{q\mathsf{SDH}}(l)$ in l in solving the q-SDH problem for q polynomial of l.

3   Secret Handshake Scheme with Request-Based-Revealing

In this section, we define the secret handshake scheme with request-based-revealing (SHRBR) and the security requirements of SHRBR.

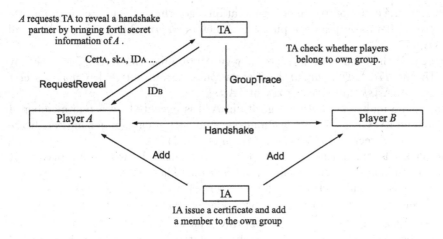

Fig. 1. A scenario for the Secret Handshake Scheme with Request-Based-Revealing

Syntax. In a secret handshake system, there exist the following four types of entities in the group G. To discuss the security against GA, we split the role of GA into the two: issue authority and trace authority. (1)Issue authority (IA): IA is responsible for adding users into his group. If a user is added to the group of IA, IA issues a certificate to the user. (2)Trace authority(TA): TA is responsible for revealing users as well as checking whether handshake players belong to his own group. TA maintains a list of member IDs. (3)Member: A member is an entity who belongs to the group. $U \in$ G means that U belongs to the group G.

Since a user sends his ID to TA in the member addition algorithm, TA has the list of member IDs in the previous SH with a handshake player tracing algorithm. TA can confirm whether a handshake player belongs to his group by revealing the ID used with a tracing algorithm. In previous SH schemes with a tracing algorithm, it seems that TA needs to reveal member ID to confirm whether a handshake player belongs to his group. Obviously, it is excessive that an ID is revealed to confirm membership, However, revealing of handshake players is useful if disputes arise.

We propose new secret handshake scheme: *Secret Handshake with Request-Based-Revealing* (SHRBR). In SHRBR system, IA and TA create the group G. IA issues a certificate to non-members and adds them to the group G. When a handshake protocol is executed, TA can check whether a handshake player belongs to G *without revealing the player's ID*. However, TA cannot reveal member's ID alone. If a handshake player A wants to know the handshake partner, A brings forth his own ID to TA and TA reveals the handshake partner by receiving A's ID and secret information from A. To implement this attractive scenario, we give formal definitions of SHRBR as follows.

Definition 4. *A SHRBR scheme consists of the following six algorithms.*

Setup: is the common parameter generation algorithm. Given a security parameter k, Setup outputs the public parameters $param$ that are common to all groups.

KeyGen: is the group public/secret key generation algorithm. KeyGen is run by IA and TA. Given $param$, KeyGen outputs a group public key gpk, a secret key of IA isk and a secret key of TA tsk.

Add: is the member addition algorithm. Add is executed by a non-member A and an IA. Given $param, gpk$ and isk, Add outputs a membership certificate ($cert_A$), a secret key (sk_A), and ID of A (ID_A).

Handshake: is the authentication protocol executed between two players A and B, based on the public input $param$. The group public keys (gpk_A and gpk_B) and certificates ($cert_A$, $cert_B$) and secret keys (sk_A, sk_B) of A and B are input to Handshake. The output of the algorithm is either rej or acc. $A \overset{Handshake}{\longleftrightarrow} B$ means the situation in which A and B execute Handshake. $\mathcal{T}_{A,B}$ means a transcript that the handshake players A and B execute Handshake. A transcript $\mathcal{T}_{A,B}$ of the handshake protocol is assumed to be known by IA and TA.

GroupTrace: is a handshake player's group trace algorithm. Given gpk, tsk and a transcript $\mathcal{T}_{A,B}$, GroupTrace outputs yes if $A, B \in G$; otherwise, GroupTrace outputs no. This algorithm is executed by TA.

RequestReveal: is the handshake player tracing algorithm. Given gpk, tsk, $cert_A$, sk_A, a transcript $\mathcal{T}_{A,B}$ and internal information that is used in Handshake by a player A, RequestReveal outputs the member B.

Security Definition. We give formal definitions of security notions for a SHRBR. We first discuss motives for the formal definitions. As in ordinary SH scheme, we need to ensure that impersonator resistance, detector resistance, and unlinkability. However, in SHRBR, we have to further ensure one type of impersonation and two types of anonymity. This relates to original motives for introducing GroupTrace and RequestReveal. (a) The introduction of GroupTrace is to guard as much as possible against imposters non-members. of the group. In more detail, SHRBR should be satisfied that if a member $A \in G$ executes a Handshake with $B \in G$ and outputs acc, GroupTrace should output yes. (b) The introduction of RequestReveal is to strengthen a handshake player's anonymity against a handshake partner and a trace authority as strongly as possible. In more detail, (b1) Even an honest member A cannot reveal a handshake partner's ID alone when A executes a Handshake. (b2) Even TA cannot reveal a handshake player's ID alone. That is, a handshake player's ID cannot be revealed without executing RequestReveal with both TA and a handshake player. We define security requirements for SHRBR as follows.

Impersonator Resistance. We define the impersonator resistance using the following game between a challenger C and a PPT adversary A.

Setup. C generates $param \leftarrow$ Setup(k) and $(gpk, isk, tsk) \leftarrow$ KeyGen($param$) and inputs $(param, gpk)$ to an adversary A.

Add member query. When A makes an add member query, C generates
$(cert_i, sk_i, ID_i) \leftarrow$ Add$(param, gpk, isk)$ and returns $cert_i, ID_i$ to A. Moreover, C stores $(cert_i, sk_i, ID_i)$ in an honest member list L_H, initially empty.

Handshake query. On inputting ID_i where $(*, *, ID_i) \in L_H$ by A. We require
that a user i is an honest user. C executes Handshake as an honest member
i with A.

Challenge query. This query is asked only once. When A makes a challenge
query, C generates $(\widetilde{cert}, \widetilde{sk}, \widetilde{ID}) \leftarrow$ Add$(param, gpk, isk)$ and executes Handshake with A using $(\widetilde{cert}, \widetilde{sk}, \widetilde{ID})$.

Finally, A wins if both A and C outputs acc in a challenge query. Now, in the
case that A impersonate an honest user i, its advantage is defined $\text{Adv}_A^{\text{IR1}}(k)$
for any probabilistic polynomial adversary A. In the case that A impersonate a
malicious user, who is not honest user i, its advantage is defined $\text{Adv}_A^{\text{IR2}}(k)$.

Definition 5 (Impersonator Resistance (IR)). *We say a SHRBR scheme
has impersonator resistance, if for any probabilistic polynomial adversary A, its
advantage both $Adv_A^{\text{IR1}}(k)$ and $Adv_A^{\text{IR2}}(k)$ are negligible.*

Detector Resistance. We define the detector resistance using the following game
between a challenger C and a PPT adversary A.

Setup. C generates $param \leftarrow$ Setup(k) and $(gpk, isk, tsk) \leftarrow$ KeyGen$(param)$
and inputs $(param, gpk)$ to an adversary A.

Add member query and Handshake query. A can make add member
queries and handshake queries as the same as IR game.

Challenge query. This query is asked only once. On inputting ID_i where
$(*, *, ID_i) \in L_H$. C picks $b \in \{0, 1\}$ randomly. If $b = 0$, C executes Handshake
as a member i with A the first time and executes Handshake as SIM$(gpk,$
$param)$ with A the second time. If $b = 1$, C executes Handshake as SIM
$(gpk, param)$ with A the first time and executes Handshake as a member i
with A the second time.

Finally, A outputs its guess $b' \in \{0, 1\}$ for b and wins the game if $b = b'$. We
define the advantage for A as $\text{Adv}_A^{\text{DR}}(k) = |\Pr[b = b'] - \frac{1}{2}|$.

Definition 6 (Detector Resistance (DR)). *We say a SHRBR scheme has
detector resistance, if for any probabilistic polynomial adversary A, its advantage
$Adv_A^{\text{DR}}(k)$ is negligible.*

Unlinkability. We define the unlinkability security using the following game between a challenger C and a PPT adversary A.

Setup. C generates $param \leftarrow$ Setup(k) and $(gpk, isk, tsk) \leftarrow$ KeyGen$(param)$
and inputs $(param, gpk)$ to an adversary A.

Add member query and Handshake query. A can make add member
queries and handshake queries as the same as IR game.

Challenge query. This query is asked only once. On inputting (ID_i, ID_j) where $(*, *, ID_i) \in L_H$ and $(*, *, ID_j) \in L_H$. C picks $\{0, 1\}$ randomly. If $b = 0$, C executes Handshake as a member i with A to the first time and executes Handshake as a member i with A to the second time. If $b = 0$, C executes Handshake as a member i with A to the first time and executes Handshake as a member j with A to the second time.

Finally, A outputs its guess $b' \in \{0, 1\}$ for b and wins the game if $b = b'$. We define the advantage for A as $\mathrm{Adv}_A^{\mathrm{Unlink}}(k) = |\Pr[b = b'] - \frac{1}{2}|$.

Definition 7 (Unlinkability (Unlink)). *We say a* SHRBR *scheme has unlinkability, if for any probabilistic polynomial adversary* A, *its advantage* $Adv_A^{\mathrm{Unlink}}(k)$ *is negligible.*

Group Traceability. We define the group traceability using the following game between a challenger C and a PPT adversary A.

Setup. C generates $param \leftarrow \mathsf{Setup}(k)$ and $(gpk, isk, tsk) \leftarrow \mathsf{KeyGen}(param)$ and inputs $(param, gpk)$ to an adversary A.

Add member query and Handshake query. A can make add member queries and handshake queries as the same as IR game.

Handshake query. On inputting ID_i where $(*, *, ID_i) \in L_H$ by A. C executes Handshake as an honest member i with A.

Challenge query. This query is asked only once. When A makes a challenge query, C chooses $(cert^*, sk^*, ID^*) \in L_H$ and executes Handshake with A using $(cert^*, sk^*, ID^*)$.

Finally, A wins if both A and C outputs acc and GroupTrace outputs no where $\mathcal{T}$ is a transcript of Handshake in a challenge query. We let $\mathrm{Adv}_A^{\mathrm{GTrace}}(k)$ denote the adversary's advantage in winning this game.

Definition 8 (GroupTraceability (GTrace)). *We say a SUPRE scheme has group traceability, if for any probabilistic polynomial adversary* A, *its advantage* $Adv_A^{\mathrm{GTrace}}(k)$ *is negligible.*

Member Anonymity. We define the member anonymity using the following game between a challenger C and a PPT adversary A.

Setup. C generates $param \leftarrow \mathsf{Setup}(k)$ and $(gpk, isk, tsk) \leftarrow \mathsf{KeyGen}(param)$ and inputs $(param, gpk)$ to an adversary A.

Add member query and Handshake query. A can make add member queries and handshake queries as the same as IR game.

Corruption query. On inputting ID_i where $(*, *, ID_i) \in L_H$. A is given sk_i and C stores $(cert_i, sk_i, ID_i)$ in a corrupted member list L_C.

Challenge query. This query is asked only once. On inputting (ID_i, ID_j) where $(*, *, ID_i) \in L_H$ and $(*, *, ID_j) \in L_H$. C picks $b \in \{i, j\}$ randomly. C executes Handshake as a member b with A.

Finally, A outputs its guess $b' \in \{i, j\}$ for b and wins the game if $b = b'$. We define the advantage for A as $\text{Adv}_A^{\text{MAnon}}(k) = |\Pr[b = b'] - \frac{1}{2}|$.

Definition 9 (Member Anonymity (MAnon)). *We say a SHRBR scheme has member authority anonymity, if for any probabilistic polynomial adversary A, its advantage $Adv_A^{\text{MAnon}}(k)$ is negligible.*

Trace Authority Anonymity. We define the trace authority anonymity using the following game between a challenger C and a PPT adversary A.

Setup. C generates $param \leftarrow$ Setup(k) and $(gpk, isk, tsk) \leftarrow$ KeyGen$(param)$ and inputs $(param, gpk, tsk)$ to an adversary A.

Add member query and Handshake query. A can make add member queries and handshake queries as the same as IR game.

Challenge query. This query is asked only once. On inputting (ID_i, ID_j) where $(*, *, ID_i) \in L_H$ and $(*, *, ID_j) \in L_H$. C picks $b \in \{i, j\}$ randomly. C executes Handshake as a member b with A.

Finally, A outputs its guess $b' \in \{i, j\}$ for b and wins the game if $b = b'$. We define the advantage of A as $\text{Adv}_A^{\text{Unlink}}(k) = |\Pr[b = b'] - \frac{1}{2}|$.

Definition 10 (Trace Authority Anonymity (TAnon)). *We say a SHRBR scheme has trace authority anonymity, if for any probabilistic polynomial adversary A, its advantage $Adv_A^{\text{TAnon}}(k)$ is negligible.*

4 Proposed Scheme

Group Signature with Message Recovery Technique. A group signature was introduced by Chaum and van Heyst [4]. A group signature allows a member who belongs to a group to sign messages without revealing his own identity. A certificate $cert_A^G$ is issued to a signer A by the manager of the group G. A generates a group signature with the message m_A using $cert_A^G$, a secret key sk_A and gpk_G and sends this signature to a verifier. A verifier checks whether the signature is valid or not using gpk_G. Also, the manager of the signer's group can reveal a group member's ID by using his secret key.

SH scheme in [8] is constructed based on a message recovery type of group signatures. We call these group signatures, group signatures with message recovery (GSMR). If A and B execute Handshake, A generates GSMR σ_A using $cert_A^G, sk_A, gpk^G$ and a message $m_A = r_A G_1$ and sends σ_A to B. B also generates σ_B using $cert_B^{G'}, sk_B, gpk^{G'}$ and a message $m_B = r_B G_1$ and sends σ_B to A. If A and B belong to the same group G and B generates σ_B using $cert_B^G$ correctly, A recovers $m_B = r_B G_1$ using gpk_G and computes $r_A r_B G_1$. Similarly, B can compute $r_A r_B G_1$. In [8], it was also pointed out that GSMR that is applied to SH must have the following properties. (1) Given gpk, anyone *can* forge a pair of signatures corresponding to a message. However, he cannot select a message. (That is, GSMR is not secure in the meaning of *existential forgery*). (2) Given gpk and a message, no one *can* forge a signature corresponding to the message.

(That is, GSMR is secure in the meaning of *universal forgery*). If GSMR does not have property (1), anyone can unmask the handshake players' groups using a public key and SH is not secure in the sense of detector resistant. If GSMR does not have property (2), anyone can forge a signature and SH is not secure in the sense of impersonator resistant. In GSMR is used in Handshake, an adversary forges a signature in the sense of existential forgery. However, an adversary cannot select r such that $m = rG_1$. Thus, GSMR satisfies the property of (2).

GroupTrace and RequestReveal are achieved using the group signatures' property in which a signer can be revealed from a group signature. In our construction, TA has a group ID and sends it to members. Handshake players should use the group ID when they generate GSMR. TA knows whether handshake players belong to his own group or not by using the group ID and a TA's secret key. Also, in Handshake, a handshake player A generates an ephemeral public/secret key and masks ID_A using the ephemeral key. Thus, TA can reveal the handshake partner of A using tsk and the ephemeral key of A.

Proposed SHRBR scheme. We show concrete SHRBR=(Setup,KeyGen, Add, Handshake,GroupTrace, RequestReveal) as follows.

Setup(k): Given a security parameter k, Setup generates $(p, \mathbb{G}_1, \mathbb{G}_2, \mathbb{G}_T, G_1, G_2, G, \psi, e)$ and chooses hash functions $\mathcal{H}_1 : \{0,1\}^* \to \mathbb{Z}_p$ and $\mathcal{H}_2 : \{0,1\}^* \to \{0,1\}^k$. Setup outputs $param = (p, \mathbb{G}_1, \mathbb{G}_2, \mathbb{G}_T, G_1, G_2, G, \psi, e, \mathcal{H}_1, \mathcal{H}_2)$.

KeyGen($param$): Given $param$, KeyGen first chooses $w, v \leftarrow_R \mathbb{Z}_p$ and $K, F \leftarrow_R \mathbb{G}_1$. KeyGen chooses $H, S, T \in \mathbb{G}_1$ and $s, t \in \mathbb{Z}_p$ where $sS = tT = H$. Next KeyGen computes $W = wG_2$ and $F_v = vF$. Finally, KeyGen outputs $isk = (w, v), tsk = (s, t, F_v)$ and $gpk = (H, W, K, F, S, T)$.

Add($param, gpk, isk$) : Add is executed between a user A and (IA,TA). First, A chooses $x_A \leftarrow_R \mathbb{Z}_p$ as a member's secret key. A sends $ID_A = x_A H, x_A F$ and proves in zero-knowledge to IA the knowledge of x_A. Although the protocol given here is only a honest verifier zero-knowledge, from this we can construct a black-box zero-knowledge protocol using the technique presented in [9]. Next, IA chooses $y_A \leftarrow_R \mathbb{Z}_p$ and computes $U_A = \frac{1}{w+y_A}(G_1 - x_A F - vF)$. IA sends (U_A, y_A, v). Finally, A checks whether $e(U_A, W)^{y_A} e(F, G_2)^{x_A + v} = e(G_1, G_2)$. Add outputs $(cert_A = (U_A, y_A, v), sk_A = x_A, ID_A = x_A H)$.

GSMR($param, gpk, cert_A, sk_A, m, s_A, K_B, H_B$): Given $(param, gpk_A, cert_A, sk_A, m, s_A, K_B, H_B)$ where $m \in \mathbb{G}_1, H_B, K_B \in \mathbb{G}_2$ and $s_A \in \mathbb{Z}_p$.
  1. GSMR computes $K_A = s_A K$, $K_{AB} = s_A K_B$ and $H_{AB} = s_A H_B$.
  2. GSMR chooses $(\alpha_A, \beta_A, \gamma_A, \delta_A) \leftarrow_R \mathbb{Z}_p$ and computes $R_1 = U_A + \alpha_A H, R_2 = \beta_A S, R_3 = \gamma_A T, R_4 = (\beta_A + \gamma_A)H + vF, R_5 = \delta_A \psi(K_{AB}) + x_A \psi(K_A)$ and $R_6 = \delta_A \psi(H_{AB})$.
  3. GSMR chooses $(r_x, r_y, r_v r_\alpha, r_\beta, r_\gamma, r_\delta, r_{y\alpha}) \leftarrow_R \mathbb{Z}_p$ and computes $R'_1 = e(R_1, G_2)^{r_y} e(F, G_2)^{-r_{y\alpha} + r_x + r_v} e(H, W)^{-r_\alpha}, R'_2 = r_\beta S, R'_3 = r_\gamma T, R'_4 = (r_\beta + r_\gamma)H + r_v F, R'_5 = r_\delta \psi(K_{AB}) + r_x \psi(K_A)$ and $R'_6 = r_\delta \psi(H_{AB})$.
  4. GSMR computes $c' = \mathcal{H}_1(param, gpk, R_1, R_2, R_3, R_4, R_5, R_6, R'_1, R'_2, R'_3, R'_4, R'_5, R'_6), c = c' \oplus m, s_x = r_x + c x_A, s_y = r_y + c y_A, s_v = r_v + $

cv, $s_\alpha = r_\alpha + c\alpha$, $s_\beta = r_\beta + c\beta$, $s_\gamma = r_\gamma + c\gamma$, $s_\delta = r_\delta + c\delta$ and $s_{y\alpha} = r_{y\alpha} + c(y_A\alpha)$. Finally, GSMR outputs $\sigma = (R_1, R_2, R_3, R_4, R_5, R_6, s_x, s_y, s_v s_\alpha, s_\beta, s_\gamma, s_\delta, s_{y\alpha}, c)$.

MR($param, gpk, \sigma, s_B, H_A, K_A$): Given $(param, gpk, \sigma, s_B, H_A, K_A)$.

1. MR computes $\hat{H} = \psi(H)$, $\hat{K} = \psi(K)$, $\hat{K_{AB}} = s_B\psi(K_A)$ and $\hat{H_{AB}} = s_B\psi(H_A)$.

2. MR computes $R_1' = e(R_1, G_2)^{s_y}e(K, G_2)^{-s_{y\alpha}+s_x+s_v}e(H, W)^{-s_\alpha}$ $(e(R_1, W)/e(G_1, G_2))^c$, $R_2' = s_\beta S - cR_2$, $R_3' = s_\gamma T - cR_3$, $R_4' = (s_\beta + s_\gamma)H + s_v F - cR_4$, $R_5' = s_\delta \hat{K_{AB}} + s_x \hat{K_A} - cR_4$ and $R_6' = s_\delta \hat{H_{AB}} - cR_5$.

3. MR computes $c' = \mathcal{H}_1(param, gpk, R_1, R_2, R_3, R_4, R_5, R_6, R_1', R_2', R_3', R_4', R_5', R_6')$ and $m = c \oplus c'$. Finally, MR outputs m.

Handshake$_{A,B}(param, (gpk_A, cert_A, sk_A), (gpk_B, cert_B, sk_B))$: Handshake is executed between two members A and B with $(gpk_A, cert_A, sk_A)$ and $(gpk_B, cert_B, sk_B)$ respectively.

1. A chooses $s_A \leftarrow_R \mathbb{Z}_p^*$ and computes $K_A = s_A K$ and $H_A = s_A H$. A sends K_A and H_A to BD

2. B chooses $r_B, s_B \leftarrow_R \mathbb{Z}_p^*$ and computes $m_B = r_B G_1$, $K_B = s_B K$ and $H_B = s_B H$. B computes $\sigma_B \leftarrow$ GSMR$(param, gpk_B, cert_B, m_B, s_B, K_A, H_A)$. B sends K_B, H_B and σ_A to AD

3. A recovers $m_B' \leftarrow$ MR$(param, gpk_A, \sigma_B, s_A, K_B, H_B)$. A chooses $r_A \leftarrow \mathbb{Z}_p^*$ and computes $m_A = r_A G_1$ and $\sigma_A \leftarrow$ GSMR$(param, gpk_A, cert_A, m_A, s_A, K_B, H_B)$ and $resp_A = \mathcal{H}_2(r_A m_B', m_A)$. A sends σ_A and $resp_A$ to BD

4. B recovers $m_A' \leftarrow$ MR$(param, gpk_B, \sigma_A, s_B, K_A, H_A)$. B computes $resp_B = \mathcal{H}_2(r_B m_A', m_B)$ and sends $resp_B$ to A. If $resp_A = \mathcal{H}_2(r_B m_A', m_A')$, B outputs acc. Otherwise B outputs rej.

5. If $resp_B = \mathcal{H}_2(r_A m_B', m_B')$, A outputs acc. Otherwise outputs rej.

GroupTrace($param, gpk, tsk, \mathcal{T}_{A,B}$): Given gpk, tsk and σ_A in $\mathcal{T}_{A,B}$, if $R_4 - (sR_2 + tR_3) = F_v$, GroupTrace outputs yes. Otherwise outputs no.

RequestReveal($param, gpk, tsk, \mathcal{T}_{A,B}, cert_A, sk_A$): Given $param, gpk, tsk, cert_A, sk_A, ID_A$, a transcript $\mathcal{T}_{A,B} = (K_A, K_B, H_A, H_B, \sigma_A, \sigma_B, resp_A, resp_B)$, and the parameters s_A used in Handshake by A. If $e(U_A, W)^{y_A}e(F, G_2)^{x_A} \neq e(G_1, G_2)$, RequestReveal outputs $\perp$, else it searches a member i by checking $e(R_{B,4}, H) = e(\psi(ID_i) + R_{B,5}, s_A K_B)$ for all $ID_i = x_i H$ where $R_{B,4}$ and $R_{B,5}$ are parameters in σ_B. Finally, RequestReveal outputs i (in this case $ID_i = ID_B = x_B H$).

Security. We describe the security of our proposed SHRBR.

Theorem 1. *Under the discrete logarithm assumption and strong Diffie-Hellman assumption, the proposed SHRBR has impersonator resistant in the random oracle model.*

Proof (Sketch). First, assume towards a contradiction that $Adv_A^{IR1}(k)$ is not negligible. Then we show that we can use A to construct another adversary B that has non-negligible discrete logarithm advantage. The construction of B is as follows. First, B is given $(param, H, Y = x^*H)$ where $H \in \mathbb{G}_1$ and $x^* \in \mathbb{Z}_p$. B chooses $w, v, \alpha \in \mathbb{Z}_p$ randomly and sets $W = wG_2, F = \alpha H$. Next B chooses $s, t \in \mathbb{Z}_p$ and $S, T \in \mathbb{G}_1$ such that $sS = tT = H$. B sets the group public key $gpk = (H, W, K, F, S, T)$, the issuer secret key $isk = (w, v)$ and the trace secret key $tsk = (s, t, F_v = vF)$. A is given $param, gpk$. When A makes an add member query, B calculates $U_i = \frac{1}{w+y_i}(G_1 - r_i\alpha Y - vF)$ and $ID_i = r_iY = r_i\alpha H$ where r_i is chosen randomly from $\mathbb{Z}_p$. B returns $cert_i = (U_i, y_i, v)$ and ID_i and stores (r_i, U_i, ID_i) into the member list L and ID_i into honest members set $\mathcal{ID}$. When A makes a handshake query, although B does not know the secret key of a user i, B is able to generate the rest of the data for the generating GSMR σ by choosing random oracle. This technique is similar to the simulation of a singing oracle for group signature schemes [5]. In challenge query, A should impersonate an honest user i where $ID_i \in \mathcal{ID}$. Our proof strategy of impersonator resistance is similar to the proof strategy of non-frameability in group signature scheme. Using the forking lemma [10], B can obtain σ_1 and σ_2 which are computed from same $(R_1, R_2, R_3, R_4, R_5, R_6, R'_1, R'_2, R'_3, R'_4, R'_5, R'_6)$ from A. B can obtain $rx^* = \frac{s_x^{(1)} - s_x^{(2)}}{c^{(1)} - c^{(2)}}$. Finally, B outputs this x^* by computing rx^* and r. If $Adv_A^{\text{IR1}}(k)$ is not negligible, B breaks the discrete logarithm problem with non-negligible probability. This contradicts discrete logarithm assumption, and thus $Adv_A^{\text{IR1}}(k)$ must be negligible.

Second, assume towards a contradiction that $Adv_A^{\text{IR2}}(k)$ is not negligible. Then we show that we can use A to construct another adversary B that has non-negligible q-SDH advantage. This proof strategy is similar to the proof strategy of traceability in group signature scheme. The construction of B is as follows. B is given $(Q_1, Q, \gamma Q, \gamma^2 Q, \ldots, \gamma^q Q)$ where $Q_1 = \psi(Q)$ and $Q_1 \in \mathbb{G}_1$. B chooses $\alpha \leftarrow_R \mathbb{Z}_p$ and $(a_i, b_i) \leftarrow_R \mathbb{Z}_p^2$ for $i = 1, \ldots, q - 1$ and $m \leftarrow_R [1, q - 1]$. Next B chooses $v \leftarrow_R \mathbb{Z}_p$ and computes $G_2 = \left[b_m \prod_{i=1, i\neq m}^{q-1}(\gamma + a_i - a_m)\right] Q + \left[\alpha \prod_{i=1}^{q-1}(\gamma + a_i - a_m)\right] Q, G_1 = \psi(G_2), F = \left[b_m \prod_{i=1, i\neq m}^{q-1}(\gamma + a_i - a_m)\right] \psi(Q)$ and sets $W = wG_2$. A is given $param, gpk$. When A makes an add member query, B obtains x_i by rewinding A and choosing other random oracles. B sets $y_i = a_i$ calculates $U_i = \frac{1}{w+y_i}(G_1 - x_iH - F_v) = \left[\alpha \prod_{i=1, i\neq m}^{q-1}(\gamma + a_i - a_m)\right] \psi(Q) + \left[(b_m - b_i) \prod_{i=1, i\neq m}^{q-1}(\gamma + a_i - a_m)\right] \psi(Q)$ and $ID_i = x_iH$. B returns $cert_i = (U_i, y_i, v)$ and ID_i and stores (r_i, U_i, ID_i) into the member list L and ID_i into honest members set $\mathcal{ID}$. If A has finished the game, honest outputs acc in Handshake. Then, using the Forking Lemma [10], B can obtain $(U^*, x^*, y^*, v^*, \alpha^*, \beta^*)$ such that $R_1 = U^* + \alpha^*H, R_2 = (\beta^*)S, R_3 = \gamma^*T$ and $R_4 = (\beta^* + \gamma^*)H + v^*F$. Here, $U^* = \frac{1}{w+y^*}(G_1 - x^*F - v^*F) = \left[\frac{\alpha\gamma - x^* - v^* + b_m}{y^* + \gamma - a_m} \prod_{i=1, i\neq m}^{q-1'}(\gamma + a_i - a_m)\right] \psi(Q)$. Here, $\alpha\gamma - x^* - v^* + b_m|y^* + \gamma - a_m$ happens with negligible probability as long as the DL problem is difficult to solve. So, B can compute $\delta_i \in \mathbb{Z}_p (i = 0, \ldots, q)$ such that $U^* = \sum_{i=0}^{q-1} \delta_i\gamma^i\psi(Q) + \frac{\delta_q}{\gamma+y^*-a_m}\psi(Q)$. B can obtain an answer of q-SDH problem as follows: $\left(\frac{1}{\delta_q}\left(U^* - \sum_{i=0}^{q-1} \delta_i\gamma^i\psi(Q)\right), y^* - a_m\right)$. If $Adv_A^{\text{IR2}}(k)$ is not negligible,

B breaks the q-strong Diffie-Hellman problem with non-negligible probability. This contradicts q-strong Diffie-Hellman assumption, and thus $Adv_A^{IR2}(k)$ must be negligible.

Theorem 2. *Under the decisional linear Diffie-Hellman (DLDH) assumption, the proposed scheme has detector resistant.*

Proof(Sketch). Assume towards a contradiction that $Adv_A^{DR}(k)$ is not negligible. Then we show that we can use A to construct another adversary B that has non-negligible DLDH advantage. The construction of B is as follows. B is given (X, Y, Z, aX, bY, cZ). B sets $X = S, Y = T, Z = H$ and generates $isk = (w, v)$ and $tsk = (s, t, F_v = vF)$. A is given $param, gpk$. In a challenge query, A outputs $ID_i = x_i H$ which is generated in add member queries. Assume that ID_i is corresponding to $cert_i = (y_i, U_i = \frac{1}{w+y_i}(G_1 - x_i F - vF), v)$ where y_i, x_i are chosen randomly from $\mathbb{Z}_p$. B picks $b \in \{0, 1\}$. If $b = 0$, B executes Handshake with A as a user i for the first time and as SIM for the second time. If $b = 1$, B executes Handshake with A as SIM for the first time and as a user i for the second time. When B executes Handshake as a user i, B sets $R_2 = aX, R_3 = bY$ and $R_4 = cZ$ in the challenge query. Finally, A outputs $b' \in \{0, 1\}$. If (X, Y, Z, aX, bY, cZ) is satisfied for $c = a + b$, A can distinguish a user i and SIM, since B can completely simulate honest user i. Then, if $b = b'$, B outputs yes, otherwise outputs no. If $Adv_A^{DR}(k)$ is not negligible, B breaks the DLDH problem with non-negligible probability. This contradicts DLDH assumption, and thus $Adv_A^{DR}(k)$ must be negligible.

Theorem 3. *Under the decisional linear Diffie-Hellman (DLDH) assumption, the proposed scheme has unlinkability.*

Proof (Sketch). First, assume towards a contradiction that $Adv_A^{Unlink}(k)$ is not negligible. Then we show that we can use A to construct another adversary B that has non-negligible DLDH advantage. The construction of B is as follows. Our proof strategy of Unlink is similar to the proof strategy of DR (Theorem 2). B is given (X, Y, Z, aX, bY, cZ). B sets $X = S, Y = T, Z = H$ and generates $isk = (w, v)$ and $tsk = (s, t, F_v = vF)$. A is given $param, gpk$. In a challenge query, A outputs $ID_i = x_i H, ID_j = x_j H$ which are generated in add member queries. Assume that ID is corresponding to $cert = (y, U = \frac{1}{w+y}(G_1 - xF - vF), v)$ where y, x are chosen randomly from $\mathbb{Z}_p$. B picks up $b \leftarrow_R \{0, 1\}$. If $b = 0$, B executes Handshake with A twice as a user i. If $b = 1$, B first executes Handshake with A as a user i and second executes Handshake with A as a user j. First time, B sets $R_2 = aX, R_3 = bY$ and $R_4 = cZ$ in the challenge query. Second time, B sets $R_2 = raX, R_3 = rbY$ and $R_4 = rcZ$ where $r \leftarrow_R \mathbb{Z}_p$. Finally, A outputs b'. If $b = b'$, B outputs yes, otherwise outputs no. If $Adv_A^{Unlink}(k)$ is not negligible, B breaks the DLDH problem with non-negligible probability. This contradicts DLDH assumption, and thus $Adv_A^{Unlink}(k)$ must be negligible.

Theorem 4. *Under the discrete logarithm assumption and q-strong Diffie-Hellman (q-SDH) assumption, the proposed scheme has group traceability in the random oracle model.*

Proof(Sketch). In this proof, we use the result of Theorem 1. That is, our SHRBR has impersonator resistance under the discrete logarithm assumption and q-SDH assumption. In order that an adversary A breaks group traceability, the following conditions are needed. (a) A and the group traceability challenger output acc. (b) GroupTrace($gpk, tsk, \mathcal{T}$) outputs no. From the result of theorem 1, in order to satisfy the condition (a), A must have valid secret key/certification pair $(sk, cert)^{1}$. So, A should execute Handshake with the challenger correctly by using valid secret key/certification pair $(sk = x, cert = (U, y, v))$ where $e(U, W)^{y} e(F, G_2)^{x+v} = e(G_1, G_2)$. Also, in order to satisfy the condition (b), $R_4 - (sR_2 + tR_3) \neq F_v$ must be satisfied. However, in the step 2 and 3 of GSMR, the handshake player should prove the equation $R_4 - (sR_2 + tR_3) = F_v$. If A can forge the GSMR σ in such a way that $R_4 - (sR_2 + tR_3) \neq F_v$, A can also break IR. From above discussion, If $Adv_A^{\text{Unlink}}(k)$ is not negligible, B breaks the DLDH problem with non-negligible probability. This contradicts impersonator resistance (the discrete logarithm and $q-$ strong Diffie-Hellman assumption), and thus $Adv_A^{\text{GTrace}}(k)$ must be negligible.

Theorem 5. *Under the linear Diffie-Hellman (DLDH) assumption, the proposed scheme has member anonymity.*

Proof (Sketch). First, assume towards a contradiction that $Adv_A^{\text{MAnon}}(k)$ is not negligible. Then we show that we can use A to construct another adversary B that has non-negligible DLDH advantage. Our proof strategy of MAnon is similar to the proof strategy of DR (Theorem 2). An algorithm B is given (X, Y, Z, aX, bY, cZ). B picks $m \leftarrow [1, q_a]$ where q_a is the total number of add member queries. A is given $param, gpk$. B chooses $s \leftarrow \mathbb{Z}_p$ and sets $F = X, H = \frac{1}{s}Y, K = \frac{1}{s}Z$ and $x_m F = aX$. B generates $isk = (w, v)$ and $tsk = (s, t, F_v = vF)$. When A makes i-th add member query, B executes Add using isk, tsk if $i \neq m$. Otherwise (that is, $i = m$), B chooses $y_m \leftarrow_R \mathbb{Z}_p$ and generates $U_m = \frac{1}{w+y_m}(G_1 - aX - vX)$ and $ID_m = aX/s$. When A makes corruption query, B can return sk with the exception of $ID_i = ID_m$. The probability that $ID_i = ID_m$ is q_c/q_a where q_c is the total number of corruption queries.

In a challenge query, A outputs $ID_i = x_i H, ID_j = x_j H$ are generated in add member queries and ID_i, ID_j are not queried to corruption queries. B picks up b $\leftarrow_R \{0, 1\}$. If b = 0, B executes Handshake with A as a user i. If b = 1, B executes Handshake with A as a user j. Now, the probability that ID_m is chosen as the challenge user in this stage is $\frac{1}{q_a}$. If ID_m is not chosen, B outputs b $\in \{0, 1\}$ randomly. Otherwise, B sends $\tilde{Y}(= sH)$ and $\tilde{Z}(= sK)$ to A and receives $\tilde{H}$ and $\tilde{K}$. Next, B sets $R_4 = \psi(cZ)$ and $R_5 = \psi(bY)$ (Here, $b = \gamma s_B$.). Finally, A outputs b' $\in \{0, 1\}$. If b' = b, B outputs yes, otherwise outputs no. If $Adv_A^{\text{MAnon}}(k)$ is not negligible, B breaks the DLDH problem with non-negligible probability. This contradicts DLDH assumption, and thus $Adv_A^{\text{MAnon}}(k)$ must be negligible.

---

[1] The result of theorem 1 means that there does not exist A who becomes successful authentication by using only certificates or forges valid secret key/certification pair without an issuer secret key.

Theorem 6. *Under the linear Diffie-Hellman (DLDH) assumption, the proposed scheme has trace authority anonymity.*

Proof (Sketch). Assume towards a contradiction that $Adv_A^{TAnon}(k)$ is not negligible. Then we show that we can use A to construct another adversary B that has non-negligible DLDH advantage. Our proof strategy of MAnon is similar to the proof strategy of Theorem 2. An algorithm B is given (X, Y, Z, aX, bY, cZ). B picks $m \leftarrow [1, q_a]$ where q_a is the total number of add member queries. B chooses $t \rightarrow_R \mathbb{Z}_p$ and sets $F = X, H = tX$. B generates $isk = (w, v)$ and $tsk = (s, t, F_v = vF)$ and. A is given $param, gpk, tsk$. When A makes i-th add member query, B executes Add using isk, tsk if $i \neq m$. Otherwise (that is, $i = m$), B chooses $y_m \leftarrow_R \mathbb{Z}_p$ and generates $U_m = \frac{1}{w+y_m}(G_1 - aX - vX)$ and $ID_m = t(aX)$. In a challenge query, A outputs $ID_i = x_i H, ID_j = x_j H$ are generated in add member queries and ID_i, ID_j are not queried to corruption queries. B picks $b \leftarrow_R \{0, 1\}$. If $b = 0$, B executes Handshake as a user i. If $b = 1$, B executes Handshake as a user j. Now, the probability that ID_m is chosen as the challenge user in this stage is $\frac{1}{q_a}$. If ID_m is not chosen, B outputs $b \in \{0, 1\}$ randomly. Otherwise, B sends $Y(= sH)$ and $Z(= sK)$ to A and receives $\tilde{H}$ and $\tilde{K}$. Next, B sets $R_4 = \psi(cZ)$ and $R_5 = \psi(bY)$ (Here, $b = \gamma s_B$.). Finally, A outputs $b' \in \{0, 1\}$. If $b' = b$, B outputs yes, otherwise outputs no. If $Adv_A^{TAnon}(k)$ is not negligible, B breaks the DLDH problem with non-negligible probability. This contradicts DLDH assumption, and thus $Adv_A^{TAnon}(k)$ must be negligible.

References

1. Ateniese, G., Blanton, M., Kirsch, J.: Secret handshakes with dynamic and fuzzy matching. In: Network and Distributed System Security Symposium (2007)
2. Balfanz, D., Durfee, G., Shankar, N., Smetters, D.K., Staddon, J., Wong, H.C.: Secret handshakes from pairing-based key agreements. In: IEEE Symposium on Security and Privacy, pp. 180–196. IEEE Computer Society (2003)
3. Castelluccia, C., Jarecki, S., Tsudik, G.: Secret Handshakes from CA-Oblivious Encryption. In: Lee, P.J. (ed.) ASIACRYPT 2004. LNCS, vol. 3329, pp. 293–307. Springer, Heidelberg (2004)
4. Chaum, D., Van Heyst, E.: Group Signatures. In: Davies, D.W. (ed.) EURO-CRYPT 1991. LNCS, vol. 547, pp. 257–265. Springer, Heidelberg (1991)
5. Furukawa, J., Imai, H.: An Efficient Group Signature Scheme from Bilinear Maps. In: Boyd, C., González Nieto, J.M. (eds.) ACISP 2005. LNCS, vol. 3574, pp. 455–467. Springer, Heidelberg (2005)
6. Jarecki, S., Kim, J.H., Tsudik, G.: Authentication for Paranoids: Multi-party Secret Handshakes. In: Zhou, J., Yung, M., Bao, F. (eds.) ACNS 2006. LNCS, vol. 3989, pp. 325–339. Springer, Heidelberg (2006)
7. Jarecki, S., Kim, J.H., Tsudik, G.: Group Secret Handshakes Or Affiliation-Hiding Authenticated Group Key Agreement. In: Abe, M. (ed.) CT-RSA 2007. LNCS, vol. 4377, pp. 287–308. Springer, Heidelberg (2006)
8. Kawai, Y., Yoneyama, K., Ohta, K.: Secret Handshake: Strong Anonymity Definition and Construction. In: Bao, F., Li, H., Wang, G. (eds.) ISPEC 2009. LNCS, vol. 5451, pp. 219–229. Springer, Heidelberg (2009)

9. Micciancio, D., Petrank, E.: Efficient and Concurrent Zero-Knowledge from any public coin HVZK protocol. In: Electronic Colloquium on Computational Complexity, ECCC (2002)
10. Pointcheval, D.: Security arguments for digital signatures and blind signatures. Journal of Cryptology 13, 361–396 (2000)
11. Sakai, R., Ohgishi, K., Kasahara, M.: Cryptosystems based on pairing. In: The Symposium on Cryptography and Information Security, SCIS 2000 (2000)
12. Sorniotti, A., Molva, R.: Secret Handshakes with Revocation Support. In: Lee, D., Hong, S. (eds.) ICISC 2009. LNCS, vol. 5984, pp. 274–299. Springer, Heidelberg (2010)
13. Tsudik, G., Xu, S.: A Flexible Framework for Secret Handshakes (Multi-Party Anonymous and Un-Observable Authentication). In: Danezis, G., Golle, P. (eds.) PET 2006. LNCS, vol. 4258, pp. 295–315. Springer, Heidelberg (2006)
14. Xu, S., Yung, M.: k-anonymous secret handshakes with reusable credentials. In: Proceedings of the 11th ACM Conference on Computer and Communications Security, pp. 158–167. ACM (2004)
15. Wen, Y., Zhang, F.: A New Revocable Secret Handshake Scheme with Backward Unlinkability. In: Camenisch, J., Lambrinoudakis, C. (eds.) EuroPKI 2010. LNCS, vol. 6711, pp. 17–30. Springer, Heidelberg (2011)

Password-Based Signatures*

Kristian Gjøsteen and Øystein Thuen

Norwegian University of Science and Technology
{kristian.gjosteen,oystein.thuen}@math.ntnu.no

Abstract. We present a digital signature scheme where users sign by using a password instead of a long secret key. Our approach uses a signing server to prevent dictionary attacks. We present two efficient and secure schemes, both based on blind signatures. Our schemes are resistant against dictionary attacks from anyone except the signing server.

Keywords: RSA signatures, blind signatures, password, bilinear pairings, CL-signatures.

1 Introduction

Digital signature schemes are useful primitives, especially as used to create legally recognized electronic signatures on electronic documents. The user has a secret signing key that is used to create valid digital signatures. A corresponding verification key is public and anyone can use this to recognize valid signatures on documents. A signature scheme is secure if it is hard to create valid signatures without knowledge of the signing key.

The main practical problem with digital signatures is for the user to keep the signing key secret while at the same time using it to create signatures. Traditionally, this is done by storing the signing key inside a special protected computer called a smart card. The smart card then talks to the user's computer and signs documents submitted by the user's computer. Unfortunately, most computers (especially mobile phones and tablets) are not equipped with smart card readers suitable for this application.

In a password-based signature scheme, the user's secret signing key is replaced by a password. The advantage of this is that since the user can remember a password, the storage problem is potentially solved. Second, since it is easy for the user to enter the password, supporting software can be quite easy to build and deploy, perhaps straight-forward Javascript for portability and browser extensions for higher security.

The most obvious approach to password-based signature schemes is to use the password as the random seed for a digital signature scheme's key generation algorithm. But we must assume that passwords have rather low entropy. Therefore, such a scheme would be vulnerable to offline password attacks since everyone has access to the verification key.

---

* Funded in part by the Norwegian Research Council's VERDIKT programme project 183195.

S. Petkova-Kikova, A. Pashalidis, G. Pernul (Eds.): EuroPKI 2011, LNCS 7163, pp. 17–33, 2012.

Another alternative [8] is to get help from a signing entity. The user authenticates to a trusted server (perhaps a bank) and this party signs on behalf of the user. The main disadvantage is that the server knows the user's secret key, and a malicious server can simply sign on behalf of any user. The problem of malicious servers can be mitigated by essentially sharing the signing key [9,10], but finding convincingly independent servers is usually not easy.

1.1 Our Contribution

We propose password-based signature schemes with a single signing server, and define natural security notions for such schemes. To show that our proposal is practical, we introduce two new schemes, based on two different blind signature schemes.

The schemes we propose are secure against attacks on the password by outsiders, but not by insiders. This design choice gives a corrupted signing server a chance to forge signatures on behalf of users, but the user can force the server to invest significant resources by using higher-entropy passwords.

The first scheme we present is based on RSA signatures. These were first used to create a blind signature scheme in [3]. The security relies on the same assumptions that blind RSA signatures rely on. This scheme is easy to implement, since the generated signatures are the same as for the RSA full-domain hash scheme, but it does not achieve our strictest security requirements.

The second scheme is less practical, but it achieves stronger security. It is based on CL-signatures introduced in [2]. A blind signature scheme was proposed from CL-signatures in [6]. We use modified CL-signatures to create a password-based signature scheme. The security on this new scheme relies on a new complexity assumption we call the *es-LRSW assumption*, which is similar to the LRSW assumption that CL-signatures rely on. The LRSW assumption was first introduced in [11] and is hard in the generic group model. We also provide confidence in our assumption by showing its hardness in the generic group model.

1.2 Related Work

Our work is mostly inspired by notions and techniques from the blind signature literature. In addition, we essentially use two-party computations on shared secrets.

Many other approaches to useable digital signatures have appeared in the literature. For instance, in [5] the authors considers the scenario where a user has access to a small computer (such as a PDA) in addition to a normal computer. Assuming that not both these computers are corrupt, they propose a scheme where the user can create signatures with the help of a signing server. The user authenticates to the server using a password. This approach has some similarities to our proposal, but the requirement that the computer and the PDA communicate may hinder deployment.

As mentioned above one can also solve the problem by using multiple signing servers working together, as proposed in for instance [9]. In this work, the authors do not blind the signatures, but this could probably be implemented if desired. One downside of this approach is that it requires a more expensive infrastructure and several rounds of computation.

2   Password-Based Signatures

2.1   Definition and Syntax of Password-Based Signatures

A password-based signature scheme consists of a set of algorithms and protocols run by a User and a Server. The outline of such a scheme is given by the following.

The underlying assumption is that the User has a secret password pw which is used in key generation and signing, and that the User and Server communicate via secure, authenticated channels.

Setup(1^k) is run by a trusted third party with the security parameter k as input. It outputs a common reference string CRS. The output contains information such as group parameters, message space, password space etc. It is assumed that all algorithms have access to the common reference string.

KeyGen is an interactive protocol between the User and the Server. The User gets a password pw as input. The protocol outputs a secret key sk_S to the Server and a public key pk to both parties.

Request(m, pk, pw) is run by the User where m is the message being signed, pk is the User's public key and pw is his password. The output is a signature request ρ and some state information $state$.

Issue(ρ, pk, sk_S) is run by the Server after it receives a signature request ρ. The output is a blinded signature $\tilde{\sigma}$, or $\perp$ if something is wrong with the signature request.

Unblind$(\tilde{\sigma}, pk, state)$ is run by the User on a blinded signature $\tilde{\sigma}$ and the corresponding state information output by the request algorithm. The outputs is a signature σ on m or $\perp$ if something is wrong with the blinded signature.

Verify(m, σ, pk) is run by a verifier. It outputs 1 if σ is a valid signature on m under pk. Otherwise it outputs 0.

We require that when the key generation protocol is run with honest parties, both parties output and they agree on the public key. When the signing process as described in Fig. 1 is run with honest parties, a valid signature is output.

Remark 1. The signing process is described in Fig. 1. While we could have allowed for more complicated protocols in our definitions, we do not believe that the restriction to simple 2-move protocols is overly strict.

Remark 2. The user's password is chosen randomly according to some process. Also, the human-memorable password is usually passed through some password-based key derivation function to get appropriate key material.

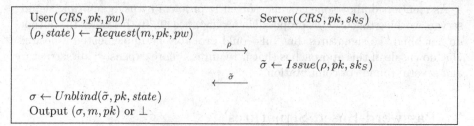

Fig. 1. Message flow during signature creation

The details of this process is not relevant to our work, so we choose a simpler model where we fix a probability space PW over some suitable set. We sample our passwords from this set, denoted by $pw \xleftarrow{r} PW$. Deriving key material from the password is modeled by a hash function G from bit strings to an appropriate set.

2.2   Security Definitions

The security definitions of a password-based signature scheme is based on those for blind signatures. *Non-forgeability* informally means that a User cannot create signatures on more distinct messages than the number of interactions he has with the Server. *Blindness* means that the Server learns nothing about the content of a message he is helping to sign.

For a password-based signature scheme we need one additional concept we call *non-frameability*. It roughly states that a Server should not be able to create a signature on behalf of a User without the User's help, unless it is willing to do at least an amount of work equivalent to finding the User's password.

The formal definitions are defined in the experiments below.

Non-forgeability. In the experiment defining non-forgeability the adversary A runs in two phases. In the first phase the adversary takes part in the *KeyGen* protocol as the role of the User, while a simulator runs the Server part. In the second phase the adversary has access to an Issue-oracle which runs the algorithm $Issue(\cdot, pk, sk_S)$ as defined in the scheme.

$\mathbf{Exp}_{PBS,A}^{nonforge}(k)$

1   $CRS \leftarrow Setup(1^k)$
2   Run the *KeyGen* with the adversary as the User to get (pk, sk_S).
3   $\{(m_i, \sigma_i)\}_{i=1}^{L} \leftarrow A^{Issue}$
4   Let l be the number of queries A made to *Issue*
5   **if** $L > l$ **and** $Verify(m_i, \sigma_i, pk, sig) = 1$ for all i
        and $m_i \neq m_j$ for all $i \neq j$
6   **then return** 1
7   **else return** 0

Define the advantage as

$$\text{Adv}^{nf}_{PBS,A}(k) = \Pr[\textbf{Exp}^{nonforge}_{PBS,A}(k) = 1].$$

We say that the scheme is non-forgeable if $\text{Adv}^{nf}_{PBS,A}(k)$ is negligible for all polynomial-time algorithms A.

Blindness. To define blindness we use the experiment $\textbf{Exp}^{blind}_{PBS,A}(k)$. We first run a key generation phase where the adversary A also selects two messages m_0 and m_1. Request-values are created and given to A in a random order. The adversary A issues blinded signatures $\tilde{\sigma}_i$. In the last phase the adversary is handed the unblinded signatures and must guess in which order the request values where sent. The password is also revealed to the adversary.

$\textbf{Exp}^{blind}_{PBS,A}(k)$

1    $CRS \leftarrow Setup(1^k)$
2    $pw \xleftarrow{r} PW$
3   Run the *KeyGen* protocol with pw as input to the User and the adversary as the Server to get pk.
4    $(m_0, m_1, st_{s1}) \leftarrow A(pw)$
5    $b \leftarrow \{0,1\}$
6    $(\rho_0, state_1) \leftarrow Request(m_0, pk, pw)$
7    $(\rho_1, state_2) \leftarrow Request(m_1, pk, pw)$
8    $(\tilde{\sigma}_0, \tilde{\sigma}_1, st_{s2}) \leftarrow A(\rho_b, \rho_{1-b}, st_{s1})$
9    $\sigma_0 \leftarrow Unblind(\tilde{\sigma}_0, pk, state_1)$
10   $\sigma_1 \leftarrow Unblind(\tilde{\sigma}_1, pk, state_2)$
11   **if** $\sigma_0 = \perp$ **or** $\sigma_1 = \perp$
12   **then return** b
13   $b' \leftarrow A(\sigma_0, \sigma_1, st_{s2})$
14   **if** $b = b'$
15   **then return** 1
16   **else return** 0

We define

$$\text{Adv}^{blind}_{PBS,A}(k) = 2 \left| \Pr[\textbf{Exp}^{blind}_{PBS,A}(k) = 1] - \frac{1}{2} \right|,$$

and a scheme satisfies blindness if $\text{Adv}^{blind}_{PBS,A}(k)$ is negligible for all polynomial-time algorithms A.

We also define restricted blindness, using the following experiment. Here the adversary only receives the request values associated to two messages of his choice, but does not receive the final signatures. The task of the adversary is to guess which order the request messages are sent. Note that the difference between blindness and restricted blindness is that the adversary does not receive the final signatures in the restricted variant.

$\mathbf{Exp}_{PBS,A}^{restricted-blind}(k)$

1   $CRS \leftarrow Setup(1^k)$
2   $pw \xleftarrow{r} PW$
3   Run the *KeyGen* protocol with pw as input to the User and the adversary as the Server to get pk.
4   $(m_0, m_1, st_{s1}) \leftarrow A(pw)$
5   $b \leftarrow \{0,1\}$
6   $(\rho_0, state_1) \leftarrow Request(m_0, pk, pw)$
7   $(\rho_1, state_2) \leftarrow Request(m_1, pk, pw)$
8   $b' \leftarrow A(\rho_b, \rho_{1-b}, st_{s1})$
9   **if** $b = b'$
10   **then return** 1
11   **else return** 0

Non-frameability. We use the experiment $\mathbf{Exp}_{PBS,A}^{nonframe}$ to define non-frameability. The adversary A is first asked to help create the public and secret key, then to create signatures σ_i on messages m_i.

The adversary has access to a Request-Unblind oracle that works as follows: Upon receipt of the ith message m, it computes $(\rho, state) \leftarrow Request(m, pk, pw)$, records $(i, m, \rho, state)$ and replies with ρ. Later, upon receipt of $(i, m, \rho, \tilde{\sigma})$ with a corresponding record $(i, m, \rho, state)$, it computes $\sigma \leftarrow Unblind(\tilde{\sigma}, pk, state)$, erases the record and replies with σ.

The adversary wins if he can create a valid signature on a message he has not queried to the Request-Unblind oracle.

$\mathbf{Exp}_{PBS,A}^{nonframe}(k)$

1   $CRS \leftarrow Setup(1^k)$
2   $pw \xleftarrow{r} PW$
3   Run the *KeyGen* protocol with pw as input to the User and the adversary as the Server to get pk.
4   $(m, \sigma) \leftarrow A^{Request-Unblind}$
5   **if** $Verify(m, \sigma, pk) = 1$ **and** m not queried to the oracles
6   **then return** 1
7   **else return** 0

We define
$$\mathrm{Adv}_{PBS,A}^{nonframe}(k) = \Pr[\mathbf{Exp}_{PBS,A}^{nonframe}(k) = 1],$$

and informally say that a scheme is non-frameable if $\mathrm{Adv}_{PBS,A}^{nonframe}(k)$ is negligibly larger than the probability of finding the password, for all polynomial-time adversaries A.

Remark 3. We could also define *outsider* security, where an adversary is allowed get signatures on arbitrary messages and to interact with an Issue-oracle, but does not know the password. It should then not be able to sign messages, except by searching for the password. However, nonframeability would imply outsider security, so we have not formalized this notion.

An even stronger notion would limit the advantage of an adversary making l queries to the Issue-oracle to be negligibly larger than the probability of guessing the password in l tries. We have not investigated such a notion.

2.3   Weak and Strong Security

Above we defined non-forgeability and non-frameability for password-based signatures. We also define weak versions of these. We say that a scheme satisfies weak non-forgeability if the scheme satisfies non-forgeability when the adversary has to reveal his secret password. Similarly for weak non-frameability the adversary has to reveal his secret key.

We note that typically a weak scheme can be modified to satisfy the strong requirements. Suppose we have a scheme satisfying the weak security requirements. Then we can modify the scheme slightly and require both the user and the Server to prove that they know their secret key, using some suitable NIZK-proofs. Assuming the NIZK-proofs are extractable, we can recover the secret key needed in the security proofs. There are well-known practical techniques for this, so we omit further discussions.

3   The Schemes

We describe two password-based signatures scheme in this section. They are both based on regular blind signature schemes, but adapted in different ways to satisfy our definitions and security requirements.

3.1   Scheme 1

Our first scheme is based on RSA blind signatures, first introduced by Chaum [3]. Recall that in blind RSA signatures we have an RSA modulus $N = pq$, public key e and signing key d. Let $H : \{0,1\}^* \to \mathbb{Z}_N^*$ be a hash function, which will be modeled as a random oracle in the proofs. To sign a message m, the User selects random $r \in \mathbb{Z}_N^*$, computes $m' \leftarrow H(m)r^e \bmod N$ and sends m' to the Server. The Server computes $s' \leftarrow m'^d \bmod N$ and sends s' to the User. The User unblinds the signature by computing $s \leftarrow s'r^{-1}$. We note that since $ed \equiv 1 \bmod \phi(N)$, we have $s \equiv H(m)^d \bmod N$, and the resulting signature is a regular RSA-signature.

We explain how we can create a password-based signature scheme from blinded RSA signatures. First, we assume that we have a standard two-party RSA key generation protocol that for a security parameter k can generate a public key (N, e) and secret shares d_1 and d_2 such that $2^{k-1} < N < 2^k$ and $e(d_1 + d_2) \equiv 1 \bmod N$. Several such methods exists, for instance [13] and [7].

Next, we assume that we have a random map G from the password space to the integer set $\{0, 1, 2, \ldots, 2^{2k} - 1\}$. Then the decryption exponent $d_1 + d_2$ can be split into the sum $G(pw) + sk$, where pw is the User's password, if the User sends $\eta = G(pw) - d_1$ to the Server, and the Server sets its decryption exponent to be $sk = d_2 - \eta$. Since G is a random map, the user does not reveal any information about d_1 to anyone who cannot guess the password.

Now the User can send the blinded message m' to the Server as usual, but the Server computes $s' \leftarrow m'^{sk}$. The User completes the signature by computing $s \leftarrow s'(H(m))^{G(pw)}r^{-1}$. We notice that $s = H(m)^{sk+G(pw)}$, and s is an RSA-signature on m under the key $d = G(pw) + sk$.

For simplicity we replace the shared RSA key generation protocol by a trusted dealer that generates a public key (N, e) and gives d_1 to the User and d_2 to the Server, where $d = d_1 + d_2 \mod \phi(N)$ and $ed \equiv 1 \mod \phi(N)$.

The complete scheme is given in Figure 2.

Setup(1^k)
1 Select a k-bit RSA modulus $N = pq$
2 Select a public key e and compute $d \leftarrow e^{-1} \mod \phi(N)$
3 Select random $d_1 \in \{0, 1, \ldots, \phi(N) - 1\}$ and set $d_2 \leftarrow d - d_1 \mod \phi(N)$
4 Select hash functions $H: \{0,1\}^* \to \mathbb{Z}_N^*$ and
   $G: \{0,1\}^* \to \{0, 1, \ldots, 2^{2k} - 1\}$
5 Send d_1 to the User, d_2 to the Server. The public key is $pk = (N, e, H, G)$.

KeyGen$_U(pk, d_1, pw)$
1 $\eta \leftarrow G(pw) - d_1$
2 **return** η

KeyGen$_S(pk, \eta, d_2)$
1 $sk \leftarrow d_2 - \eta$
2 **return** sk

Request(pk, m, pw)
1 $r \xleftarrow{r} \mathbb{Z}_N^*$
2 $\rho \leftarrow H(m)r^e \mod N$
3 $state \leftarrow (\rho, r, pw)$
4 **return** $(state, \rho)$

Issue(pk, sk, ρ)
1 $\tilde{\sigma} \leftarrow \rho^{sk} \mod N$
2 **return** $\tilde{\sigma}$

Unblind$(pk, \tilde{\sigma}, state)$
1 Interpret $state$ as (ρ, r, pw)
2 $\sigma \leftarrow \tilde{\sigma}\rho^{G(pw)}r^{-1} \mod N$
3 **if** $Verify(pk, m, \sigma) = 1$
4   **then return** σ
5   **else return** $\perp$

Verify(pk, m, σ)
1 **if** $H(m) \equiv \sigma^e \mod N$
2   **then return** 1
3   **else return** 0

Fig. 2. Password-Based Signatures from RSA signatures

3.2 Scheme 2

The second password-based signature scheme we present is based on the blind signature scheme by Ghadafi and Smart [6]. This scheme is again based on Camenisch and Lysyanskaya's signature scheme from [2]. We will call the underlying signatures for CL-signatures.

The original CL-signatures where designed using a symmetric pairing. By using a type 3 pairing instead, we can create shorter signatures. A type 3 pairing is on the form

$$e : \mathcal{G}_1 \times \mathcal{G}_2 \to \mathcal{G}_3$$

where there is no known isomorphism between $\mathcal{G}_2$ and $\mathcal{G}_1$. Such pairings that can be efficiently computed are well-known.

CL-signatures using Type 3 pairings

KeyGen(1^k): Select a bilinear pairing $e : \mathcal{G}_1 \times \mathcal{G}_2 \to \mathcal{G}_3$ where the groups have order p and $\log p = k$. Select generators $g_1 \in \mathcal{G}_1$ and $g_2 \in \mathcal{G}_2$ and $x, y \in \mathbb{Z}_p$. The secret key is $sk = (x, y)$, while the verification key is $vk = (X, Y) = (g_2^x, g_2^x)$.

Sign(sk, m): Select random $a \in \mathbb{Z}_p$. The signature is given by the pair $(A, C) \leftarrow (g_1^a, g_1^{ax+amy})$.

Verify(vk, m, (A, C)): If $e(C, g_2) = e(A, X)e(A, Y)^m$ holds, return 1. Otherwise return 0.

Note that only verification requires the computation of the pairing. This will also be true for our password-based signature scheme.

Blind Signatures from CL-signatures. Ghadafi and Smart proposed to use CL-signatures to create Blind Signatures in [6]. The scheme uses the standard method of creating blind signatures from normal signatures: The User commits to a message and the commitment is sent to the Server. The Server signs the commitment and sends this signature, along with some additional information, back to the User. The User finally unblinds the signature and rerandomizes it. The result is a regular CL-signature that can be verified as normal.

Password-Based Signatures from CL-signatures. Recall that in the CL-scheme the keys are on the form $sk = (x, y)$ and $vk = (X, Y) = (g_2^x, g_2^y)$. Again, we assume that we have a random function $G : \{0, 1\}^* \to \mathbb{Z}_p \times \mathbb{Z}_p$. In the password-based signature scheme these keys are shared between the User and the Server. The Server has (x_1, y_1) and the User $(x_2, y_2) = G(pw)$ such that $x = x_1 + x_2$, $y = y_1 + y_2$. The corresponding public values are then $(X, Y) = (g_2^{x_1} g_2^{x_2}, g_2^{y_1} g_2^{y_2})$. The scheme is shown in Figure 3. The scheme produces regular CL-signatures which can be verified under vk.

4   Complexity Assumptions

The first complexity assumption we present is the *simplified LRSW assumption*. This assumption is closely related to the assumption introduced in [11]. The security of the CL-signatures rely on this assumption.

Setup(1^k)
1 Select a pairing $e : \mathcal{G}_1 \times \mathcal{G}_2 \to \mathcal{G}_3$
    where the groups have prime order p and $\log p = k$
2 Select generators $g_1, Z \in \mathcal{G}_1, g_2 \in \mathcal{G}_2$
3 Select a hash function $G : \{0,1\}^* \to \mathbb{Z}_p \times \mathbb{Z}_p$
4 **return** $CRS \leftarrow (p, e, g_1, g_2, Z)$

KeyGen$_{U1}(pw)$
1 $(x_2, y_2) \leftarrow G(pw)$
2 $X_2 \leftarrow g_2^{x_2}$
3 $Y_2 \leftarrow g_2^{y_2}$
4 $state_k \leftarrow (X_2, Y_2, x_2, y_2)$
5 $\eta \leftarrow (X_2, Y_2)$
6 **return** $(state_k, \eta)$

KeyGen$_S(\eta)$
1 Interpret η as (X_2, Y_2).
2 $x_1 \xleftarrow{r} \mathbb{Z}_p$
3 $y_1 \xleftarrow{r} \mathbb{Z}_p$
4 $X_1 \leftarrow g_2^{x_1}$
5 $Y_1 \leftarrow g_2^{y_1}$
6 $X \leftarrow X_1 X_2$
7 $Y \leftarrow Y_1 Y_2$
8 $pk \leftarrow (X, Y)$
9 $sk_S \leftarrow (x_1, y_1)$
10 $\tau \leftarrow (X_1, Y_1)$
11 **return** (pk, sk_S, τ)

KeyGen$_{U2}(\tau, pk, state_k)$
1 $X \leftarrow X_1 X_2$
2 $Y \leftarrow Y_1 Y_2$
3 $pk' \leftarrow (X, Y)$
4 Verify that pk'
    matches pk

Request(pk, pw, m)
1 $r \xleftarrow{r} \mathbb{Z}_p$
2 $\rho \leftarrow g_1^m Z^r$
3 $state \leftarrow (pw, m, r)$
4 **return** $(state, \rho)$

Issue(ρ, pk, sk_S)
1 $a \xleftarrow{r} \mathbb{Z}_p \backslash \{0\}$
2 $A \leftarrow g_1^a$
3 $C \leftarrow g_1^{ax_1} \rho^{ay_1}$
4 $D \leftarrow Z^{ay_1}$
5 **return** (A, C, D)

Unblind$((A, C, D), pk, state)$
1 Interpret $state$ as (pw, m, r)
2 $(x_2, y_2) \leftarrow G(pw)$
3 $C \leftarrow C/D^r$
4 $C \leftarrow CA^{x_2 + my_2}$
5 **if** $Verify(pk, m, (A, C)) = 0$
6   **then return** $\perp$
7 $t \xleftarrow{r} \mathbb{Z}_p$
8 $A \leftarrow A^t$
9 $C \leftarrow C^t$
10 **return** (A, C)

Verify$(pk, m, (A, C))$
1 **if** $A \neq 0$ **and**
    $e(C, g_2) = e(A, X)e(A, Y)^m$
2   **then return** 1
3   **else return** 0

Fig. 3. Password-Based Signatures from CL-signatures

Definition 1 (s-LRSW). *Let* $e : \mathcal{G}_1 \times \mathcal{G}_2 \to \mathcal{G}_3$ *be a type 3 pairing of order* p. *Let* $g_1 \in \mathcal{G}_1$ *and* $g_2 \in \mathcal{G}_2$ *be generators. Fix elements* g^x *and* g^y. *Define an oracle that on input* $m \in \mathbb{Z}_p$, *outputs* (g_1^a, g_1^{ax+amy}) *for random* $a \in \mathbb{Z}_p \backslash 0$. *The problem is given* $(e, p, g_1, g_2, g_2^x, g_2^y)$, *to compute a tuple* (m, A, A^{x+my}) *for any* m *not queried to the oracle and any non-trivial element* A *from* $\mathcal{G}_1$. *The simplified LRSW assumption is that no efficient algorithm exists that can solve this with non-negligible probability.*

The second assumption we need is also based on the LRSW assumption. We call this the *extended simplified LRSW assumption*, es-LRSW assumption. It is closely related to the E-LRSW assumption from [6]. In Section 7 we show that it is hard in the generic group model.

Definition 2 (es-LRSW). *Let* $e : \mathcal{G}_1 \times \mathcal{G}_2 \to \mathcal{G}_3$ *be a type 3 pairing. Let* $g_1 \in \mathcal{G}_1$ *and* $g_2 \in \mathcal{G}_2$ *be generators and let the groups have order* p. *Let* $x, y, z \in \mathbb{Z}_p$. *Define an oracle* $\mathcal{O}$ *that on input* $M = g_1^m$, *outputs a tuple on the form* $(g_1^a, g_1^{ax+amy}, g_1^{ayz})$ *for some random* $a \in \mathbb{Z}_p \backslash \{0\}$. *Then the es-LRSW problem is given*

$$(g_1, g_2, e, p, g_2^x, g_2^y, g_1^z)$$

and q *queries to* $\mathcal{O}$, *compute*

$$\{(m_i, A_i, A_i^{x+m_i y})\}_{i=1}^{q+1}$$

where $A_i \in \mathcal{G}_1 \backslash \{Id\}$ *and all* m_i *are distinct.*

We say that the *es-LRSW assumption* holds if no polynomial-time algorithm can solve the above problem with non-negligible probability.

5   Security Results for Scheme 1

Given an RSA public key (N, e) and L randomly chosen elements $x_1, x_2, \ldots, x_L$ from $\mathbb{Z}_N^*$, the *RSA known-target inversion* problem is to find eth roots of $l + 1$ of the given random elements. To help with this task, the adversary is allowed l queries to an inversion oracle that on input $x \in \mathbb{Z}_N^*$ outputs $y \in \mathbb{Z}_N^*$ such that $y^e = x$. Note that the inversion oracle is not restricted to queries among the given L random elements.

Theorem 1. *If the RSA known-target inversion problem is hard, then Scheme 1 satisfies weak non-forgeability in the Random Oracle Model.*

Proof. Our solver for the RSA known-target inversion problem is given an RSA public key (N, e) and L elements $x_1, \ldots, x_L \in \mathbb{Z}_N^*$.

First, we must simulate the trusted dealer that generates the shared RSA key. It is enough to choose an appropriate random value d_1 and give this to the adversary as his share of the decryption exponent. During key generation, the adversary replies with η. Note that we do not know the second share of the decryption exponent, but we know that it is $d_2 = d - d_1$, so with $sk = d_2 - \eta$, we know that $sk = d - d_1 - \eta$.

To simulate the Issue oracle, we need to compute ρ^{sk}. Our simulator has access to the RSA inversion oracle, so it can compute ρ^d, from which it is easy to compute

$$\rho^{sk} = \rho^d \rho^{-d_1 - \eta}.$$

Finally, we need to simulate the hash H. For the ith message, we reply with x_i.

Now suppose the adversary computes $l + 1$ valid signatures on $l + 1$ distinct messages. This will certainly happen with negligible probability unless the adversary has queried H at every message. This means that the adversary has computed the eth roots of $l + 1$ of the elements $x_1, \dots, x_L$, which means that our solver succeeds.

Theorem 2. *Scheme 1 satisfies restricted blindness.*

Proof. The adversary only sees values on the form $\rho = H(m)r^e \bmod N$ for random r. Such a value is uniformly distributed in $\mathbb{Z}_N^*$ and leaks no information about m.

The password guessing game is a game played between a simulator and a guesser. The simulator first samples a password. The guesser then sends password guesses to the simulator until it guesses the correct password. The interesting metric associated with this game is the number of guesses before the game stops. For an (l, ϵ)-guesser, the probability that the game stops after at most l guesses is ϵ.

Theorem 3. *If RSA inversion is hard, Scheme 1 satisfies weak non-frameability.*

Proof. Suppose we have a non-frameability adversary with advantage ϵ.

We first consider the possibility that an adversary recovers the secret exponent d by guessing the password. Since we model the hash function G as a random oracle, this cannot happen unless the adversary queries G at the correct password. Suppose the adversary makes at most l queries to the random oracle G and has probability ϵ' for guessing the password. In that case, we can trivially convert the adversary into an (l, ϵ')-guesser for the password, which means that we are done unless ϵ is non-negligibly larger than ϵ'.

Otherwise, the adversary does not guess the password with probability $\epsilon - \epsilon'$, but still succeeds in creating a forgery. It is well known that the RSA full domain hash (RSA-FDH) is secure [1,4] if RSA inversion is hard. We will show that an adversary againt non-frameabilty can be used to create a forger for RSA-FDH.

An RSA-FDH forger gets the RSA public key as input. It is allowed to query a signature oracle with messages to be signed. Eventually, it must present a valid signature on a message that has not been a query to the signing oracle.

Our forger plays the trusted dealer, and invents a secret exponent d_2 that it sends to the adversary. It then sends the adversary η as part of the key generation protocol, and remembers $sk = d_2 - \eta$.

The Request-Unblind oracle sends the adversary a random value ρ. It then checks if the adversary replies with the correct value ρ^{sk}. If it is correct, it queries its signature oracle for m, then outputs the valid signature. If it is incorrect, it reports unblinding failure.

It is clear that as long as the adversary does not guess the password, the simulation is perfect. If the adversary creates a forgery, this will be a forgery for RSA-FDH and our forger will be successful with probability at least $\epsilon - \epsilon'$.

6   Security Results for Scheme 2

Theorem 4. *Scheme 2 satisfies blindness.*

Proof. We start the proof by examining the distribution of the signatures. Let (x, y) be the secret key. For a message m, the valid signatures are all on the form $(A, C = A^{x+my})$, where $A \in \mathcal{G}_1 \setminus \{Id\}$. If we randomize such a signature, by computing (A^r, C^r) for random r, we get a new signature of m. Such a rerandomizing selects a new signature in a uniformly random way from the set of all valid signatures.

The second observation is that $\rho = g_1^m Z^r$ reveals no information about m. If r is selected uniformly from $\mathbb{Z}_p$, then ρ will be uniformly selected from $\mathcal{G}_1$.

From these two facts it is clear that Scheme 2 satisfies blindness. The input of ρ_i to the adversary gives no information about the messages and the final signatures are not related to the blinded signatures the adversary provide.

Theorem 5. *If the es-LRSW assumption holds, then Scheme 2 satisfies weak non-forgeability.*

Proof. Let A be an adversary that plays $\mathbf{Exp}^{nf}_{PBS,A}$. We create an adversary against es-LRSW. We notice that in the weak case, the adversary has to reveal the password pw.

$\mathbf{B}^{\mathcal{O}}(p, e, g_1, g_2, X_1, Y_1, Z)$
1   $CRS \leftarrow (p, e, g_1, g_2, Z)$
2   $(X_2, Y_2, pw, st) \leftarrow A(CRS)$
3   $(x_2, y_2) \leftarrow pw$
4   $pk \leftarrow (X_1, Y_1, X_2, Y_2)$
5   $\{(m_i, A_i, C_i)\}_{i=1}^L \leftarrow A^{Issue}(X_1, Y_1, st)$
6   **return** $\{(m_i, A_i, C_i A_i^{-x_2 - my_2})\}_{i=1}^L$

Here the oracle Issue uses the oracle provided by the es-LRSW problem. We note that we need the secret key of the adversary to transform the signatures into appropriate signatures for the es-LRSW problem.

We note that if A wins the experiment, B solves es-LRSW.

Theorem 6. *If the s-LRSW assumption holds, then Scheme 2 satisfies weak non-frameability.*

Proof. Let A be an algorithm that plays $\mathbf{Exp}^{nonframe}_{PBS,A}$. We create an algorithm B, against s-LRSW.

$\mathbf{B}^{\mathcal{O}}(p, e, g_1, g_2, X_2, Y_2)$
1   $z \xleftarrow{r} ZZ_p$
2   $CRS \leftarrow (p, e, g_1, g_2, g_1^z)$
3   $(X_1, Y_1, x_1, y_1, st) \leftarrow A(CRS, X_2, Y_2)$
4   $pk \leftarrow (X_1, Y_1, X_2, Y_2)$
5   $(m, A, C) \leftarrow A^{Request, Unblind}(st)$
6   **return** $(m, A, CA^{-x_1 - my_1})$

Here the oracle *Request* is the normal request algorithm and *Unblind* is given below.

$\mathbf{Unblind}(A, C, D, m, r, x_1, y_1)$
1   $(A_2, C_2) \leftarrow \mathcal{O}(m)$
2   $(A, C) \leftarrow (A_2, C_2 A_2^{x_1 + my_1})$
3   **return** (m, A, C)

If A returns a valid signature on a message he has not sent to the request oracle, this message has also not been queried to the oracle $\mathcal{O}$. Thus if A is successful, then so is B.

However, if the adversary guesses the user's password, the above may fail. But as for the RSA case we can construct a password guesser.

7   es-LRSW in the Generic Group Model

We prove that es-LRSW is hard in the Generic Group Model. The GGM used is an extension of Shoup's model from [14]. We model all groups generically. We note that the hardness of s-LRSW follows from es-LRSW.

Theorem 7. *Let a generic algorithm try to solve the es-LRSW problem. Assume the adversary does q_G group operations, q_P pairing operations and q queries to the $\mathcal{O}$ oracle. Define $q_t = 6 + q_G + q_P + 3q$. Then the probability that the generic adversary solves the es-LRSW problem is bounded by $O(q_t^3/p)$.*

Proof. This proof follows the structure and notation of the GGM proof of E-LRSW from [6].

A GGM adversary has access to the group operations and other operations through oracles. Let $\mathcal{G}_1, \mathcal{G}_2$ and $\mathcal{G}_3$ be three lists of pairs (s, F) where $s \in \mathcal{S}$ is a random encoding of a group element and F is a polynomial in $\mathbb{F}_p[X, Y, Z, A_1, \ldots, A_q]$. Here $\#\mathcal{S} > 3p$, to ensure that different group elements correspond to different random encodings.

To each list we define an *Update* operator. *Update* takes as input a list $\mathcal{G}$ and a polynomial F. If an element (s, F) exists on the list, s is returned. Otherwise a random $s \in \mathcal{S}$, distinct from all previous, is selected and (s, F) is added to $\mathcal{G}$. Then s is returned to the adversary. Note that the adversary only ever sees the first entry on the lists.

Before the simulation begins, the following update operations are performed:

$$Update(\mathcal{G}_1, 1), Update(\mathcal{G}_1, Z),$$
$$Update(\mathcal{G}_2, 1), Update(\mathcal{G}_2, X), Update(\mathcal{G}_2, Y),$$
$$Update(\mathcal{G}_3, 1)$$

The adversary can now interact using the following oracles.

Group operations: The adversary has access to group operations in each of the three groups, using $\mathcal{O}_1, \mathcal{O}_2, \mathcal{O}_3$. On a query $\mathcal{O}_i(s_1, s_2)$ the simulator searches the list $\mathcal{G}_i$ for entries on the form (s_1, F_1) and (s_2, F_2) for some polynomials. If a match is found for both entries, $Update(\mathcal{G}_i, F_1 - F_2)$ is performed. Otherwise $\perp$ is returned.

Pairing operation: The adversary has access to a pairing oracle, $\mathcal{O}_P$. Let $\mathcal{O}_P(s_1, s_2)$ be called. If the list $\mathcal{G}_1$ has an entry (s_1, F) and $\mathcal{G}_2$ has an entry (s_2, G), then $Update(\mathcal{G}_3, F \cdot G)$ is called. Otherwise $\perp$ is returned.

es-LRSW oracle: The adversary can call this oracle q times, on input $\mathcal{O}(s)$. Let this be the ith query. If no entry on the form (s, F) exists in cG_1, return $\perp$. Otherwise the following is called: $Update(\mathcal{G}_1, A_i)$, $Update(\mathcal{G}_1, A_i X + A_i Y F)$, $Update(\mathcal{G}_1, A_i Y Z)$.

If we let q_G be the number of group operations, q_P the number of pairing operations and q the number of calls to the es-LRSW oracle, the total number of elements in the lists $\mathcal{G}_1, \mathcal{G}_2$ and $\mathcal{G}_3$ is bounded by $q_t = 6 + q_G + q_P + 3q$.

If the adversary is successful in solving es-LRSW, it outputs a set of $q + 1$ tuples on the form

$$(m_i, s_A^{(i)}, s_C^{(i)})$$

where $m_i \in \mathbb{F}_p \backslash \{0\}$ are distinct and $s_A^{(i)}, s_C^{(i)} \in S$ and encodings in the list $\mathcal{G}_1$. Let $F_A^{(i)}$ and $F_C^{(i)}$ be their corresponding polynomials. We now select a tuple of elements $(x, y, z, a_1, \ldots, a_q)$ from $\mathbb{F}_p$. If the adversary is successful, this equation will hold for every i:

$$(X F_A^{(i)} + m_i Y F_A^{(i)} - F_C^{(i)})(x, y, z, a_1, \ldots, a_q) = 0$$

We now show that the adversary cannot do this, with more than negligible probability.

Part A: We first need to show that the above equations cannot be identically zero. That is, we show that we cannot have $X F_A^{(i)} + m_i Y F_A^{(i)} - F_C^{(i)}$ for all i.

Let $F_A^{(i)}, F_C^{(i)}$ be in $\mathcal{G}_1$ and corresponding to the ith answer from the adversary. We first claim that $F_A^{(i)}$ cannot contain terms of X. If $F_A^{(i)}$ contains X, it must contain $A_k X$ for some value k, since the only way to produce terms with X, is to ask the oracle $\mathcal{O}$. However if $F_A^{(i)}$ contains $A_k X$, $F_C^{(i)}$ must contain $A_k X^2$. But the oracle $\mathcal{O}$ does not use X in a way to create X^2, and this cannot happen. Thus $F_A^{(i)}$ does not contain any terms with X. Similar arguments works for Y and Z.

We can write

$$F_A^{(i)} = \sum_{j=1}^{q} r_{ij} A_j + r_{i0}$$

for $r_{ij} \in \mathbb{F}_p$. Since this could be a valid response, it follows that we must have

$$F_C^{(i)} = \sum_{j=1}^{q} r_{ij} A_j (X + m_i Y) + r_{i0}(X + m_i Y).$$

However $F_C^{(i)}$ must be constructed using the provided oracle operations. We note that only input to $\mathcal{O}$ on the form $g_j + h_j Z$ gives output that fits the above equation. We can write

$$F_C^{(i)} = \sum_{j=1}^{q} s_{ij} A_j (X + (g_j + h_j Z)Y) + t_{ij} A_j Y Z.$$

From these two equations of $F_C^{(i)}$, we get

$$r_{i0} = 0$$
$$r_{ij} = s_{ij}$$
$$r_{ij} m_i = s_{ij} g_j$$
$$s_{ij} h_j + t_{ij} = 0$$

If for any i, $r_{ij} = 0$ for all j, then $F_A^{(i)} = 0$, which is not allowed. Therefore for any i, there exists at least one index j_i such that $r_{ij_i} \neq 0$. Then $m_i = g_{j_i}$ and this must lead to a collision, since there are more i's than j's. It follows that there must exist two indices i_0 and i_1 such that $m_{i_0} = m_{i_1}$. But this contradicts the assumption that the adversary outputs a valid answer, and Part A holds.

Part B: If the adversary could tell that he was interacting with a simulator and not the real GGM model, there would be polynomials such that $F_1 = F_2$ when assigned with values to the variables. This cannot happen identically. Using Lemma 1 from Shoup's paper[14], the probability for a single assignment is bounded by d/p, where d is the maximal degree of the polynomials involved. We note that $d \leq 2q + 2$. Since the total number of polynomials is less that q_t the probability of the adversary discovering the simulation is bounded by $O(q_t^2 d/p)$.

Part C: In a similar way, we must bound the probability that the adversary outputs an answer that on assignment matches the requirements. We have $(q+1)$ equations that must all be satisfied, in degree less than $2q+3$. The chance of this happening is bounded by $O((q/p)^q)$, again using Lemma 1 from Shoup's paper.

The probability now follows from Part B and the theorem is proven.

References

1. Bellare, M., Rogaway, P.: The Exact Security of Digital Signatures - How to Sign with RSA and Rabin. In: Maurer, U.M. (ed.) EUROCRYPT 1996. LNCS, vol. 1070, pp. 399–416. Springer, Heidelberg (1996)

2. Camenisch, J.L., Lysyanskaya, A.: Signature Schemes and Anonymous Credentials from Bilinear Maps. In: Franklin, M. (ed.) CRYPTO 2004. LNCS, vol. 3152, pp. 56–72. Springer, Heidelberg (2004)
3. Chaum, D.: Blind signatures for untraceable payments. In: CRYPTO 1982, pp. 199–203 (1982)
4. Coron, J.-S.: On the Exact Security of Full Domain Hash. In: Bellare, M. (ed.) CRYPTO 2000. LNCS, vol. 1880, pp. 229–235. Springer, Heidelberg (2000)
5. Damgård, I., Mikkelsen, G.L.: On the Theory and Practice of Personal Digital Signatures. In: Jarecki, S., Tsudik, G. (eds.) PKC 2009. LNCS, vol. 5443, pp. 277–296. Springer, Heidelberg (2009)
6. Ghadafi, E., Smart, N.P.: Efficient two-move blind signatures in the common reference string model. Cryptology ePrint Archive, Report 2010/568 (2010), http://eprint.iacr.org/
7. Gilboa, N.: Two Party RSA Key Generation. In: Wiener, M. (ed.) CRYPTO 1999. LNCS, vol. 1666, pp. 116–129. Springer, Heidelberg (1999)
8. Gjøsteen, K.: Weaknesses in BankID, a PKI-substitute deployed by Norwegian banks. In: Mjølsnes, et al. (eds.) [12], pp. 196–206
9. He, Y.-Z., Wu, C.-K., Feng, D.-G.: Server-aided digital signature protocol based on password. In: Security Technology, CCST 2005, pp. 89–92 (2005)
10. Landrock, P.: New PKI protocols using tamper resistant hardware. In: Mjølsnes, et al. (eds.) [12], pp. 1–16
11. Lysyanskaya, A., Rivest, R.L., Sahai, A., Wolf, S.: Pseudonym Systems. In: Heys, H.M., Adams, C.M. (eds.) SAC 1999. LNCS, vol. 1758, pp. 184–199. Springer, Heidelberg (2000)
12. Mjølsnes, S.F., Mauw, S., Katsikas, S.K. (eds.): EuroPKI 2008. LNCS, vol. 5057. Springer, Heidelberg (2008)
13. Poupard, G., Stern, J.: Generation of Shared RSA Keys by Two Parties. In: Ohta, K., Pei, D. (eds.) ASIACRYPT 1998. LNCS, vol. 1514, pp. 11–24. Springer, Heidelberg (1998)
14. Shoup, V.: Lower Bounds for Discrete Logarithms and Related Problems. In: Fumy, W. (ed.) EUROCRYPT 1997. LNCS, vol. 1233, pp. 256–266. Springer, Heidelberg (1997)

Isolating Partial Information
of Indistinguishable Encryptions

Jean Lancrenon and Roland Gillard

Institut Fourier (Université Joseph Fourier), St Martin d'Hères, France

Abstract. In this paper we present a new notion of indistinguishability of encryptions that is proven equivalent to *ind-cpa*-security and separates the encryptions from whatever partial information about the plaintexts accompanies them. We then proceed to show its use in an authentication scheme setting.

Keywords: provable security, indistinguishable encryptions, partial information, authentication scheme.

1   Introduction

This paper contains a new characterization of indistinguishability of encryptions (under a chosen plaintext attack) for a public-key encryption scheme. The notion was stumbled upon by the author during attempts to prove the security of remote authentication protocols using encryption to achieve confidentiality. Such schemes are considered here to demonstrate the usefulness of this notion.

In section 2 we briefly recall current notions of security in the attack-game language that will be used for the rest of the paper. We discuss first semantic security, then indistinguishability of encryptions. Section 3 presents our main contribution, which is a new definition of indistinguishability that takes into account the possible presence of partial information derived from the plaintext. We also prove that this notion is equivalent to the ones recalled in section 2. Finally, section 4 shows an application of our definition to remote authentication. We first treat the case of a general protocol, and then look at a specific (toy) instance of this protocol.

1.1   Related Work

Formalizing and strengthening notions of security for encryption schemes first began with Goldwasser and Micali's paper [11] in which semantic security and indistinguishability of encryptions were presented along with probabilistic encryption. Since then, a wide plethora of security notions for encryption have appeared, with the objective to capture the power of stronger and stronger adversaries. The most powerful one considered nowadays is indistinguishability under a chosen ciphertext attack, which was first formulated in [16] and strengthened afterwards in [17]. In the public-key setting, which is that of this

S. Petkova-Kikova, A. Pashalidis, G. Pernul (Eds.): EuroPKI 2011, LNCS 7163, pp. 34–48, 2012.

paper, semantic security is actually equivalent to indistinguishability under a chosen plaintext attack. A good survey of these notions and the relations between them in the public-key setting is [2]. Work establishing similar relations and separations in the private-key case can be found in [15]. Also, in [1] it is proved that in the public-key setting security is maintained when a polynomial number of public keys and messages are treated with the same encryption infrastructure. More recently, notions of security for encryption schemes taking into account the knowledge of various partial information on the secret key have been defined and investigated in [7] and [6].

The results here are in [12]. The authentication schemes that provided the motivation for this work are also in [12], as well as in other related works ([13] and [14]). These schemes are themselves inspired by various schemes devised by Bringer *et al.* in [3] and [4].

1.2   Some Notations for the Rest of the Paper

We place ourselves in the uniform model of computation. Consequently, all adversaries are probabilistic polynomial-time algorithms (PPTA in the sequel). Also, P will always designate a positive polynomial.

We will essentially be looking at secure public-key encryption. For the rest of the paper, an encryption scheme $\mathcal{CS}$ is defined as being a triple of PPTAs $(\mathcal{K}, \mathcal{E}, \mathcal{D})$ with the following properties:

• $\mathcal{K}$ is the key generator, which takes as input 1^n for $n \in \mathbb{N}$ and outputs a public key/secret key pair (pk, sk);

• $\mathcal{E}$ is the encryption algorithm. It takes as input the public key pk and a message m, and outputs a ciphertext c;

• $\mathcal{D}$ is the decryption algorithm, taking as input the secret key sk and a ciphertext c, and outputting a plaintext message;

• **Soundness assumption:** for all $n \in \mathbb{N}$, all $(pk, sk) \in \mathcal{K}(1^n)$, and all messages m:

$$\mathcal{D}\big(sk, \mathcal{E}(pk, m)\big) = m$$

In the sequel, $\mathcal{E}(pk, m)$ and $\mathcal{D}(sk, c)$ will be denoted respectively $\mathcal{E}_{pk}(m)$ and $\mathcal{D}_{sk}(c)$.

2   Classical Notions of Security

2.1   Semantic Security

In [11] Goldwasser and Micali defined two important security notions for encryption schemes: *semantic security* and *indistinguishability of encryptions*. The latter will be more discussed in the next section. Semantic security roughly states that whatever can be efficiently computed from a ciphertext can be efficiently computed without it, i.e. the ciphertext provides no useful information in reasonable time. Formally, it can be described in terms of attack games. The following definition comes from [10].

Let $\mathcal{M}$ be a message generating PPTA taking as input 1^n for $n \in \mathbb{N}$ and let $h : \{0,1\}^* \longrightarrow \{0,1\}^*$ be a polynomially computable function. For any two PPTAs $\mathcal{A}$ and $\mathcal{A}'$, and all $n \in \mathbb{N}$ we define:

$$\mathbf{Exp}^{sem}_{\mathcal{CS},\mathcal{M},h,\mathcal{A}}(n)$$
$$(pk, sk) \leftarrow \mathcal{K}(1^n)$$
$$m \leftarrow \mathcal{M}(1^n)$$
$$c \leftarrow \mathcal{E}_{pk}(m)$$
$$\gamma \leftarrow \mathcal{A}(pk, c, h(m))$$
$$\text{Return } \gamma$$

$$\mathbf{Exp}^{sem}_{\mathcal{M},h,\mathcal{A}'}(n)$$
$$m \leftarrow \mathcal{M}(1^n)$$
$$\gamma' \leftarrow \mathcal{A}'(h(m), 1^{|m|})$$
$$\text{Return } \gamma'$$

Let $f : \{0,1\}^* \longrightarrow \{0,1\}^*$ be a polynomially bounded function and set:

$$Adv^{f-sem}_{\mathcal{CS},\mathcal{M},h,\mathcal{A}}(n) = \mathbb{P}\big[\gamma = f(m)\big]$$

and

$$Adv^{f-sem}_{\mathcal{M},h,\mathcal{A}'}(n) = \mathbb{P}\big[\gamma' = f(m)\big]$$

Definition 1. *The encryption scheme $\mathcal{CS}$ is said to be **semantically secure** if for every PPTA $\mathcal{A}$, there exists a PPTA $\mathcal{A}'$ such that for all $\mathcal{M}$, h, and f as above, for every (positive) polynomial P, $n \in \mathbb{N}$ sufficiently large implies:*

$$Adv^{f-sem}_{\mathcal{CS},\mathcal{M},h,\mathcal{A}}(n) \leq Adv^{f-sem}_{\mathcal{M},h,\mathcal{A}'}(n) + \frac{1}{P(n)}$$

2.2 Indistinguishability of Encryptions

We now turn our attention to indistinguishability of encryptions. An encryption scheme $\mathcal{CS}$ is said to have such encryptions if it is infeasable to tell apart the encryptions of two distinct messages. To give a formal definition, let $\mathcal{M}$ be a PPTA that on input 1^n outputs a triple (m_0, m_1, z) where m_0 and m_1 are messages of the same length, and z is some partial information. For any PPTA $\mathcal{A}$, any n, and $\beta \in \{0,1\}$, we define:

$$\mathbf{Exp}^{ind-\beta}_{\mathcal{CS},\mathcal{M},\mathcal{A}}(n)$$
$$(pk, sk) \leftarrow \mathcal{K}(1^n)$$
$$(m_0, m_1, z) \leftarrow \mathcal{M}(1^n)$$
$$c \leftarrow \mathcal{E}_{pk}(m_\beta)$$
$$\gamma_\beta \leftarrow \mathcal{A}(pk, c, z)$$
$$\text{Return } \gamma_\beta$$

and set:
$$Adv_{CS,\mathcal{M},\mathcal{A}}^{ind}(n) = \left| \mathbb{P}[\gamma_0 = 1] - \mathbb{P}[\gamma_1 = 1] \right|$$

Definition 2. *The encryption scheme CS is said to have **indistinguishable encryptions**, or be ind-secure, if for every PPTA $\mathcal{A}$ and every PPTA $\mathcal{M}$, for every polynomial P, $n \in \mathbb{N}$ sufficiently large implies:*

$$Adv_{CS,\mathcal{M},\mathcal{A}}^{ind}(n) \le \frac{1}{P(n)}$$

It has been shown that semantic security and *ind*-security are in fact equivalent, i.e.:

Theorem 1. *An encryption scheme is semantically secure if and only if it is ind-secure.*

For the proof, see [10]. $\qquad\qquad\qquad\qquad\qquad\qquad\qquad\qquad\qquad$ □

This has important practical applications as it is usually easier to prove that an encryption scheme is *ind*-secure than to prove that it is semantically secure.

2.3 Indistinguishability under a Chosen Plaintext Attack

The previous notions of security are nowadays considerably reinforced by giving potential adversaries access to more information during an attack simulation, so as to capture as many situations as possible. The first example of this is *indistinguishability of encryptions under a chosen plaintext attack.* Let $\mathcal{A} = (\mathcal{A}_1, \mathcal{A}_2)$ be a PPTA running in two stages such that on input any pk from $\mathcal{K}(1^n)$, $\mathcal{A}_1$ outputs triples of the form (m_0, m_1, e) where m_0 and m_1 are messages of equal length and e is state information. For $n \in \mathbb{N}$ and $\beta \in \{0,1\}$ we define:

$$\mathbf{Exp}_{CS,\mathcal{A}}^{ind-cpa-\beta}(n)$$
$$(pk, sk) \leftarrow \mathcal{K}(1^n)$$
$$(m_0, m_1, e) \leftarrow \mathcal{A}_1(pk)$$
$$c \leftarrow \mathcal{E}_{pk}(m_\beta)$$
$$\gamma_\beta \leftarrow \mathcal{A}_2(m_0, m_1, e, c)$$
$$\text{Return } \gamma_\beta$$

where the advantage of $\mathcal{A}$ is:
$$Adv_{CS,\mathcal{A}}^{ind-cpa}(n) = \left| \mathbb{P}[\gamma_0 = 1] - \mathbb{P}[\gamma_1 = 1] \right|$$

Definition 3. *We say that CS has **indistinguishable encryptions under a chosen plaintext attack**, or is ind-cpa-secure, if for every PPTA $\mathcal{A}$ running in two phases as above, for every polynomial P, $n \in \mathbb{N}$ sufficiently large implies:*

$$Adv_{CS,\mathcal{A}}^{ind-cpa}(n) \le \frac{1}{P(n)}$$

It is of this notion that we give, and apply, a new characterization of.

3   Indistinguishability and Partial Information

The following new definition of security lies in flavor somewhere between the original definition of semantic security and the practical indistinguishability definitions that are common today. It borrows from the former the presence of partial information accompanying the encryptions and specifically attributed to the corresponding plaintexts, and from the latter the indistinguishability format. This way of defining security has proven useful for us in providing confidentiality in settings where:

a) the crucial information to protect is not necessarily the plaintext itself, but rather information derived from that plaintext;

b) partial information specifically related to the plaintext exists alongside the ciphertext.

The current notion of security that encryption schemes are required to satisfy is in an adaptive chosen-ciphertext context (*ind-cca*-2-security). Here, we define and examine a notion that we prove to be equivalent to *ind-cpa*-security as defined above.

3.1   Chosen Partial Information and Attributed Partial Information

Let $\mathcal{A} := (\mathcal{A}_1, \mathcal{A}_2)$ and $\mathcal{A}' := (\mathcal{A}'_1, \mathcal{A}'_2)$ be PPTAs that operate in two stages, where $\mathcal{A}_1$ and $\mathcal{A}'_1$ output triples of the form (z_0, z_1, e) with e again being state information. Let $\mathcal{MPI}$ be a PPTA that takes as input (z_0, z_1) and outputs quadruples of the form (m_0, m_1, y_0, y_1), with m_0 and m_1 having equal length.

We define the following experiments for $n \in \mathbb{N}$, $\beta \in \{0,1\}$, and $\beta' \in \{0,1\}$:

$$\text{Exp}_{\mathcal{CS},\mathcal{MPI},\mathcal{A}}^{ind-cpi-api-\beta}(n)$$

$$(pk, sk) \leftarrow \mathcal{K}(1^n) \qquad \text{Exp}_{\mathcal{MPI},\mathcal{A}'}^{ind-cpi-api-\beta'}(n)$$

$$(z_0, z_1, e) \leftarrow \mathcal{A}_1(pk) \qquad (z_0, z_1, e') \leftarrow \mathcal{A}'_1(1^n)$$

$$(m_0, m_1, y_0, y_1) \leftarrow \mathcal{MPI}(z_0, z_1) \quad (m_0, m_1, y_0, y_1) \leftarrow \mathcal{MPI}(z_0, z_1)$$

$$c \leftarrow \mathcal{E}_{pk}(m_\beta) \qquad \gamma'_{\beta'} \leftarrow \mathcal{A}'_2(e', y_{\beta'}, 1^{|m_{\beta'}|})$$

$$\gamma_\beta \leftarrow \mathcal{A}_2(e, y_\beta, c) \qquad \text{Return } \gamma'_{\beta'}$$

$$\text{Return } \gamma_\beta$$

where the advantages of $\mathcal{A}$ and $\mathcal{A}'$ are defined respectively as:

$$Adv_{\mathcal{CS},\mathcal{MPI},\mathcal{A}}^{ind-cpi-api}(n) = \left| \mathbb{P}[\gamma_0 = 1] - \mathbb{P}[\gamma_1 = 1] \right|$$

and

$$Adv_{\mathcal{MPI},\mathcal{A}'}^{ind-cpi-api}(n) = \left| \mathbb{P}[\gamma'_0 = 1] - \mathbb{P}[\gamma'_1 = 1] \right|$$

Definition 4. *An encryption scheme $\mathcal{CS}$ is said to have **indistinguishable encryptions under a chosen partial information and attributed partial***

information attack, or is ind-cpi-api-secure, if for every PPTA $\mathcal{A}$ as above, there exists a PPTA $\mathcal{A}'$ as above such that for every PPTA $\mathcal{MPI}$ as above, for every polynomial P, if $n \in \mathbb{N}$ is sufficiently large then:

$$Adv_{CS,\mathcal{MPI},\mathcal{A}}^{ind-cpi-api}(n) \leq Adv_{\mathcal{MPI},\mathcal{A}'}^{ind-cpi-api}(n) + \frac{1}{P(n)}$$

The intuition behind this definition is also a mix of the intuitions behind semantic security and (chosen plaintext) indistinguishability. What is truly interesting is the attributed partial information. Semantic security states that whatever can be efficiently computed from the ciphertext and the partial information accompanying it can be efficiently computed from the partial information alone. The above definition formalizes this idea in the indistinguishability setting with the attributed partial information (y_0, y_1): it is attributed in the sense that for $i \in \{0, 1\}$, y_i accompanies c_i. In the classical definition of indistinguishability, z represents partial information, but this information accompanies both c_0 and c_1. Hence, what the above definition says is:

If messages consisting of ciphertexts accompanied by attributed partial information are efficiently distinguishable, then what makes them so is the attributed partial information alone.

3.2 Particularizations

Before giving a practical characterization of *ind-cpi-api*-security, it is interesting to see what can be obtained from it in terms of security definitions alone, by varying the output of $\mathcal{MPI}$.

● **Varying the effect of the chosen partial information:**
Suppose that $\mathcal{MPI}$ completely ignores $\mathcal{A}$'s output and chooses m_0 and m_1 as it wants. In this case, $\mathcal{A}$ has no control over the messages that are encrypted.

At the other end of the spectrum, suppose that $\mathcal{MPI}$ sets $m_0 = z_0$ and $m_1 = z_1$. In this case, the chosen partial information is optimal: the setting is one of a completely chosen plaintext attack.

● **Varying the effect of the attributed partial information:**
Suppose that $\mathcal{MPI}$ returns quadruples (m_0, m_1, y_0, y_1) where $y_0 = y_1$. In this specific case, the underlying probability distributions of $\mathcal{A}_2'(e', y_0, 1^{|m_0|})$ and $\mathcal{A}_2'(e', y_1, 1^{|m_1|})$ are identical (remembering that $|m_0| = |m_1|$). Hence, $Adv_{\mathcal{MPI},\mathcal{A}'}^{ind-cpi-api}$ is identically zero and we are left with the inequality:

$$Adv_{CS,\mathcal{MPI},\mathcal{A}}^{ind-cpi-api}(n) \leq \frac{1}{P(n)}$$

In other words, we recover another part of the classical definition of indistinguishable encryptions.

These particularizations namely show that *ind-cpi-api*-security implies *ind-cpa*-security: this follows by taking $\mathcal{MPI}$ as returning $(m_0, m_1, 0, 0)$ on input (m_0, m_1). The main theorem of this paper is that the converse is also true.

3.3   Main Theorem

We now state and prove the main theorem of this paper:

Theorem 2. *A public-key encryption scheme CS is ind-cpi-api-secure if and only if it is ind-cpa-secure.*

That *ind-cpi-api*-security implies *ind-cpa*-security is trivial (see above), so we treat the opposite implication. Let $A = (A_1, A_2)$ be a PPTA operating in two stages designed to play against CS in $Exp_{CS,MPI,A}^{ind-cpi-api-\beta}$. We define a two-stage PPTA $A' := (A_1', A_2')$ in the following way:

Description of A_1': For all $n \in \mathbb{N}$, A_1' takes input 1^n, invokes $K(1^n)$ to obtain pk, invokes $A_1(pk)$ to obtain (z_0, z_1, e), sets $e' = e$, and returns (z_0, z_1, e').

Description of A_2': For all $(z_0, z_1, e') \in A_1'(1^n)$, all $(m_0, m_1, y_0, y_1) \in MPI$ (z_0, z_1), and all $\beta' \in \{0, 1\}$, A_2' takes input $(e', y_{\beta'}, 1^{|m_{\beta'}|})$, gets pk from $e' = e$, invokes $\mathcal{E}_{pk}(1^{|m_{\beta'}|})$ to obtain c, invokes $A_2(e, y_{\beta'}, c)$ to obtain γ, and returns γ.

That A' is a PPTA is obvious as it calls PPTAs a constant number of times. Furthermore, the construction of A' depends solely on A as required by the definitions. We must now show that for all MPI, and every polynomial P, if n is sufficiently large then:

$$Adv_{CS,MPI,A}^{ind-cpi-api}(n) \leq Adv_{MPI,A'}^{ind-cpi-api}(n) + \frac{1}{P(n)}$$

Let MPI be a PPTA as specified above and P be a polynomial. We define two more two-stage PPTAs A^i, for $i \in \{0, 1\}$, as follows:

Description of A_1^i: For all $n \in \mathbb{N}$ and all $(pk, sk) \in K(1^n)$, A_1^i takes input pk, invokes $A_1(pk)$ to obtain (z_0, z_1, e), invokes $MPI(z_0, z_1)$ to obtain (m_0, m_1, y_0, y_1), sets $e^i = (e, y_i)$, and returns $(m_i, 1^{|m_i|}, e^i)$.

Description of A_2^i: For all $(m_i, 1^{|m_i|}, e^i) \in A_2^i(pk)$, all $m \in \{m_i, 1^{|m_i|}\}$, and all $c \in \mathcal{E}_{pk}(m)$, A_2^i takes (e^i, c) as input, obtains e and y_i from e_i, invokes $A_2(e, y_i, c)$ to obtain γ, and returns γ.

Again, that A^i is a PPTA is clear. Furthermore, A^i is designed to play against CS in $Exp_{CS,A^i}^{ind-cpa-\beta}$. Since CS is *ind-cpa*-secure by hypothesis, if $n \in \mathbb{N}$ is sufficiently large then on one hand we obtain for all $i \in \{0, 1\}$:

$$\left| \mathbb{P}\left[A_2^i(e^i, \mathcal{E}_{pk}(m_i)) = 1 \right] - \mathbb{P}\left[A_2^i(e^i, \mathcal{E}_{pk}(1^{|m_i|})) = 1 \right] \right| \leq \frac{1}{2P(n)}$$

On the other hand, A^0 and A^1 are constructed in such a way that with the notations of $Exp_{CS,MPI,A}^{ind-cpi-api-\beta}$ and $Exp_{MPI,A'}^{ind-cpi-api-\beta'}$ used above we have for all n and $i \in \{0, 1\}$:

$$\mathbb{P}\left[A_2^i(e^i, \mathcal{E}_{pk}(m_i)) = 1 \right] = \mathbb{P}\left[A_2(e, y_i, \mathcal{E}_{pk}(m_i)) = 1 \right]$$

and

$$\mathbb{P}\Big[\mathcal{A}_2^i(e^i, \mathcal{E}_{pk}(1^{|m_i|})) = 1\Big] = \mathbb{P}\Big[\mathcal{A}_2(e, y_i, \mathcal{E}_{pk}(1^{|m_i|})) = 1\Big] = \mathbb{P}\Big[\mathcal{A}_2'(e', y_i, 1^{|m_i|}) = 1\Big]$$

Thus, for n sufficiently large and $i \in \{0, 1\}$ we obtain:

$$\left| \mathbb{P}\Big[\mathcal{A}_2(e, \mathcal{E}_{pk}(m_i), y_i) = 1\Big] - \mathbb{P}[\mathcal{A}_2'(e', y_i, 1^{|m_i|}) = 1] \right| \le \frac{1}{2P(n)}$$

which in turn implies that for n sufficiently large:

$$\left| \mathbb{P}\Big[\mathcal{A}_2(e, \mathcal{E}_{pk}(m_0), y_0) = 1\Big] - \mathbb{P}\Big[\mathcal{A}_2(e, \mathcal{E}_{pk}(m_1), y_1) = 1\Big] \right| \le$$

$$\left| \mathbb{P}[\mathcal{A}_2'(e', y_0, 1^{|m_0|}) = 1] - \mathbb{P}[\mathcal{A}_2'(e', y_1, 1^{|m_1|}) = 1] \right| + \frac{1}{P(n)}$$

Since this is exactly the equation required, the proof of the theorem is complete.   □

3.4 Multi-user, Multi-message

Before moving on to a possible application of *ind-cpi-api*-security, it is worth mentioning that the proof can be adapted in a straightforward manner to the following two important practical cases:

• The multi-user setting, i.e. in the presence of a polynomial number of public keys;

• The multi-message setting, i.e. when one key encrypts a polynomial number of messages.

Hence in the sequel we shall consider these cases as having been treated as well. Combined with the results of [1] and remembering that our encryption scheme is public-key we can state:

Theorem 3. *A public-key encryption scheme CS is ind-cpi-api-secure in the multi-user and multi-message setting if and only if it is ind-cpa-secure (in the single-user, single-message setting).*

4 An Application to Remote Authentication

In this section we show how to apply *ind-cpi-api*-security directly to prove anonymity in an authentication scheme setting. To illustrate how partial information arises within a protocol, we show how to protect the identity of an entity seeking to authenticate itself from a specific internal system component: the authentication server. We place ourselves first in a general setting, for which we will only describe enough structure to consider this internal component an adversary, and then we will examine a concrete toy authentication scheme.

4.1 A General Setting

System Components. We consider an authentication scheme having the following architecture:

- $\mathcal{U}$ is the entity trying to authenticate itself. We make the assumption that it is possible to extract from $\mathcal{U}$ a fingerprint bitstring that characterizes it (such as the biometric of an individual like in [3] and [4] or the morphometric fingerprint of an object considered in [8] or [9]), and that this entity also possesses a system-dependent identity;
- $\mathcal{R}$ is a reader. It has the ability to extract the aforementioned bitstring from $\mathcal{U}$ as well as $\mathcal{U}$'s identity;
- $\mathcal{AS}$ is an authentication server. Its role is to decide on the authenticity of $\mathcal{U}$ during the protocol. It does so by computing the Hamming distance between the freshly extracted fingerprint sent by the reader and a reference fingerprint obtained from a database;
- $\{\mathcal{C}\}_\mathcal{C}$ is a set of components that interact with $\mathcal{AS}$ to help $\mathcal{AS}$ make its decision. They collectively have knowledge of a database $\mathcal{DB}$ containing the list of reference fingerprints indexed by affiliated entities' identities. We shall assume that there are N registered entities, that each identity is an integer i between 1 and N, and that the fingerprints are of length ℓ. The reference fingerprint related to i is denoted f_i.

System parameters. In such a system, we distinguish two sides: the *client side* consisting of the reader and user, and the *server side*, consisting of the authentication server and additional components. We suppose that all components in the system share a public-key encryption scheme $\mathcal{CS}$ in the following sense: $\mathcal{K}(1^n)$ is invoked as many times as necessary independently to provide each $\mathcal{C}$ with a public key/secret key pair $(pk_\mathcal{C}, sk_\mathcal{C})$. The reader and authentication server have no keying material other then the public keys of the rest of the components.

The authentication process. Let $\mathcal{U}'$ be some entity trying to authenticate itself under the identity $ID_\mathcal{U}$. The authentication round proceeds as follows:

1) $\mathcal{R}$ extracts from $\mathcal{U}'$ a fingerprint f' and obtains $ID_\mathcal{U}$ from $\mathcal{U}'$;

2) $\mathcal{R}$ runs a randomized algorithm to produce information $\left(m_\mathcal{C}(ID_\mathcal{U})\right)_\mathcal{C}$ related to the identity for the $\mathcal{C}$ components, and information $m_{\mathcal{AS}}(f')$ related to the extracted fingerprint for $\mathcal{AS}$. It computes $c_\mathcal{C} \leftarrow \mathcal{E}_{pk_\mathcal{C}}\left(m_\mathcal{C}(ID_\mathcal{U})\right)$ for each $\mathcal{C}$, and sends $(m_{\mathcal{AS}}(f'), (c_\mathcal{C})_\mathcal{C})$ to $\mathcal{AS}$;

3) $\mathcal{AS}$ forwards $c_\mathcal{C}$ to $\mathcal{C}$ for all $\mathcal{C}$;

4) The $\mathcal{C}$ components each decrypt $m_\mathcal{C}(ID_\mathcal{U})$ and compute some information related to the reference fingerprint $X_\mathcal{C}(f_{ID_\mathcal{U}})$ that is sent back to $\mathcal{AS}$;

5) $\mathcal{AS}$ uses some function $\mathcal{F}$ to compute $\mathcal{F}\left(m_{\mathcal{AS}}(f'), \left(X_\mathcal{C}(f_{ID_\mathcal{U}})\right)_\mathcal{C}\right) = hw(f' \oplus f_{ID_\mathcal{U}})$ and decides on the authenticity of $\mathcal{U}'$ based on this hamming weight.

Providing confidentiality against a malicious authentication server.
We consider our adversary to be the authentication server. It is malicious in the
following way: it tries to infer identity information from the messages it receives
during an authentication round. Since our starting point is a security notion
that gives the adversary choosing power, it seems reasonable to quantify $\mathcal{AS}$'s
ability to distinguish two authentication rounds using the following game, where
$\mathcal{A} := (\mathcal{A}_1, \mathcal{A}_2)$ is a two-phase PPTA, $n \in \mathbb{N}$, and $\beta \in \{0, 1\}$:

$$\mathbf{Exp}_{\mathcal{CS},\mathcal{A}}^{ind-ID-\beta}(n)$$

$$(pk_C, sk_C)_C \leftarrow \mathcal{K}(1^n)\#\{C\}_C$$

$$(N, \ell, \{f_i\}_i, i_0, i_1, \kappa, e) \leftarrow \mathcal{A}_1((pk_C)_C)$$

$$\left(m_{\mathcal{AS}}(f_{i_\beta} \oplus \kappa), (m_C(i_\beta))_C\right) \leftarrow \mathcal{R}(i_\beta, N, \ell)$$

$$(X_C(f_{i_\beta}))_C \leftarrow \left(\mathcal{C}(N, \ell, \{f_i\}_i, m_C(i_\beta))\right)_C$$

$$(c_C)_C \leftarrow (\mathcal{E}_{pk_C}(m_C(i_\beta)))_C$$

$$\gamma_\beta \leftarrow \mathcal{A}_2\left(e, m_{\mathcal{AS}}(f_{i_\beta} \oplus \kappa), (X_{C\beta}(f_{i_\beta}))_C, (c_C)_C\right)$$

Return γ_β

Here, the advantage of $\mathcal{A}$ is defined as:

$$Adv_{\mathcal{CS},\mathcal{A}}^{ind-ID}(n) = |\mathbb{P}[\gamma_0 = 1] - \mathbb{P}[\gamma_1 = 1]|$$

This game basically simulates two authentication rounds performed on input
a database $(N, \ell, \{f_i\}_i)$ and pair of identities (i_0, i_1) that are chosen by the
adversary, and gives the information that $\mathcal{AS}$ would normally receive to $\mathcal{A}$.
The adversary now has the task of telling these sets of messages apart. The
string $\kappa \in \{0, 1\}^\ell$ is chosen by the adversary as well; it simulates the error
term by which an extracted bitstring and reference bitstring may differ. (This
error can be for instance due to reading variations that are common in biometric or morphometric settings. It could also simply be due to the fact that the
entity $\mathcal{U}'$ is trying to impersonate $\mathcal{U}$.) The same string κ is used on f_{i_0} and
f_{i_1} to ignore the situation in which the adversary could distinguish two rounds
simply by choosing different errors, a possibility that has nothing to do with
identities.

We now turn to considering the security of this scheme. Let $\mathcal{A}' := (\mathcal{A}'_1, \mathcal{A}'_2)$
be a two-stage PPTA. We need to consider one more game. Let $n \in \mathbb{N}$ and
$\beta' \in \{0, 1\}$:

$$\mathbf{Exp}_{\mathcal{A}'}^{ind-ID-\beta'}(n)$$

$$\left(N, \ell, \{f_i\}_i, i_0, i_1, \kappa, e'\right) \leftarrow \mathcal{A}_1'(1^n)$$

$$\left(m_{\mathcal{AS}}(f_{i_{\beta'}} \oplus \kappa), (m_\mathcal{C}(i_{\beta'}))_\mathcal{C}\right) \leftarrow \mathcal{R}(i_{\beta'}, N, \ell)$$

$$\left(X_{\mathcal{C}\beta'}(f_{i_{\beta'}})\right)_\mathcal{C} \leftarrow \left(\mathcal{C}(N, \ell, \{f_i\}_i, m_\mathcal{C}(i_{\beta'}))\right)_\mathcal{C}$$

$$\gamma'_{\beta'} \leftarrow \mathcal{A}_2'\left(e', m_{\mathcal{AS}}(f_{i_{\beta'}} \oplus \kappa), \left(X_{\mathcal{C}\beta'}(f_{i_{\beta'}})\right)_\mathcal{C}\right)$$

Return $\gamma'_{\beta'}$

The advantage of $\mathcal{A}'$:

$$Adv_{\mathcal{A}'}^{ind-ID}(n) = \left|\mathbb{P}[\gamma'_0 = 1] - \mathbb{P}[\gamma'_1 = 1]\right|$$

This game measures the same advantage as the other game except that the adversary does not get the encrypted messages, i.e. it needs to rely only on the accompanying partial information. With these notations, we have:

Proposition 1. *Suppose that $\mathcal{CS}$ is ind-cpa-secure and let $\mathcal{A}$ be a PPTA designed to play against the above authentication scheme in the game $\mathbf{Exp}_{\mathcal{CS},\mathcal{A}}^{ind-ID}$. There exists a PPTA $\mathcal{A}'$ designed to play against this authentication scheme in the game $\mathbf{Exp}_{\mathcal{A}'}^{ind-ID}$ such that for every polynomial P, if $n \in \mathbb{N}$ is sufficiently large then:*

$$Adv_{\mathcal{CS},\mathcal{A}}^{ind-ID}(n) \le Adv_{\mathcal{A}'}^{ind-ID}(n) + \frac{1}{P(n)}$$

In other words, $\mathcal{AS}$ can only efficiently exploit the accompanying messages to attempt distinguishing between (equal error) authentication rounds. Let $\mathcal{MPI}$ be a PPTA that takes as input $(N, \ell, \{f_i\}_i, i_0, i_1, \kappa)$, and first runs $\mathcal{R}(i_0, N, \ell)$ and $\mathcal{R}(i_1, N, \ell)$ to obtain:

$$\left(m_{\mathcal{AS}}(f_{i_0} \oplus \kappa), (m_\mathcal{C}(i_0))_\mathcal{C}\right) \text{ and } \left(m_{\mathcal{AS}}(f_{i_1} \oplus \kappa), (m_\mathcal{C}(i_1))_\mathcal{C}\right)$$

Next, $\mathcal{MPI}$ runs $\mathcal{C}(N, \ell, \{f_i\}_i, m_\mathcal{C}(i_0))$ and $\mathcal{C}(N, \ell, \{f_i\}_i, m_\mathcal{C}(i_1))$ for all $\mathcal{C}$ to obtain:

$$\left(X_{\mathcal{C}0}(f_{i_0})\right)_\mathcal{C} \text{ and } \left(X_{\mathcal{C}1}(f_{i_1})\right)_\mathcal{C}$$

Finally, $\mathcal{MPI}$ outputs (m_0, m_1, y_0, y_1), where for $j \in \{0,1\}$:

$$m_j := (m_\mathcal{C}(i_j))_\mathcal{C} \text{ and } y_j := \left(m_{\mathcal{AS}}(f_{i_j} \oplus \kappa), (X_{\mathcal{C}j}(f_{i_j}))_\mathcal{C}\right)$$

We now see that $\mathbf{Exp}_{\mathcal{CS},\mathcal{A}}^{ind-ID-\beta}(n) = \mathbf{Exp}_{\mathcal{CS},\mathcal{MPI},\mathcal{A}}^{ind-cpi-api_\beta}(n)$ with $\mathcal{MPI}$ as just described (in the multi-user setting). Also, we clearly have:

$$Adv_{\mathcal{CS},\mathcal{A}}^{ind-ID}(n) = Adv_{\mathcal{CS},\mathcal{MPI},\mathcal{A}}^{ind-cpi-api}(n)$$

Since CS is *ind*-secure, we know that it is *ind-cpi-api*-secure by theorem 2. Hence, there exists a PPTA $\mathcal{A}'$ designed to play against CS in $\mathbf{Exp}^{ind-cpi-api}_{\mathcal{MPI},\mathcal{A}'}$ such that for every polynomial P, if $n \in \mathbb{N}$ is sufficiently large then:

$$Adv^{ind-cpi-api}_{CS,\mathcal{MPI},\mathcal{A}}(n) \leq Adv^{ind-cpi-api}_{\mathcal{MPI},\mathcal{A}'}(n) + \frac{1}{P(n)}$$

Deconstructing $\mathcal{MPI}$ back into $\mathcal{R}$ and $\{\mathcal{C}\}_\mathcal{C}$ then shows that $\mathcal{A}'$ is the desired algorithm.   □

4.2   A Toy Authentication Scheme

In this paragraph, we describe a concrete toy authentication scheme and apply proposition 1 to prove confidentiality at the authentication server.

Structure and parameters. The components of the system are:

- The reader $\mathcal{R}$ and server $\mathcal{AS}$, as in the general setting above;
- $\mathcal{DB}_a$ and $\mathcal{DB}_b$, which are copies of a database containing reference bitstrings indexed by the identities of system-affiliated users. As above, the number of stored bitstrings is N, their length is ℓ, and bitstring associated to identity i is f_i. These are the only $\mathcal{C}$ components we need.

All of the components in the system share one public-key encryption scheme CS. The key generator $\mathcal{K}$ is invoked three times to produce public key/secret key pairs $(pk_\mathcal{AS}, sk_\mathcal{AS})$, (pk_a, sk_a), and (pk_b, sk_b) for $\mathcal{AS}$, $\mathcal{DB}_a$, and $\mathcal{DB}_b$ respectively, while $\mathcal{R}$ has no secret keying information of its own.

The scheme that we are going to describe is one of several found in [12], where a more complete security model (that also treats authenticity of communications in between the reader and the server) is given and studied. Here we make no mention of outside adversaries or other internal adversaries so as to focus on the authentication server, but it is worth mentioning that the presence of encryption in between $\mathcal{R}$ and $\mathcal{AS}$ and the use of a private information retrieval protocol devised by Kushilevitz *et al.* in [5] address these issues.

We need an additional notation to use the PIR protocol: if E is a set and x some element, $E \oplus \{x\}$ is $E - \{x\}$ if $x \in E$ and $E \cup \{x\}$ if $x \notin E$.

The authentication round. As before, $\mathcal{U}'$ is an entity trying to authenticate itself under the identity $ID_\mathcal{U}$ through $\mathcal{R}$:

1) $\mathcal{R}$ extracts from $\mathcal{U}'$ a fingerprint f' and obtains $ID_\mathcal{U}$ from $\mathcal{U}'$;

2) $\mathcal{R}$ chooses $S_a \subseteq \{1, ..., N\}$ uniformly at random, computes $S_b := S_a \oplus \{ID_\mathcal{U}\}$, chooses two masks M_a and M_b in $\{0,1\}^\ell$ uniformly at random, computes $c_a \leftarrow \mathcal{E}_{pk_a}(S_a || M_a)$, $c_b \leftarrow \mathcal{E}_{pk_b}(S_b || M_b)$, and $c_\mathcal{AS} \leftarrow \mathcal{E}_{pk_\mathcal{AS}}(f' \oplus M_a \oplus M_b)$, and sends $(c_a, c_b, c_\mathcal{AS})$ to $\mathcal{AS}$;

3) $\mathcal{AS}$ forwards c_a to $\mathcal{DB}_a$ and c_b to $\mathcal{DB}_b$, and computes $g' := f' \oplus M_a \oplus M_b$ by decrypting $c_\mathcal{AS}$;

4) $\mathcal{DB}_a$ (resp., $\mathcal{DB}_b$) computes S_a and M_a (resp., S_b and M_b) by decrypting c_a (resp., c_b), computes $X_a := M_a \oplus \bigoplus_{i \in S_a} f_i$ (resp., $X_b := M_b \oplus \bigoplus_{i \in S_b} f_i$), and sends X_a (resp,. X_b) to $\mathcal{AS}$;

5) $\mathcal{AS}$ computes $h := g' \oplus X_a \oplus X_b$ and outputs its answer based on the Hamming weight of h.

4.3   Security at the Authentication Server

Proposition 2. *Suppose that* CS *is ind-cpa-secure and that* $\mathcal{AS}$ *plays against the above toy scheme in the game* $\mathbf{Exp}_{CS,\mathcal{AS}}^{ind-ID}$. *For every polynomial P, if* $n \in \mathbb{N}$ *is sufficiently large then:*

$$Adv_{CS,\mathcal{AS}}^{ind-ID}(n) \leq \frac{1}{P(n)}$$

This essentially says that $\mathcal{AS}$ cannot distinguish the messages between two equal error authentication rounds. To prove the proposition, we apply proposition 1: there exists a PPTA $\mathcal{A}' = (\mathcal{A}'_1, \mathcal{A}'_2)$ such that for all P, if n is sufficiently large we have:

$$Adv_{CS,\mathcal{AS}}^{ind-ID}(n) \leq Adv_{\mathcal{A}'}^{ind-ID}(n) + \frac{1}{P(n)}$$

We now study $Adv_{\mathcal{P},\mathcal{A}'}^{ind-ID}$. By definition, this quantity is equal to:

$$\left| \mathbb{P}[\mathcal{A}'_2(e', M_{a0} \oplus M_{b0} \oplus f_{i_0} \oplus \kappa, X_{a0}, X_{b0}) = 1] - \mathbb{P}[\mathcal{A}'_2(e', M_{a1} \oplus M_{b1} \oplus f_{i_1} \oplus \kappa, X_{a1}, X_{b1}) = 1] \right|,$$

where M_{a0}, M_{b0}, M_{a1}, and M_{b1} are masks chosen independently, uniformly at random. This implies that the triples:

$$(M_{a0} \oplus M_{b0} \oplus f_{i_0} \oplus \kappa, X_{a0}, X_{b0}) \text{ and } (M_{a1} \oplus M_{b1} \oplus f_{i_1} \oplus \kappa, X_{a1}, X_{b1})$$

are identically distributed over the set of elements $(u, v, w) \in \{0,1\}^\ell \times \{0,1\}^\ell \times \{0,1\}^\ell$ such that $u \oplus v \oplus w = \kappa$. It follows that:

$$\mathbb{P}[\mathcal{A}'_2(e', M_{a0} \oplus M_{b0} \oplus f_{i_0} \oplus \kappa, X_{a0}, X_{b0}) = 1] = \mathbb{P}[\mathcal{A}'_2(e', M_{a1} \oplus M_{b1} \oplus f_{i_1} \oplus \kappa, X_{a1}, X_{b1}) = 1]$$

Thus, $Adv_{\mathcal{A}'}^{ind-ID}$ is identically zero, and all that we are left with for sufficiently large n is:

$$Adv_{CS,\mathcal{AS}}^{ind-ID}(n) \leq \frac{1}{P(n)},$$

as claimed. $\square$

5 Conclusion and Future Work

We have given a new characterization of semantic security in the public-key model that separates encryptions from attributed partial information, and demonstrated its use in partially securing authentication schemes having a certain structure. The notion presented here suffers from not being in the chosen ciphertext model; future work should provide such a definition and an expected characterization result. Also, the work presented here is in the public-key model. Aside from the fact that *ind-cpa*-security implies multi-party and multi-message *ind-cpa*-security in the public-key setting, this assumption does not seem crucial for our results. Hence, writing the secret-key version should be done as well.

Acknowledgements. We would like to thank the Rhônes-Alpes region (France) for funding the first author's Phd thesis from 2007 to 2010. We would also like to thank the Institut Fourier in Grenoble (France) for providing us with excellent working conditions. Finally, we would like to thank the anonymous reviewers for the many helpful comments.

References

1. Bellare, M., Boldyreva, A., Micali, S.: Public-key Encryption in a Multi-user Setting: Security Proofs and Improvements. In: Preneel, B. (ed.) EUROCRYPT 2000. LNCS, vol. 1807, pp. 259–274. Springer, Heidelberg (2000)
2. Bellare, M., Desai, A., Pointcheval, D., Rogaway, P.: Relations Among Notions of Security for Public-key Encryption Schemes. In: Krawczyk, H. (ed.) CRYPTO 1998. LNCS, vol. 1462, pp. 26–46. Springer, Heidelberg (1998)
3. Bringer, J., Chabanne, H., Izabachène, M., Pointcheval, D., Tang, Q., Zimmer, S.: An Application of the Goldwasser-Micali Cryptosystem to Biometric Authentication. In: Pieprzyk, J., Ghodosi, H., Dawson, E. (eds.) ACISP 2007. LNCS, vol. 4586, pp. 96–106. Springer, Heidelberg (2007)
4. Bringer, J., Chabanne, H.: An Authentication Protocol with Encrypted Biometric Data. In: Vaudenay, S. (ed.) AFRICACRYPT 2008. LNCS, vol. 5023, pp. 109–124. Springer, Heidelberg (2008)
5. Chor, B., Goldreich, O., Kushilevitz, E., Sudan, M.: Private Information Retrieval. In: Proceedings of the 36th Annual IEEE Conference on Foundations of Computer Science, pp. 41–50. IEEE, New York (1995)
6. Dodis, Y., Goldwasser, S., Tauman Kalai, Y., Peikert, C., Vaikuntanathan, V.: Public-Key Encryption Schemes with Auxiliary Inputs. In: Micciancio, D. (ed.) TCC 2010. LNCS, vol. 5978, pp. 361–381. Springer, Heidelberg (2010)
7. Dodis, Y., Kalai, Y., Lovett, S.: On Cryptography with Auxiliary Input. In: STOC, pp. 621–630 (2009)
8. Fournel, T., Coltuc, D., Becker, J.-M., Boutant, Y.: Multiscale extraction of uncompressive bitstrings from speckle patterns. In: Proc. Workshop on Information Optics 2008. JPCS, p. 139 (2008)
9. Fournel, T., Gillard, R., Becker, J.-M., Boutant, Y.: Morpho-cryptography: a new way for securing both information and storage media. In: Proc. SAR-SSI 2007, Annecy, June 12-15 (2007)

10. Goldreich, O.: Foundations of Cryptography II: Basic Applications. Cambridge University Press (2004)
11. Goldwasser, S., Micali, S.: Probabilistic Encryption and How to Play Mental Poker Keeping Secret All Partial Information. In: Proceedings of the 14th Annual ACM Symposium on Theory of Computing, San Francisco, pp. 365–377. ACM, New York (1982)
12. Lancrenon, J.: Authentification d'Objets à Distance, Phd thesis, Université Joseph Fourier (June 2011)
13. Lancrenon, J., Gillard, R., Fournel, T.: Remote Object Authentication: Confidence Model, Cryptosystem, and Protocol. In: Dasarathy, B.V. (ed.) Data Mining, Intrusion Detection, Information Security and Assurance, and Data Network Security 2009. Proceedings of SPIE, vol. 7344, p. 20 (2009)
14. Lancrenon, J., Gillard, R., Fournel, T.: Remote Object Authentication Against Counterfeiting Using Elliptic Curves. To appear in the Proceedings of the SPIE Defense, Security, and Sensing 2011 Conference in Orlando, Fl., USA (2011)
15. Katz, J., Yung, M.: Characterization of Security Notions for Probabilistic Private-Key Encryption. Journal of Cryptology 19(1), 67–96 (2006)
16. Naor, M., Yung, M.: Public-key Cryptosystems Provably Secure Against Chosen Ciphertext Attacks. In: Proceedings of the 22nd Annual Symposium on Theory of Computing. ACM (1990)
17. Rackoff, C., Simon, D.: Non-interactive Zero-Knowledge Proof of Knowledge and Chosen Ciphertext Attack. In: Feigenbaum, J. (ed.) CRYPTO 1991. LNCS, vol. 576, pp. 433–444. Springer, Heidelberg (1992)

A Universal Client-Based Identity Management Tool

Haitham S. Al-Sinani and Chris J. Mitchell

Information Security Group
Royal Holloway, University of London
Egham, Surrey TW20 0EX, UK
Haitham.Al-Sinani.2009@rhul.ac.uk, me@chrismitchell.net

Abstract. A wide variety of identity management systems have been
introduced to improve the security and usability of user authentication;
however, password-based authentication remains the dominant technology despite its well known shortcomings. In this paper we describe a
client-based identity management tool we call IDSpace, designed to address this problem by providing a single user interface and user experience for user authentication, whilst supporting a range of existing
identity management technologies. The goal is to simplify the use of
the wide range of existing technologies, helping to encourage their use,
whilst imposing no additional burden on existing service providers and
identity providers. Operation of IDSpace with certain existing systems
is described.

1 Introduction

1.1 The Need for Authentication

Authentication of human users is a fundamental security requirement; indeed, it
could be argued that it is *the* fundamental requirement. Despite its importance,
it is almost universally acknowledged that providing user authentication remains
a huge practical problem. In practice, as many observers have noted (see, for example, Herley et al. [1]), we are still using passwords almost universally. Again
as widely acknowledged, the use of passwords has many shortcomings, not least
because users today have so many Internet relationships, all requiring authentication. In such a context, password re-use and use of weak passwords are almost
inevitable.

A common approach to addressing this problem is to propose yet another new
way of achieving user authentication, possibly involving a Public Key Infrastructure (PKI) [2]. However, there are already many good technological solutions.
Perhaps the real problem is the insufficiently broad adoption of the solutions we
already have. If so, this is partly a business and sociological issue, but perhaps
it is also a problem which requires new technical thinking.

It is easy for those of us providing technological solutions to claim that this is
not our problem. We provide the technology, and the business and commercial

S. Petkova-Kikova, A. Pashalidis, G. Pernul (Eds.): EuroPKI 2011, LNCS 7163, pp. 49–74, 2012.
© Springer-Verlag Berlin Heidelberg 2012

world should just get on with adopting it. However, real life is not so simple. We in the academic world should be thinking about how to devise technological solutions which are easier to adopt. As always, key issues for easy adoption are transparency, ease of use, and backward compatibility, and these factors have played a large part in the design of the system we describe here.

1.2 Identity Management

Identity (ID) management systems [3–6] have been designed to simplify user authentication. An ID management system enables an Identity Provider (IdP) to support authentication of a User (and assertion of user attributes) to a Service Provider (SP). Recent years have seen the emergence of a wide range of such systems, including OpenID [7, 8], Liberty[1] [9], Shibboleth [10, 11], CardSpace [12, 13] and OAuth [14]. Each system has its own set of protocols governing communications between the main parties. As well as its own protocols, each system may also have a unique supporting infrastructure, including public key certificates, shared keys, passwords, etc. Some systems have gained a limited amount of traction recently, e.g. the use of OpenID in some sectors and Facebook's adoption of OAuth (Facebook Connect). However, the systems that have been most widely used also possess the most significant security issues (e.g. phishing vulnerabilities), and no system has broad penetration into the user community.

Many ID management systems are susceptible to phishing attacks, in which a malicious (or fake) SP redirects a user browser to a fake IdP. The user then reveals to the fake IdP secrets that are shared with a genuine IdP. This arises because, in the absence of a system-aware client agent, schemes rely on browser redirects.

A further problem faced by an end user is that the user experience of every ID management system is different. It is widely acknowledged that users fail to make good security decisions, even when confronted with relatively simple decisions [15]. The lack of consistency is likely to make the situation much worse, with users simply not understanding the complex privacy- and security-relevant decisions that they are being asked to make.

Finally, when using third party IdPs which provide assertions about user attributes, there is a danger that a user will damage their privacy by revealing attributes unintentionally to an SP. This is a particular threat when using systems like OAuth (e.g. as instantiated by Facebook Connect). In general, getting privacy settings right is highly non-trivial.

1.3 A New Approach

It is tempting to try to devise another new scheme which has the practical advantages of OAuth and OpenID, but yet provides robust protection against phishing and privacy loss. That is, we might wish to devise a client-based scheme

---

[1] The Liberty Alliance specifications have been input to the Kantara Initiative (http://kantarainitiative.org/).

with the user convenience of other systems, but which somehow avoids the fate of CardSpace[2]. However, it seems that a new solution is highly unlikely to succeed when others have failed (especially given that systems such as CardSpace have had the support of a large corporation and incorporate very attractive features). Moreover, a new system is likely to create yet another different user experience, increasing the likelihood of serious mistakes by end users. This suggests that devising yet another new system may not be the right approach.

The goal of this paper is to propose a new approach to the user authentication problem. It does not involve proposing any new protocols or infrastructures. The goal is to try to make it easier to use existing systems, and also to make their use more secure (including resistance to phishing) and privacy-enhancing (not least through the provision of a consistent user interface and an explicit user consent procedure).

The scheme we propose involves a client-based user agent. This is a single tool which supports a wide range of ID management systems yet provides a single interface to the user. The consistent user interface should maximise user understanding of what is happening and thereby reduce the risk of errors and increase user confidence. It also avoids the need for passive browser redirects, hence mitigating phishing attacks.

1.4   CardSpace

One motivation for the novel scheme arises from consideration of CardSpace (and related schemes such as Higgins (www.eclipse.org/higgins). Before proceeding we thus need to briefly describe CardSpace.

CardSpace acts as a client-based agent, and provides a consistent card-based user interface known as the *Identity Selector*. That is, sets of user credentials (relationships with IdPs) are represented to users as cards. CardSpace also defines a set of protocols for interactions between IdPs, Clients (user machines) and SPs. The user, interacting with a browser via the identity selector, may have identities issued by one or more IdPs. Each identity is represented by an *InfoCard* held by the identity selector, and this InfoCard is the means by which the user interacts with the identity selector to choose which identity to use. Each IdP runs a Security Token Service (STS), to generate security tokens. A Self-issued Identity Provider running on the client platform is also provided to allow use of self-issued tokens.

Before issuing a token, an IdP will typically need to authenticate the user. This user authentication takes place via the local CardSpace software. There are two key advantages of such an approach: it provides a consistent user experience, and it helps to limit the possibility of phishing attacks.

The user interface of CardSpace and the underlying communications protocols are not inherently tied together. It is thus possible in principle to keep the simple/intuitive user interface, and use it as the front end for a tool which manages

---

[2] Despite its adoption as an OASIS standard [16], in early 2011 Microsoft made a statement (http://blogs.msdn.com/b/card/archive/2011/02/15/beyond-windows-cardspace.aspx) implying that the project will not be pursued further.

user credentials in a consistent way regardless of the underlying ID management system. Credential sets can then identify with which ID management system (or systems) they should be used. For example, each credential set could be stored as a self-describing XML document. Indeed, these credential sets could include username/password pairs. This series of observations provides the basis for the IDSpace scheme, which we describe next.

2   IDSpace

We now describe IDSpace, the name of which pays homage to CardSpace. IDSpace is an architecture for a client-based ID management tool that operates in conjunction with a client web browser. A tool conforming to the architecture provides a user-intuitive and consistent means of managing a wide range of types of digital identities and credentials for user web activities. The IDSpace architecture is designed to support all existing ID management protocols, and can be used to replace existing ID management client software, including the CardSpace [12, 13], and Higgins[3] clients, Liberty-enabled client software [17], and client-based password managers.

It is important to observe that IDSpace is not an ID management system, at least in the normal sense of the term. Instead it is an architecture for a client system which enables the use of a multiplicity of ID management protocols with maximal transparency to the user (avoiding the need to install multiple ID management clients). The IDSpace architecture is designed so that conformant tools are able to work with all existing Internet SPs and IdPs without any changes to their current operation. That is, the system is transparent to all third parties.

The IDSpace architecture is designed to be platform-independent, and a prototype implementation is being developed (a partial Windows-based prototype is already operational). Implementations should be capable of being deployed on Windows, Unix, Mac, and smart phone-based platforms with minimal changes. Key parts of the system can be instantiated as browser add-ons, e.g. written in C++ and/or JavaScript, thereby maximising portability.

As with any ID management tool, the primary purpose is to enable an end user to access a protected resource. Once installed on a user device, IDSpace will execute whenever a user wishes to access a protected service using a web browser. It allows the user to select a particular ID management system from amongst those supported by the SP. It also allows the user to choose which set of credentials is to be used with this SP, where the network interactions with the SP and IdP will conform to the chosen ID management system.

An IDSpace system interacts with the user via a key component known as the *Card Selector*. This provides a visual representation of user credential sets in the form of 'virtual cards', referred to here as *credential cards* (*cCards*). The operation of this component is motivated by the CardSpace's identity selector

---

[3] http://www.eclipse.org/higgins/

(whose virtual cards are known as InfoCards or iCards). Higgins, which originated as an open source implementation of a CardSpace-like system, also uses the term InfoCards.

A cCard can represent any of a wide range of types of user credential, including:

- ready-to-use credential tokens including 'password manager' tokens containing a username/password pair, referred to as *local cCards*; and
- a pointer to a remote, credential-issuing party (an IdP), referred to as *remote cCards*.

Whilst IDSpace has a similar user interface to CardSpace and Higgins, it is also important to note certain fundamental differences. Both CardSpace and Higgins support just one set of protocols for web interactions between the user platform and third party systems. If future versions of these systems support additional protocols, then this will require corresponding modifications to SPs and/or IdPs. IDSpace, by contrast, is designed to work with almost any conceivable ID management protocol suite, and its adoption does not require any changes to third party systems (including IdPs and SPs).

IDSpace is made up of a set of self-contained components interacting with each other in a pre-defined way, thus enabling modular implementation. Such an architectural design enables new ID management protocols to be supported in a simple way by adding new software modules to an existing implementation.

3   High-Level Architecture

3.1   Context of Use

As stated above, IDSpace provides a user-intuitive means for managing digital identities and credentials for user web activities, consistent across underlying ID management systems. The intended context of use is shown in Figure 1.

The parties involved, as shown in the figure, include the following.

1. The *user* interacts with a *user platform* or *hardware platform* (e.g. a PC or mobile device) in order to access services provided across the Internet. This user platform is equipped with an *operating system (OS)* on which applications execute.
2. The *IdP* provides identity services to the user. This typically involves issuing a user-specific identity token for consumption by an SP (where, although the token is intended for use by a specific user, the user's identity will not necessarily be revealed to the SP). This token will provide the SP with assurance regarding certain attributes of the user, e.g. the user identity. The IdP is located either remotely or locally on the user platform; in the latter case the IdP is referred to as a *local identity provider (LIP)*. Examples of possible IdPs include Facebook and Google.

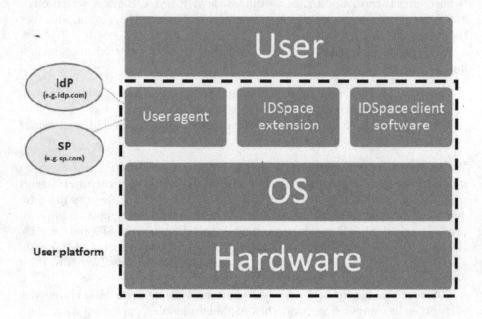

Fig. 1. IDSpace Context

3. The *SP* provides services which the user wishes to access. In order to allow the user to access a protected resource, the SP will wish to be provided with verifiable statements regarding certain attributes of the user. This is typically achieved by supplying the SP with a user-specific credential or identity token issued by a local or remote IdP. (In some contexts the SP is known as a *relying party (RP)*). Examples of possible SPs include YouTube, Amazon, Facebook and Google (some parties may act as both IdPs and SPs).

4. The *user agent* (UA) is a software component employed by a user to manage interactions between the user/user platform and remote entities (IdPs and SPs). This will typically be instantiated as a web browser, such as Internet Explorer or Firefox; indeed, for the sake of simplicity, in some subsequent discussions we refer to a web browser rather than a UA. The UA processes protocol messages on behalf of the user, and prompts the user to make decisions, provide secrets, etc.

5. The *IDSpace client software*, implementing part of the IDSpace architecture, interacts with the user via a graphical user interface (GUI). This GUI allows the user to select a particular credential set (represented as a cCard) for use in a specific transaction with an SP. The application also interacts with a web browser, and, where necessary, with remote entities.

6. The *IDSpace extension* (or the *IDSpace browser extension*), implementing part of the IDSpace architecture, supplements the functionality of the UA. It is made up of a set of modules performing specific tasks, e.g. scanning

a webpage for a username-password login form. The IDSpace extension exchanges data with the client software via the browser, and, where necessary, interacts with the user.

3.2 IDSpace Components

Figure 2 shows the relationships between the main components of IDSpace, including the primary information flows. The dotted line shows the limits of the browser extension. Note that, although shown as part of the browser extension, the *Activator* could also be implemented as an independent component. This is because, in certain ID management systems e.g. CardSpace, the SP webpage must implement certain X/HTML tags to enable this component to perform its task (see below). However, it is also possible for a browser extension to add such tags.

The remaining components, apart from the 'web browser' and 'remote IdP', represent the IDSpace *client software*. Note that the boxes marked 'Other ...' refer to other IDSpace components, which, although covered in the text, are not shown in the figure.

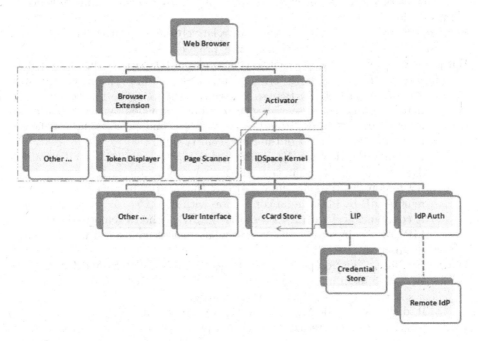

Fig. 2. IDSpace Components

The two primary elements of the IDSpace architecture, i.e. the IDSpace client software and the IDSpace extension (as introduced in section 3.1), are now discussed in greater detail.

Client Software. The client software, a stand-alone application, is made up of the following components.

cCards. A cCard is a (relatively non-sensitive) XML document corresponding to a set of user credentials (or, more generally, to a set of user private information). A cCard indicates the types of personal information in the set, and also the type (or types) of ID management system with which the cCard can be used. However, it does not contain the personal information itself. cCards can be *local*, in which case they are generated by the LIP, or *remote*, in which case they are generated by a remote IdP.

cCard Store. This is a protected local store for *cCards*. The nature of the protection provided for stored cCards will depend on the implementation environment. For example, protection could involve the use of cryptography, physical protection and/or logical protection (as provided by the OS).

Credential Store. This is a protected local store for sensitive data, such as personal information, certificates, user passwords, etc., associated with local cCards. It is used by the LIP. Note that, in practice, the *Credential Store* and the *cCard Store* could be combined. As is the case for the cCard store, the nature of the protection provided will be implementation-dependent, and could involve the use of cryptography, physical protection and/or logical protection.

Settings Store. This is a local store for (relatively) non-sensitive data such as system state, system/user settings, user preferences, etc.

IDSpace Kernel. This is the central component of IDSpace. It runs locally on the user platform, handling communications with and between other components of IDSpace. In particular, it performs the following functions.

- It receives and processes the security policy provided by the *Activator*.
- It retrieves the cCards from the *cCard Store*, and checks which of them meet the requirements of the SP's security policy.
- It invokes the IDSpace *User Interface* in a private desktop window, and displays the cCards that meet the SP's policy requirements.
- If a remote cCard is chosen, it retrieves the security policy of the relevant remote IdP by initiating a connection with it.
- It communicates with the user-selected IdP (either a remote IdP or the LIP) to obtain an identity token, where necessary using the *IdP Auth* component.

User Interface. This component, which incorporates the **IDSpace Card Selector**, is the main means by which an end user interacts with the IDSpace client software. Its tasks include the following.

- It displays the identity of the SP website to the user, and indicates whether the website has been visited previously. If the website is being visited for the first time then it allows the user to either continue or terminate.
- It displays the available cCards (it might display all the cards and highlight those that meet the SP site policy, or it might only display those meeting the policy). Note that the cCards are displayed in the *Card Selector*.

- It allows the user to review the contents of a cCard.
- It allows the, user to generate and modify 'local' cCards (as opposed to 'remote' cCards generated by remote IdPs) — in doing so it provides an interface to some of the functions of the LIP.
- It allows the user to import a cCard provided by a remote IdP.
- It asks a user for explicit consent before providing potentially sensitive information to an SP.
- It allows the user to set preferences for future operation of the system. These preferences are stored in the *Settings Store*.

LIP. This provides the functionality of an IdP, but is resident on the user platform. Like any IdP, the LIP can generate identity tokens. These tokens can be retrieved by the *IDSpace Kernel*. The LIP stores user-attribute values and other sensitive user data in the *Credential Store*.

IdP Auth. This authenticates the user to a remote IdP, if a remote cCard is selected. It uses the *User Interface* to prompt the user to enter the required credentials, e.g. username and password, and then submits them to the IdP.

By doing so it enables a consistent and simple user authentication interface to be provided to the user, even when a range of different identity protocols are being used. It also supports IdP-specific protocol interactions, e.g. to create requests for specific types of token.

Networker. This initiates a direct online connection between the client software and a remote server (i.e. not involving the browser).

Browser Extension. The IDSpace extension, typically implemented as a browser add-on, includes the following modules.

Page Scanner. This browser extension module scans the SP website login page in order to discover the identity system(s) it supports. It passes the results of the scan to the *Identity System Selector*.

Activator. This is a (logical) bridge between the client browser and the *IDSpace Kernel*. Its tasks include the following.
- It informs the user that the IDSpace system can be used.
- It enables the user to activate the Card Selector.

Identity System Selector. This browser extension module enables the user to select the identity management system to be used from amongst those supported by the SP website. The precise operation of this component will depend on the implementation of the IDSpace architecture.

If more than one identity system is available, the Identity System Selector could ask the user to either choose an identity system immediately or defer the selection until the point at which a cCard is selected (using the *IDSpace Card Selector*). It might also provide a means to store the user answer (in the *Settings Store*) for future authentication attempts.

It passes the user response to the *Data Transporter*.

Data Transporter. This browser extension module provides the means to exchange data between components of the IDSpace architecture, including the following.

- It is responsible for the transfer of metadata regarding the SP page (e.g. the discovered and selected identity system(s), the identity of the SP, the SP website policy requirements, etc.), to the *IDSpace Kernel*. For example, if the user indicates that IDSpace is to be used, it passes the security policy of the SP website to the IDSpace Kernel.
- It transfers data from the IDSpace Kernel to the browser. For example, if IDSpace obtains or generates an identity token during the authentication process, it gives the token to the browser which dispatches it to the SP website.

Token Displayer. This browser extension module displays an indication of the contents of an IdP-generated identity token to the user. This helps the user to decide whether or not to allow the token to be passed to the SP. This function can only be provided if the token is not:

- encrypted in such a way that only the SP can read it (e.g. using an SP's public key); and
- transmitted via a (direct) IdP-SP channel, i.e. the token must pass via the client platform.

4   Supporting Functionality

We next discuss a number of key functions that an IDSpace-conformant system must provide. For many of these functions we outline multiple approaches to implementation.

4.1   Identity System Discovery

IDSpace must be able to determine which ID management systems are supported by an SP website. This can be accomplished in a number of different ways, including the following.

1. IDSpace could scan the visited page for HTML/XHTML tags that are associated with specific ID management systems. For example, the string:
   - 'application/x-informationCard' indicates support for CardSpace; and
   - 'openid_url' and/or 'openid_identifier' indicates support for OpenID.

   The benefits of such an approach include complete transparency, albeit at the cost of performance (because IDSpace must scan every web page).
2. IDSpace could ask the user which ID management systems the page currently supports. The benefits of such an approach include accuracy and higher performance, at the cost of transparency and user convenience (although the user's choice could be stored in the *Settings Store* for future logins).
3. IDSpace could employ a hybrid approach based on a combination of the above two options, e.g. so that if the first option fails then it resorts to the second option.

4.2   Identity System Selection

Having learnt which ID management system(s) an SP supports, IDSpace must allow the user to select which system to use for the current transaction. Such a process could take place before or after invocation of the *IDSpace Card Selector*. We next consider these options in greater detail.

1. **Prior to selector invocation.** IDSpace could allow the user to choose the ID management system in one of the following ways.
   - IDSpace could embed a descriptive icon (logo, image, link or button) in the web page for each available system, and require the user to select one (e.g. by clicking the selected icon). Whilst this approach is intuitive and transparent, it could damage the appearance of the page, particularly if there are many logos to embed.
   - IDSpace could ask the user which system they wish to use by embedding forms in the page or by triggering pop-up boxes. The benefits of such an approach would include accuracy and higher performance, at the cost of minor user convenience.
   - IDSpace could add an ID management system selection option to the in-page context menu (i.e. the menu that appears as a result of right-clicking). Once such an option is selected, a list of ID management systems would be displayed, allowing the user to select one. Whilst this might be transparent, it might not be so intuitive to end users.
   - IDSpace could extend the browser frame[4], e.g. by adding a browser icon, bar or menu. Once the added icon (or bar or menu) has been selected, the user could choose one of the systems currently supported by the SP. Whilst this may be transparent, modifying the browser frame could be somewhat intrusive to the end user.

2. **After selector invocation.** The IDSpace Card Selector could display the currently supported ID management systems, allowing the user to select one. This choice could be combined with a display of the available cCards (if any) associated with each of the systems. In the latter case, the selector window could be partitioned so that each section displays an ID management system along with a previously used cCard for that system; a clickable option could be used to request the display of other available cCards. This approach would be transparent, convenient and would avoid making changes to web browsers or web pages. However, it would require more processing, and hence could adversely affect client platform performance.

---

[4] Both the browser frame and the browser-displayed web page could be extended. Browser extensions could, for example, create lightweight buttons, menu extensions, and in-process browser helper objects. The browser frame could be extended using band objects, and the web page content could be enhanced with, for example, ActiveX Controls or similar technologies [18].

4.3   Card Selector Invocation

In response to a user action, IDSpace must be able to invoke the IDSpace card selector. This involves embedding IDSpace support in the SP web page using a browser extension (see above).

4.4   IdP Discovery

IDSpace must help the user discover an IdP from which the user can obtain a suitable identity token. This process varies considerably depending on the ID management system in use. Specific approaches must therefore be devised for each supported system. The primary goal of the architecture is to allow this to take place in a way that is both as user-transparent as possible and gives a view of the process to the user that is consistent across ID management systems.

4.5   cCard Storage

The format of cCards must be sufficiently flexible and self-contained in order to allow cCard storage in a variety of locations, and to support portability. We assume that cCards will be protected while stored (where, as stated previously, the nature of this protection will be implementation-dependent).

cCards could be stored on various media, including:

- local file systems, which would give good performance and allow fast retrieval;
- remote web servers ('the cloud'), which would give a roaming capability;
- portable user devices such as mobile phones or smart cards, which would also provide a roaming capability.

4.6   cCard Format

Each cCard will contain an identifier indicating the ID management system with which it can be used (in principle a cCard could have many such identifiers). We suppose here that cCards are encoded using XML (as is the case for CardSpace InfoCards). A single XML schema could be devised encompassing all supported ID management systems. This would have the advantage that the identity system identifier (discussed immediately above) could form part of the encoding of a cCard. Other methods of encoding could also be used, such as JSON (http://www.json.org/).

4.7   cCard Content

The content of a cCard will vary depending on the ID management system with which it is to be used. However, the types of content listed below are likely to be contained in almost all cCards.

1. **A list of supported attribute types**, e.g. age, password, first name, last name, the values of which are known by the IdP, and for which the IdP will be prepared to generate an identity token. The actual claim values are not stored by the Card Selector; they are either stored by the remote IdP or by the LIP. The LIP will store the values in the protected Credential Store. Protection could, for example, involve implementing the Credential Store on a separate device such as a smart card, or using a Trusted Platform Module (TPM) [19] to provide encrypted storage.

2. **A list of supported token type(s)**, indicating which type(s) of identity token (e.g. SAML, username-password) the IdP(s) associated with the card are capable of issuing.

3. **IdP location**, including the URI/URL address(es) of the (remote or local) IdP(s).

4. **IdP authentication method(s)**, specifying the method(s) employed by the IdP to authenticate the user.

5. **Display information**, e.g. an image and or a name for the cCard.

4.8   Process Isolation

Where possible, the IDSpace processes should be isolated from other processes to maximise the security and privacy of data handled by IDSpace. For example, on a Windows platform the IDSpace Card Selector could be invoked in a private desktop session.

4.9   Authentication Methods

The IDSpace architecture allows the user to be authenticated to an IdP using a wide range of different authentication methods. The ease with which additional methods can be supported depends on precisely how user authentication to a remote IdP is supported by IDSpace. We consider three main possibilities.

1. IDSpace could control all communications between the user and the remote IdP. That is, all requests for authenticating information by the IdP could be made to the user by IDSpace (specifically by the *IdP Auth* component, as described in section 2), and the supplied information could then be forwarded by IDSpace to the remote IdP. Adding a new authentication method would require adding functionality to the implementation of IDSpace executing on the user platform. This is the approach adopted by CardSpace, currently deployed versions of which support four authentication methods.

   New user authentication techniques could be added in a modular fashion, as and when they are required. Whilst this would clearly add to the cost of deploying and maintaining an IDSpace implementation, for a widely deployed system this does not seem such an unreasonable approach (given that the number of authentication methods seems unlikely to grow very rapidly). Such an approach would have the advantage of user transparency and would enable the provision of a consistent user interface for the authentication process, and is hence the preferred option.

2. IDSpace could cause the task of user authentication to be performed at the IdP rather than via the IDSpace User Interface (i.e. using the IdP Auth component). That is, whenever a remote IdP requires user authentication (e.g. prior to issuing an identity token), IDSpace would redirect the UA (web browser) to the IdP, allowing the IdP to directly authenticate the user using a method of the IdP's choice. Although such a simple approach would minimise the maintenance cost for IDSpace, the user would lose the consistent experience provided by the IDSpace User Interface.

3. IDSpace could employ a hybrid approach. The default would be the first approach outlined above. IDSpace could support a set of widely-adopted (possibly standardised) authentication methods; new methods could be added as and when it is deemed appropriate. However, if an IdP wishes to use a technique not supported by IDSpace, then IDSpace could redirect the UA (web browser) to the IdP for 'direct' authentication.

5   IDSpace Operation

5.1   Initialisation

Prior to use of IDSpace, the following preparatory steps must be performed.

- The IDSpace components, including the browser extension and the client software, must be installed on the user platform.
- The user must install cCards in the cCard Store on the user platform. As noted above, these cCards can be created by either a local or a remote IdP. We briefly consider the two cases.
  - Local cCards are created using the LIP. Once it has created a cCard, the LIP will insert it in the cCard Store, and the corresponding user data will be added to the Credential Store. A user could also choose to create a local cCard during use of IDSpace.
  - Remote cCards are created by remote IdPs. Typically the creation of such a cCard will occur via an 'out of band' process, i.e. a process completely independent of the operation of IDSpace, perhaps involving the user completing a registration process using the IdP website. The resulting cCard will be provided to the user, and the user can then arrange for it to be imported into IDSpace using the IDSpace User Interface.
- For ease of identification, the user can personalise a cCard, e.g. by giving the card a meaningful name, and/or uploading an image representing the card to be displayed by the User Interface.

5.2   Protocol Flows

We now describe the operation of IDSpace. It is important to note that some parts of the operation of IDSpace will vary depending on the specific ID management system in use. The operation of IDSpace in the case of two widely discussed ID management systems is described in the next section.

1. UA → SP: HTTP/S GET Request. A user employs the UA to navigate to an SP login page.
2. SP → UA: HTTP/S Response. A login page is returned to the UA.
3. IDSpace Browser Extension→ UA: Page Processing. Certain IDSpace browser extension modules (as described below) perform the following processes on the login page provided by the SP.

    (a) Page Scanner → UA: Page Scanning. The Page Scanner module scans the login page to discover which ID management system(s) are supported by the SP (from amongst those supported by IDSpace). It passes the identifiers of the supported systems to the Identity System Selector. If no ID management system is identified, the Page Scanner could embed an icon in the browser frame to allow the user to inform IDSpace if there is an SP-supported ID management system available that has been missed.

    (b) Identity System Selector → UA. The Identity System Selector module uses the results passed to it by the Page Scanner. If more than one ID management system is discovered, then (depending on the implementation) the Selector could ask the user to select one. Alternatively, the decision could be deferred and made using the *IDSpace Card Selector*. The advantages and disadvantages of the two approaches are discussed in section 4.2. A further alternative approach would involve the user deciding at which stage to make a choice.

    The module might also offer to store any choices made by the user (in the *Settings Store*) for managing future authentication attempts. The module finally reports all the results to the *Data Transporter* module (see below).

    (c) Activator ⇌ UA: Card Selector Activation. The *Activator* module provides a means for the user to activate the IDSpace Card Selector. How this is achieved is implementation specific (options are discussed in sections 4.2 and 4.3). This involves embedding IDSpace-enabling tags and an IDSpace security policy in the login page. The embedded policy is subsequently used by the IDSpace User Interface to help it decide which cCards should be displayed for possible use.

4. User → UA: Card Selector Invocation. The user performs an action which invokes the IDSpace Card Selector. The precise way in which this occurs is implementation specific (options are discussed in section 4.2).
5. Data Transporter → IDSpace Kernel: Passing Metadata. The Data Transporter module passes the necessary metadata (e.g. the identified and/or selected identity system(s), the SP identity, the SP policy requirements, etc.) to the IDSpace Kernel.
6. IDSpace Kernel ⇌ Card Selector: SP Identity. The IDSpace Kernel examines the SP identity (as received from the Data Transporter module in the previous step), including noting whether or not the SP uses HTTPS and whether or not the user has visited this particular SP before. The IDSpace Kernel uses the IDSpace Card Selector to:

    (a) identify the SP to the user; and

(b) ask the user whether to continue or terminate the protocol.

Depending on the user answer, IDSpace either continues or terminates the protocol. To assist in user decision-making, the Card Selector could indicate key security-relevant features of the SP to the user, e.g. using visual cues. In particular, it could indicate whether or not the SP:
- uses HTTPS;
- possesses an extended evaluation certificate;
- has been visited before; and/or
- requires a large number of, or particularly sensitive, user attributes.

The Card Selector could also offer the user a recommendation as to whether or not to continue, based on user policy settings and the SP's security properties.

7. IDSpace Kernel $\rightleftharpoons$ IDSpace Components. The IDSpace Kernel evaluates the received metadata in order to learn which actions to take. If the user has already chosen an ID management system, then the following processes take place.

(a) IDSpace Kernel $\rightleftharpoons$ cCard Store: cCards Retrieval. The IDSpace Kernel retrieves the appropriate cCards (possibly none) by comparing the received metadata with the available cards. Note that the retrieved cards are specific to the user-selected ID management system.

(b) IDSpace Kernel $\rightarrow$ Selector: Displaying cCards. The IDSpace Kernel passes the retrieved cCards to the Card Selector so that they can be displayed to the user. cCards previously used with this SP (if any) could be displayed more prominently than the others.

If the user has not yet chosen an ID management system, then the following processes take place.

(a) IDSpace Kernel $\rightleftharpoons$ cCard Store: cCard Retrieval. The IDSpace Kernel retrieves the appropriate cCard(s) by comparing the received metadata with the available cards. Note that cards will be retrieved for all the SP-supported ID management systems.

(b) IDSpace Kernel $\rightarrow$ Card Selector: Displaying SP-supported ID Management Systems + cCards. The Kernel passes the SP-supported ID management systems, along with the matching cCards (if any), to the Card Selector to be displayed to the user. The Card Selector displays the list of supported ID management systems, together with the available cCards, indicating which cards have been used previously with this SP (it could also indicate which ID management systems have been previously used with this SP).

Depending on the implementation and the number of systems and cards to be displayed, the Card Selector might only display the cards previously used. In such a case it would need to indicate that other cards are also available, and would need to provide a means to retrieve them.

In both cases, the Card Selector should also allow the user to create a new local cCard (if the relevant ID management system supports such cards).

8. User $\rightarrow$ Card Selector: Selecting/Creating cCards. The user selects (or creates) a cCard.

9. Card Selector → IDSpace Kernel: User Action Results. The Card Selector reports the results of the user actions back to the IDSpace Kernel.

10. IDSpace Kernel ⇌ IDSpace Components. The IDSpace Kernel evaluates the results received from the Card Selector, and takes the appropriate steps.

If the user has chosen to select an existing cCard, then the following processes take place.

(a) The IDSpace Kernel determines whether an IdP (local or remote) needs to be contacted. If not, control is passed to step 13. If so, the protocol continues.

(b) The IDSpace Kernel determines the IdP (local or remote) that must be contacted in order to enable the user to obtain the identity token required by the SP. This also includes determining the nature of the information regarding the user (e.g. login credentials) that must be supplied to this IdP.

(c) IDSpace Kernel ⇌ Card Selector: Display IdP Identity. If this IdP has not previously been used, or if it does not use HTTPS, the IDSpace Kernel uses the Card Selector to obtain user consent before sending the IdP any information. This step is designed to mitigate the risks of phishing attacks. In such a case the Card Selector reports the user response back to the Kernel.

(d) If user consent has been obtained, the Kernel now passes a token request to the IdP. The token request may have been received from the SP, or, if necessary, the IDSpace Kernel creates the request.

If the user has chosen to create a local cCard, the following processes take place.

(a) IDSpace Kernel ⇌ Selector GUI. The Kernel invokes a special Card Selector window to allow the user to enter the necessary data. This would typically include allowing the user to personalise the cCard, e.g. uploading a card image, entering a card name, etc. Such steps would enable the card to be readily recognisable.

(b) IDSpace Kernel ⇌ Card Creation Module (in the LIP): Card Creation. The Kernel instructs the Card Creation module to create an XML-based cCard using the user-inserted data. The Card Creation module returns the newly-created card to the Kernel.

(c) IDSpace Kernel ⇌ cCard Storage Module: Card Storage. The Kernel sends the cCard to the Card Storage module for permanent storage; the Card Storage module reports back to the Kernel whether or not the operation has been successful.

(d) IDSpace Kernel ⇌ Card Selector. The Kernel treats the newly-created cCard as a user-selected cCard and step 10a repeats.

11. IDSpace Kernel ⇌ IdP. One of the following processes takes place, depending on whether the selected IdP is local or remote.

– If a remote IdP is selected, and if such information is required by the IdP (and is not already stored by IDSpace) then the IDSpace Kernel prompts the user to enter the relevant IdP credentials using a special credential screen. If this fails, e.g. if the Kernel does not support the IdP authentication method, or if the user-selected ID management system dictates that the UA must be redirected to the IdP, then the Kernel redirects the UA (web browser) to the remote IdP along with an authentication request. In the latter case the IdP can authenticate the user directly using an authentication method of its choice.

If user authentication is successful, the IdP issues an identity token.

– If a local IdP is selected, then the Kernel constructs a token request and sends it to the LIP. The LIP responds with an appropriate identity token.

12. Token Displayer Module $\rightleftharpoons$ User. If an ID management system other than CardSpace is in use, then the Token Displayer module intercepts, analyses, and displays information about the identity token before releasing it to the SP, and seeks user consent for release. If consent is denied, then the protocol is terminated. Note that this assumes that the token is not end-to-end encrypted to the SP and that it is not sent via a direct IdP-SP channel.

If CardSpace is in use, then the CardSpace IdP will send back a display token along with the real token, which the Kernel can instruct the Card Selector to display to the user, prior to obtaining user consent.

13. IDSpace Kernel $\rightarrow$ UA $\rightarrow$ SP: Passing Identity Token. The identity token is passed to the UA, which forwards it to the SP.

14. SP $\rightarrow$ User: Grant/Deny Access. The SP validates the token, and, if satisfied, grants access to the user.

6   Mapping Specific Protocol Architectures onto IDSpace

ID management systems can be classified according to how the SP communicates via the client with the IdP. There are two main ways in which this can be achieved, namely by using an HTTP redirect or involving an active client.

1. **Redirect-Based Systems.** In such a scheme, the UA is redirected by an SP to an IdP (and vice versa). In such a case the UA is essentially passive, and does not need to be aware of the ID management system in use. One major disadvantage is that a malicious SP can redirect the UA to a malicious IdP impersonating an expected IdP (e.g. to fraudulently obtain user credentials). Example systems of this type include OpenID, Liberty (browser-post profile), Shibboleth, and Facebook Connect.

2. **Active Client-Based Systems.** In schemes of this type, the UA must incorporate an 'active client', which acts as an intermediary between SPs and IdPs, and which must be aware of the ID management system in use. Typically all communications between an SP and an IdP occur via this active client, and there is no need for direct SP-IdP communication. Depending on the details of the system in use, the active client can prompt the user to select a digital identity, choose an IdP, review (and perhaps modify) an identity token created by the IdP, and approve a transaction. Phishing attacks

are mitigated since an SP cannot redirect the UA to an IdP of its choosing. The active client can also provide a consistent user experience, and its existence helps to give the user a greater degree of control. Examples include CardSpace and Liberty (when using a Liberty-enabled client (LEC)).

We now describe how two specific examples of ID management systems can be mapped onto the IDSpace architecture. We consider OpenID [7, 8] and Liberty (using a LEC) [20] since they are widely discussed examples of the above two models. We also briefly look at CardSpace support. These descriptions are intended as examples; this is not the only way in which the systems concerned could be supported using IDSpace.

6.1   IDSpace and OpenID

cCards. Either prior to, or during, use of IDSpace, the user must create an OpenID-specific cCard. This cCard must contain one required field, and may also contain one optional field, as follows.

1. The single **required field** must contain the user's OpenID.
2. The **optional field** contains the identifier of the user's OpenID IdP.

The cCard contains a unique, OpenID-specific identifier, and is stored in the secure cCard store, possibly in an OpenID-specific location (e.g. to allow faster look-up/retrieval).

Protocol. We now describe one way in which IDSpace could support OpenID. Steps 3b, 4–9, 10a–d (second series), 13 and 14 of the IDSpace-OpenID-specific protocol are the same as steps 3b, 4–9, 10a–d (second series), 13 and 14, respectively, of the generic IDSpace protocol given in section 5.2, and hence are not described here. Whenever prompted to select/create/import a cCard, it is assumed that the user will select/create/import an OpenID-specific cCard.

1. UA → SP: HTTP/S GET Request. A user navigates to an OpenID-enabled SP.
2. SP → UA: HTTP/S Response. A login page is returned containing an OpenID form.
3. IDSpace Browser Extension→ UA: Page Processing. The browser extension performs the following processes on the login page provided by the SP.
    (a) Page Scanner Module → UA: Page Scanning. The Page Scanner module searches the login page for an OpenID login form; such a form can be identified by searching for an input field named 'openid_url' and/or 'openid_identifier'. (The Page Scanner module also scans the page for triggers for any other ID management systems supported by IDSpace.) Finally, the module passes the search results to the Identity System Selection module.
    (c) Activator ⇌ UA: Selector Activation. The *Activator* module performs the following processes.

     i. It embeds IDSpace-enabling tags in the SP-provided login page, including a security policy statement in the format required by IDSpace. This policy statement must request OpenID-specific cCards.

    ii. It adds a special function to the SP-provided login page to intercept the identity token that will later be returned by the IDSpace Kernel.

   iii. It employs certain (implementation-dependent) means to enable the user to activate the IDSpace Card Selector (see sections 4.2 and 4.3); e.g. it might cause a special icon to appear above the submit button with the property that clicking this icon invokes the selector.

10. IDSpace Kernel $\rightleftharpoons$ IDSpace Components. The IDSpace Kernel evaluates the results (as provided by the Card Selector) in order to take appropriate actions. If the user has chosen to select an existing OpenID-specific cCard, then the following steps are performed.

(a) The IDSpace Kernel retrieves the cCard and passes it to the UA.

(b) The Browser Extension parses the received cCard, retrieving the value of the user's OpenID and (if present) the OpenID IdP.

(c) The Browser Extension temporarily stores the OpenID IdP value.

(d) The Browser Extension adds the user's OpenID identifier to the OpenID form, and submits the form back to the SP.

(e) The SP performs an IdP discovery process. Once the OpenID IdP has been discovered, the SP generates an OpenID authentication request and attempts to redirect the user's browser to the IdP.

(f) The Browser Extension intercepts the SP-initiated OpenID authentication request, and compares the value of the OpenID IdP in this request with the OpenID IdP value it stored in step 10c. If they match, the process continues (with redirection of the UA to the IdP). If not, the Browser Extension could either terminate or warn the user of a possible phishing threat and ask whether or not to continue.

(g) From this point on, OpenID operates as it would do in the absence of IDSpace, except for the final check in step 12 (see also the discussion below). In particular the user experience is OpenID-specific, and the user will see the OpenID IdP's authentication page.

11. OpenID IdP $\rightleftharpoons$ User. If necessary (authentication may be unnecessary if an IdP-user session already exists), the OpenID IdP authenticates the user. If successful, the OpenID IdP requests permission from the user to send the OpenID assertion token to the SP.

12. Token Displayer $\rightleftharpoons$ User. When the OpenID IdP attempts to redirect the UA back to the SP, the Token Displayer module intercepts, analyses, and displays the OpenID identity token to the user before releasing it to the SP. If user consent is obtained, then the protocol continues; otherwise it terminates. Note that this is possible since the OpenID token provided by the IdP is not encrypted.

The above example describes only a partial integration of OpenID with IDSpace. We believe it is possible to replace direct authentication of the user by the OpenID IdP with a process mediated by IDSpace (specifically using the *IdP*

Auth module). This would enhance the user experience by making the user authentication process consistent across different ID management systems. However, whilst the system described above has been successfully prototyped, the latter enhancement has not been implemented, and hence its practicality remains untested.

6.2   IDSpace and Liberty (LEC)

LECcards. Either prior to, or during, use of IDSpace, the user must create a Liberty-specific cCard. This cCard must contain one required field, and may also contain one or more optional fields, as follows.

1. The single **required field** must contain the identifier of the user's Liberty IdP.
2. The **optional field(s)**, could contain other alternative 'backup' Liberty IdPs.

The cCard contains a unique, LEC-specific identifier, and is stored in the secure cCard store, possibly in a Liberty (LEC)-specific location (e.g. to allow faster look-up/retrieval).

IdP Auth Functionality. The *IdP Auth* module is part of the client software. When supporting Liberty (LEC profile) its functionality includes the ability to handle token requests in Liberty format (received from Liberty SPs and sent to Liberty IdPs) and also the means to parse and process token messages received from a Liberty IdP. It makes use of the *Networker* module to communicate with the IdP and SP.

Protocol. We now describe one way in which IDSpace could act as a Liberty client.

Steps 3(b,c), 4–9, 10a–d (second series), 13 and 14 of the IDSpace-LEC-specific protocol are the same as steps 3(b,c), 4–9, 10a–d (second series), 13 and 14, respectively, of the generic IDSpace protocol given in section 5.2, and hence are not described here. Whenever prompted to select/create/import a cCard, it is assumed that the user will select/create/import a Liberty-specific cCard.

1. UA → SP: HTTP/S GET Request. A user navigates to a LEC-enabled SP.
2. SP → UA: HTTP/S Response. A login page is returned containing an option (e.g. a button, link, or image) to use Liberty (we use Liberty here and below to mean Liberty using the LEC profile).
3. IDSpace Browser Extension→ UA: Page Processing. The Browser Extension performs the following processes on the login page provided by the SP.
   (a) Page Scanner Module → UA: Page Scanning. The Page Scanner module searches the login page for a distinguishing feature that indicates support for Liberty. (The Page Scanner module also scans the page for triggers

for any other ID management systems currently supported by IDSpace.) Finally, the module passes the search results to the Identity System Selection module.

10. IDSpace Kernel $\rightleftharpoons$ IDSpace Components. The IDSpace Kernel evaluates the search results (as provided by the Card Selector) in order to take appropriate actions. If the user has chosen to select an existing Liberty-specific cCard, then the following steps are performed.

   (a) The IDSpace Kernel retrieves the cCard, and passes it to the *IdP Auth* module.

   (b) The IdP Auth module parses the received cCard, retrieving the values of the LEC IdP(s) and temporarily stores them.

   (c) IDSpace IdP Auth $\rightarrow$ SP: HTTP Request. The IdP Auth module issues an HTTP request to the SP containing a Liberty-enabled header (or with a Liberty-enabled entry in the *User-Agent* header).

   (d) SP $\rightarrow$ IdP Auth: HTTP Response + Authentication Request. The SP generates a Liberty authentication request and sends it to the IdP Auth module in the body of the HTTP response. The SP could choose to include a list of IdPs it knows about in the request.

   (e) The IdP Auth compares the received list of IdPs (if present) with the LEC IdP(s) retrieved from the selected cCard. If there is a non-empty intersection, then a cCard-specified IdP is contacted (this shall be the 'primary' IdP if possible); if not, then either the protocol terminates or the user could be asked to choose an IdP from amongst those in the SP list. The user could also be offered the choice to store the selected IdP (in the *Settings Store*) for future authentication attempts. If the SP does not specify a list of IdPs, then the cCard-associated IdP is contacted.

   (f) IdP Auth $\rightarrow$ IdP: Authentication Request. The IdP Auth module issues an HTTP POST to submit a SOAP-based [21] Liberty authentication request message to the appropriate IdP. Note that this request must contain the authentication request as received from the SP.

11. Liberty IdP $\rightleftharpoons$ User. If necessary, the IdP authenticates the user. Ideally this process would be mediated by the IDSpace system (using the *IdP Auth* module), in order to provide a user experience that is consistent across ID management systems. If successful, the IdP generates a SOAP-based, signed Liberty authentication response message and sends it to the IdP Auth module via an SSL/TLS channel.

12. Token Displayer $\rightleftharpoons$ User. If the token is not end-to-end encrypted, the Token Displayer module displays the token and requests user consent to proceed. If consent is granted, the protocol continues; otherwise it terminates.

6.3   IDSpace and CardSpace

During or prior to use of IDSpace, the user must create a CardSpace-specific cCard (using the LIP) and/or import a CardSpace-managed InfoCard. The IDSpace generic protocol given in section 5.2, excluding step 12, could then be used to provide the functionality of CardSpace [12, 13].

7 Concluding Remarks

We have described an architecture for a client-based, platform-independent, protocol-agnostic ID management tool that operates in conjunction with a client web browser. A tool conforming to the architecture provides a user-intuitive means of managing digital identities and credentials for all user web activities.

7.1 Relationship to the Prior Art

CardSpace and Higgins. The Microsoft CardSpace system shares certain features in common with IDSpace. In particular, it too is client-based and operates in conjunction with a web browser. However, CardSpace requires the IdPs and SPs to implement a specific set of protocols for inter-communication (we refer to these as the 'CardSpace protocols', although many are based on WS-* standards). Although CardSpace supports a wide range of security token formats, these tokens must be sent using a very specific protocol suite.

This gives rise to a classic 'chicken and egg problem' — without an established identity infrastructure of IdPs, there is no (or little) incentive for SPs to make the changes necessary to support CardSpace. Similarly, without any customer SPs, there is no (or little) incentive to set up a CardSpace-specific IdP infrastructure.

By contrast, IDSpace gives the convenience and intuitive user experience of CardSpace, without requiring SPs and IdPs to change the way they work. That is, IDSpace enables convenient and more secure operation by end users, without any changes to the existing identity infrastructures or service providers. Moreover, once deployed, IDSpace will enable much simpler deployment of more sophisticated systems such as the CardSpace protocols (and the many other systems currently emerging).

The Higgins system (which originated with the goal of providing CardSpace-like functionality on non-Windows platforms) has somewhat similar objectives to IDSpace.

Other Schemes. In previous work [22, 23] we have described how to build browser extensions which enable CardSpace/Higgins selectors to support password management without requiring any changes to the SPs or to the identity selector. Operational, open-source prototypes[5] have also been described. These prototypes demonstrate the workability of certain aspects of the IDSpace system.

7.2 Novel Features

The main novel feature of IDSpace, as intimated above, is the proposal of an architecture for a client-based system which supports multiple ID management systems transparently to SPs and IdPs. That is, it combines the convenience and intuitiveness of the CardSpace user interface with support for multiple systems,

---

[5] http://iescripts.org/view-scripts-808p1.htm and/or
http://sourceforge.net/projects/passcard/

without requiring any changes to existing SPs and IdPs. To our knowledge, the only previous work permitting client-based support for multiple ID management systems requires the SPs and IdPs to adopt new protocols.

The IDSpace architecture incorporates novel components, including the *Page Scanner*, *Activator*, *Identity System Selector* and *Token Displayer*, which are not found in the CardSpace or Higgins architectures. While much simpler versions of some of these novel components (notably the Page Scanner and Activator) have previously been described, [22–26], they have only been discussed in very specific contexts, and not in the general way in which they are used in IDSpace. Key elements of the architecture have been successfully prototyped.

7.3 Future Work

Our main initial goal is to complete an operational prototype of IDSpace, which we plan to make available for public scrutiny and testing. We intend that the initial version should support all the ID management systems discussed in this paper.

A variety of future directions for this research present themselves, a few of which we briefly mention.

- Apart from the ID management schemes mentioned previously, it would also be desirable if IDSpace could provide support for protocols providing a high degree of privacy protection for end users, notably U-Prove [27] and idemix [28]. This remains a topic of ongoing research.
- In previous work [25, 29], we have investigated using a client-based tool to support interoperation between different ID management systems, and a series of prototypes have been developed. It would be attractive (and straightforward) to build this functionality into an IDSpace implementation.
- Finally, in future work we intend to study variants of the architecture presented here to further enhance the security and privacy of user authorisation, whilst maintaining transparency to third parties.

References

1. Herley, C., van Oorschot, P.C., Patrick, A.S.: Passwords: If We're So Smart, Why Are We Still Using Them? In: Dingledine, R., Golle, P. (eds.) FC 2009. LNCS, vol. 5628, pp. 230–237. Springer, Heidelberg (2009)
2. Adams, C., Lloyd, S.: Understanding PKI: Concepts, Standards, and Deployment Considerations, 2nd edn. Addison-Wesley (2002)
3. Alrodhan, W.: Privacy and Practicality of Identity Management Systems: Academic Overview. VDM Verlag Dr. Müller GmbH, Germany (2011)
4. Bertino, E., Takahashi, K.: Identity Management: Concepts, Technologies, and Systems. Artech House Publishers, Norwood (2011)
5. Williamson, G., Yip, D., Sharoni, I., Spaulding, K.: Identity Management: A Primer. MC Press, Big Sandy (2009)

6. Windley, P.J.: Digital Identity. O'Reilly Media, Sebastopol (2005)
7. Recordon, D., Rae, L., Messina, C.: OpenID: The Definitive Guide. O'Reilly Media, Sebastopol (2010)
8. Surhone, L.M., Timpledon, M.T., Marseken, S.F. (eds.): OpenID: Authentication, Login, Service, Digital Identity, Password, User, Software System, List of OpenID Providers, Yadis, Shared Secret. Betascript Publishing (2010)
9. Surhone, L.M., Timpledon, M.T., Marsaken, S.F.: Security Assertion Markup Language: Security Domain, Single Sign-on, Identity Management, Access Control, OASIS, Liberty Alliance, SAML 1.1, SAML 2.0. Betascript Publishing (2010)
10. Internet2: Shibboleth Architecture — Technical Overview (2005)
11. Internet2: Shibboleth Architecture — Protocols and Profiles (2005)
12. Bertocci, V., Serack, G., Baker, C.: Understanding Windows CardSpace: An Introduction to the Concepts and Challenges of Digital Identities. Addison-Wesley, Reading (2008)
13. Mercuri, M.: Beginning Information Cards and CardSpace: From Novice to Professional. Apress, New York (2007)
14. IETF: Internet draft-ietf-oauth-v2-20: The OAuth 2.0 Authorization Protocol (2011)
15. Leach, J.: Improving user security behaviour. Computers & Security 22, 685–692 (2003)
16. OASIS: Identity Metasystem Interoperability Version 1.0, IMI 1.0 (2009)
17. Liberty Alliance Project: Liberty ID-FF protocols and schema specification (2005)
18. Crowley, M.: Pro Internet Explorer 8 & 9 Development: Developing Powerful Applications For The Next Generation Of IE. Apress, New York (2010)
19. Gallery, E.: An overview of trusted computing technology. In: Mitchell, C.J. (ed.) Trusted Computing, pp. 29–114. IEE Press, London (2005)
20. Liberty Alliance Project: Liberty ID-FF bindings and profiles specification (2004)
21. W3C: W3C Recommendation: SOAP Version 1.2 Part 1: Messaging Framework (2007)
22. Al-Sinani, H.S., Mitchell, C.J.: Implementing PassCard — a CardSpace-based password manager. Technical Report RHUL-MA-2010-15, Department of Mathematics, Royal Holloway, University of London (2010)
23. Al-Sinani, H.S., Mitchell, C.J.: Using CardSpace as a Password Manager. In: de Leeuw, E., Fischer-Hübner, S., Fritsch, L. (eds.) IDMAN 2010. IFIP AICT, vol. 343, pp. 18–30. Springer, Heidelberg (2010)
24. Al-Sinani, H.S.: Browser extension-based interoperation between OAuth and information card-based systems. Technical Report RHUL-MA-2011-15, Department of Mathematics, Royal Holloway, University of London (2011)
25. Al-Sinani, H.S., Mitchell, C.J.: Client-based CardSpace-Shibboleth interoperation. Technical Report RHUL-MA-2011-13, Department of Mathematics, Royal Holloway, University of London (2011)
26. Al-Sinani, H.S., Mitchell, C.J.: Client-based CardSpace-OpenID interoperation. In: Gelenbe, E., Lent, R., Sakellari, G. (eds.) Proceedings of ISCIS 2011 — the 26th International Symposium on Computer and Information Sciences, September 26-28. LNEE, pp. 387–394. Springer, London (2011), Full version available at: http://www.ma.rhul.ac.uk/techreports/2011/RHUL-MA-2011-12.pdf
27. Brands, S.A.: Rethinking Public Key Infrastructures and Digital Certificates: Building in Privacy. MIT Press, Cambridge (2000)

28. Camenisch, J., Van Herreweghen, E.: Design and implementation of the idemix anonymous credential system. In: Atluri, V. (ed.) Proceedings of the 9th ACM Conference on Computer and Communications Security, CCS 2002, Washington, DC, USA, November 18-22, pp. 21–30. ACM, New York (2002)
29. Al-Sinani, H.S., Alrodhan, W.A., Mitchell, C.J.: CardSpace-Liberty integration for CardSpace users. In: Klingenstein, K., Ellison, C.M. (eds.) Proceedings of the 9th Symposium on Identity and Trust on the Internet, IDtrust 2010, Gaithersburg, Maryland, USA, April 13-15, pp. 12–25. ACM, New York (2010)

Design and Evaluation of a Privacy-Preserving Architecture for Vehicle-to-Grid Interaction

Mark Stegelmann[1] and Dogan Kesdogan[1,2]

[1] Centre for Quantifiable Quality of Service in Communication Systems*,
Norwegian University of Science and Technology, Trondheim, Norway
mark.stegelmann@q2s.ntnu.no

[2] Research Group for IT Security, FB5, University of Siegen, 57068 Siegen, Germany
kesdogan@uni-siegen.de

Abstract. Charging battery-electric vehicles can pose a significant load to the power grid. Letting a central instance control vehicle charging processes can reduce the grid load and allows for vehicles to be used as distributed grid resources. It is commonly assumed that vehicle owners are willing to reveal their driving patterns to the control instance. As we show, current privacy-preserving technologies can be used to construct an architecture that reduces the need to reveal such sensitive information. Yet, we identify limitations to such an approach and demonstrate how an adversary can use information inherent to the context to decrease vehicle owner privacy. As a concrete case, we discuss an adversary algorithm based on travel times and show how to obtain anonymity sets for individual vehicles. This allows us to make an important step towards understanding and quantifying privacy achievable in practice.

Keywords: vehicle-to-grid interaction, privacy-preserving architecture, privacy-enhancing technologies, quantification of privacy.

1 Introduction

In recent years, battery-electric vehicles have gained attention due to some of the benefits they offer. They can, for instance, be recharged using any energy source that feeds the power grid. However, recharging a large number of electric vehicles can pose a significant load for the grid. To address this issue, a central control instance could be allowed to communicate with the vehicles and to control their charging processes. Furthermore, energy could be allowed to flow back, i.e., from vehicles to the grid, in a controlled way such that connected vehicles could form a distributed grid resource [1]. The operators of vehicle charging stations could manage the charging processes for their respective charging stations. As so-called aggregators, they could then sell services that help grid operators with balancing

---

* "Centre for Quantifiable Quality of Service in Communication Systems, Centre of Excellence" appointed by The Research Council of Norway, funded by the Research Council, NTNU and UNINETT. http://www.q2s.ntnu.no

S. Petkova-Kikova, A. Pashalidis, G. Pernul (Eds.): EuroPKI 2011, LNCS 7163, pp. 75–90, 2012.

out energy supply and demand [1–4]. Vehicle owners, in turn, could be payed for providing their vehicle as a resource.

The communication between aggregators and electric-drive vehicles is central for such an approach. An aggregator that would like to be able to offer services to a grid operator needs to know about what types of vehicles are available at which locations at what times. It is commonly assumed that vehicle owners will be willing to communicate such information to aggregators [1, 2, 5, 6]. However, vehicle owners put their privacy at risk by doing so [7, 8]. Regularly parking, e.g., in the vicinity of a rehabilitation clinic or at a defence lawyer's office can reveal sensitive details, e.g., about a person's financial status, habits, social network, or health situation. Without such a system, such information would not be collected and be readily available to aggregators. Anonymising vehicle-to-grid (V2G) interactions and data using existing privacy-enhancing technologies might be a solution. However, we show that this is non-trivial in this context and that further research is needed in order to find a balance between anonymity, the possibility to plan V2G interaction, and accountability for malicious behaviour.

In this work, we discuss how current privacy-preserving technologies can be used to construct a privacy-preserving architecture that aims at addressing these requirements and reduces the need to reveal sensitive information. Yet, we also show how curious aggregators can still exploit information inherent to the context to decrease vehicle owner anonymity. As a concrete example, we present an adversary algorithm that is based on vehicle travel times. It allows aggregators observing connection and disconnection events at their charging stations to relate such events based on the fact that vehicles need a certain time to travel between two such stations. We investigate how to obtain individual vehicle anonymity sets and make an important step towards both understanding and quantifying the privacy achievable in such practical scenarios.

The remainder of this work is structured as follows. In Sect. 2, we introduce the reader to the V2G concepts relevant for this work and discuss a general model for V2G interaction. Thereafter, we elaborate in Sect. 3 on the interests of the concerned parties and the according key security and privacy requirements. After describing work related to this work's focus in Sect. 4, we discuss in Sect. 5 the design of an architecture addressing the identified requirements based on current privacy-preserving technologies. In Sect 6, we discuss how to evaluate privacy in this context and provide an adversary algorithm and necessary optimisations to determine individual vehicle anonymity sets. We conclude in Sect. 7 by summarising our contributions and by pointing out future research directions.

2   Background and Model

As depicted in Fig. 1, V2G interaction concerns four parties: a grid operator, an energy service provider, an aggregator, and a vehicle owner. First and foremost, a vehicle owner connects his vehicle to the power grid via a charging station. A set of such charging stations is geographically dispersed across a city and operated by an aggregator. The aggregator takes the role of a middleman. On the one hand, he buys energy from energy service providers and resells it to the vehicle owner. On the other hand, the aggregator sells ancillary services to the grid operator [3, 9]. The latter can use these ancillary services when balancing energy supply and demand in the grid during the course of a day.

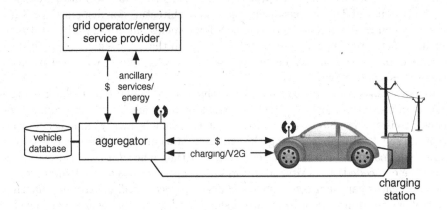

Fig. 1. V2G interaction model including communication paths

Different V2G interaction models are used in the literature. Depending on the respective work's focus, a model can additionally include parties such as a battery supplier and a parking facility [2], or omit, e.g., an explicit energy service provider [6]. We choose to keep the model simple, yet, to include the logical entities and service exchanges needed for V2G interactions. Another key aspect, where V2G interaction models differ is the assumed communication infrastructure between the aggregator and vehicles. Two distinct approaches can be identified. As shown in Fig. 1, in the first, communication is routed through an infrastructure provided by the aggregator (e.g., through the charging station). This is depicted by the solid line leading from the aggregator through the charging station to the vehicle. In this model, the communication channel to the charging station's vicinity can be chosen by the aggregator based on, e.g., availability, performance and, cost factors at the respective location. The local communication to vehicles is then realised using a short-range communication standard such as Bluetooth, power line communication (PLC), ZigBee, or a member of the IEEE 802.11 standards family. In the second approach, communication is *not* routed through the aggregator's infrastructure. Instead, the vehicle uses long-range wireless communication such as a cellular network or an Internet connection over a cellular connection to contact the aggregator (see, e.g., [6, 9]). If an additional communication path between the charging station and the vehicle is necessary depends on if intelligence is placed in the charging station.

As mentioned before, communication is of key importance for V2G interaction. When connecting to a charging station, a vehicle reveals different information to an aggregator. Guille and Gross, which assume an aggregator-provided infrastructure, propose a unique alphanumeric identifier for each vehicle, a binary charging connection status, the vehicle owner's charging preferences/constraints, the battery's current State of Charge (SoC), and signed power flow measurements [2]. Kempton and Tomić consider the second architecture for dispersed V2G interactions and list unique identifiers both for vehicles and for charging stations, certified meter readings, an electronic verification that the vehicle is plugged in a connection of known kW capacity, and electronic "offer" and "acceptance" messages for spot power contracts [9].

In both cases, the aggregator can use the vehicle's identifier to look up the vehicle in his database. There, he keeps track on a vehicle's configuration, movement profiles, the charging preferences of the vehicle owner, and accounting information. Furthermore, using the charging station's identifier he can determine the location of the V2G interaction and thus where in the grid energy is available or needed [10]. After all information has been exchanged successfully, the aggregator can plan the vehicle's charging process and control its charging controller by sending according control signals. When a vehicle leaves, it disconnects from the charging station and the aggregator updates the vehicle owner's account balance in his database. To be able to check their account's balance and to update their preferences in the aggregator's database, vehicle owners can be offered a user interface such as, e.g., a web page [6].

The information revealed in the models used in the literature allows aggregators to uniquely identify individual vehicle owners, e.g., for billing purposes [2, 6]. Furthermore, aggregators are given the ability to link distinct V2G interactions. This allows them to build detailed movement profiles even if such profiles are not explicitly communicated. The aspect of vehicle owner privacy is not considered in these models and vehicle owners need to trust aggregators both to not abuse the information known to them and to keep it confidential from third parties.

3 Requirements Analysis

Let us now investigate what steps are necessary to reduce the level of trust needed towards the aggregator and what is necessary to preserve the vehicle owners' privacy while retaining the security interests of the concerned parties.

The aggregators would like to resell energy to the vehicles and to control V2G interactions so that they can offer ancillary services to grid operators. To minimise their risk of being unable to perform according to contracts made with the grid operator, they need to know about resource, respectively vehicle, availability. In other words, they need to know, in advance, both about about a vehicle's availability as a resource as well as respective usage constraints. Thus, they are interested in information about what types of vehicles are available at which locations at what times and which V2G interactions are permissible.

Vehicle owners would like to have their vehicle charged according to their driving needs, to get payed for providing their vehicle as a resource, and to preserve their privacy. For both parties it holds that they would like to receive payments for provided services and services for 'made payments. This applies both to providing energy and to offering a vehicle as a resource.

Let us discuss the aspect of privacy, the main focus of this work, in more detail. For this we consider a strong adversary namely we assume that all aggregators collude with each other and pool their knowledge. They act honest but curious. In other words, they do not deviate from any protocols, but try to analyse the information that they can observe at the charging stations. They are interested in learning about the past, present, and future locations of individual vehicle owners. This passive adversary behaviour minimises the aggregators' risk of their actions being detected. During the operation of their charging stations, aggregators observe and record all information that they legitimately learn during V2G interactions. They then analyse this information and try to identify individual vehicle owners for V2G interactions.

They can trivially do so if unique identifiers linked to individual vehicle owners as those discussed in Sect. 2 are used. Consequently, anonymous or respectively pseudonymous service usage needs to be possible. However, even if pseudonyms are used, if they are fixed, V2G interactions are linkable and movement profiles can be created. It is likely that over time in such profiles home and work locations will appear with a higher frequency than other locations and thus become identifiable. In [11], Golle and Partridge show that an individual's pair of home and working location can reveal a person's identity with high probability. Therefore, we require distinct V2G interactions to be unlinkable to prevent the anonymity from being removed over time. This concerns not only unlinkability on the application-layer but also on lower communication layers.

However, the prospect of anonymity must not encourage misbehaviour and prevent the other security requirements from being addressed. Neither aggregators nor a vehicle owner should be able to gain an unfair advantage in a service for payment exchange. That is to say, providing a service must imply matching payments and if no service is rendered no payment must be implied. We can distinguish two service types for which this must hold: charging services, i.e., charging a vehicle, and V2G services, i.e., providing a vehicle as a resource.

Note that correct billing also depends on the quality of rendered services. As we discussed in Sect. 2, vehicles communicate information to aggregators that regards service quality. It is therefore necessary to ensure the integrity of claimed properties that influence the assessment of a service's quality. They should be verifiable by the party receiving the service. If integrity violations can not be prevented or mitigated as such, but only be detected after the fact, then accountability should be established. For the latter, it is necessary to ensure both the integrity of claimed identities and the non-repudiation of messages sent. Furthermore, the integrity of messages needs to be guaranteed.

Last but not least, we require that the content of messages is kept confidential from all parties except the respective senders and the intended recipients. All adversaries are assumed to be computationally bounded and unable to break cryptographic primitives based on computationally hard problems.

4   Related Work

The issue of smart grid privacy is actively being researched in the area of smart metering. Here, fine-grained meter readings passed to energy providers for billing purposes can reveal the use of individual devices [7, 12]. Moreover, such readings can make it possible to learn, e.g., about the number of persons present in a house, their activities and habits, and the devices that they own or use. In V2G interaction, every service use implies the use of an individual device and as we will show additional privacy issues arise due to the linkability of different service instances and their associated location information.

The importance of securing grid communication in the context of V2G interactions is acknowledged in [13]. However, the work's focus lies on encryption standards commonly used in combination with different communication standards. In [5], a cryptographic protocol for V2G interaction is put forward. The protocol's focus is authentication. Both works assume a benevolent aggregator and do not consider the issue of vehicle owner privacy.

International standardisation efforts both by the International Electrotechnical Commission (IEC) and the International Organization for Standardization (ISO) exist in the area of electrically propelled vehicles [14]. For security, IEC TC57 WG15 develops data and communications security standards for power industry communication protocols that are published in the IEC 62351 series. IEC/ISO JWG V2G focuses on V2G communication and is expected to publish their results in late 2011. A commonality of these standardisation efforts is their provider focus and that they do not evaluate privacy issues. This is also mirrored by the fact that the short-range communication standards used do not prevent charging station operators from linking distinct communication instances based on network-layer identifiers.

Another related body of research investigates location privacy issues related to vehicles. In Vehicular Ad-hoc Networks (VANETs) vehicles reveal their locations regularly to nearby peers by broadcasting messages (e.g., to report traffic conditions). To prevent vehicles from being tracked over time, changing pseudonyms and so called vehicular mix zones are used [15–17]. Basic vehicular mix zones are street crossings where vehicles change their pseudonyms to confuse an adversary attempting to track them based on transmitted messages. Due to their intended application area, VANETs exhibit both differing requirements, communication architectures, and adversary models than those relevant for V2G interaction.

5   Privacy-Preserving Architecture

We will now sketch the steps necessary to address the requirements identified in Sect. 3. Figure 2 shows the structure of the according architecture for privacy-preserving V2G interaction. Both a vehicle connected to a charging station and the aggregator operating the station are depicted.

The first step we discuss is making V2G interactions anonymous and ensuring that different V2G interactions remain unlinkable. For this, no fixed identifiers

must be used for distinct V2G interactions. This concerns both identifiers revealed as part of a V2G application-layer protocol and any fixed network-layer
identifiers part of lower level communication protocols.

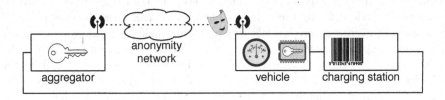

aggregator   vehicle   charging station

Fig. 2. Architecture for privacy-preserving V2G interaction

The standard technique to provide network-layer anonymity are low-latency
anonymity networks [18]. As described in Sect. 2, there exist two possible
communication paths between aggregators and vehicles. The bi-directional short-
range communication standards for communication between vehicle and an aggregator's infrastructure require the use of fixed network-layer identifiers and,
thus, allow aggregators to link distinct V2G communication instances. In the
second communication model, vehicles can contact the aggregator through an
anonymity network as depicted in Fig. 2 and hide their network-layer identifiers
from the aggregator. Remember from Sect. 2 that it is necessary for vehicles to
communicate with the aggregator's infrastructure to learn the charging station's
identifier. Reading an RFID tag in the charging station can realise this information exchange with the aggregator's infrastructure without the need to reveal
any vehicle identifiers.

Let us now investigate how to achieve fair service exchanges while preserving
anonymity. To establish accountability and the integrity and non-repudiation of
sent messages, digital signatures in combination with a public key infrastructure
(PKI) are the standard approach. Here, the role of certificate authority (CA)
can, e.g., be taken by a public authority. Aggregators need to register their
respective public key with the CA. An anonymous credential system, such as
Idemix, preserves the vehicle owner's anonymity, yet, achieves accountability by
supporting optional anonymity revocation [19]. Vehicle owners register with the
CA by establishing a pseudonym and proving that the used pseudonym was
generated using a matching master secret key. The master secret key can be
stored in a tamper-resistant cryptographic module in their respective vehicle.

Based on these cryptographic building blocks, the communication partners
can mutually authenticate each other for V2G interactions. While the aggregator
uses his public key, the vehicle uses a newly generated cryptographic pseudonym
for every connection. By using these cryptographically unlinkable pseudonyms,
the vehicle can stay anonymous and distinct V2G interactions unlinkable. During
communication, the parties encrypt messages using a shared secret key to keep
eavesdroppers from learning the content of exchanged messages.

As discussed in Sect. 3, for fair service exchanges, the integrity of claimed service qualities is of importance. Depending on the type of information revealed (see Sect. 2), different integrity protection mechanisms can be employed. The integrity of static vehicle attributes such as battery capacity can be ensured by having a trusted third party, e.g., the Ministry of Transport, issue according anonymous credentials to the vehicle. The vehicle can then demonstrate the possession of according credentials to aggregators using zero-knowledge proofs [20]. The integrity of physical connection measurements can be ensured by the use of a certified, tamper-resistant energy meter built into the vehicle. This meter provides vehicle owners with the possibility both to verify charging services that they paid for and to demonstrate the quality of provided V2G services to an aggregator. For billing of services itself, an anonymous electronic cash scheme can be used (see, e.g., [21]).

Based on the above-described building blocks, higher-level cryptographic protocols can be designed that satisfy both the anonymity and the fairness requirements. Note that a detailed specification of the architecture is ongoing work. For the main focus of this work, the privacy aspect of V2G interaction, the architecture sketched above provides a sufficient basis for an initial privacy evaluation.

6   Privacy Evaluation

After having discussed both how to achieve network-layer and application-layer anonymity and unlinkable interactions, let us now focus on evaluating anonymity and unlinkability. While anonymity means that an adversary cannot identify a subject within a set of subjects, the latter denotes the inability of an adversary to determine if two items of interest are related or not [22]. The basic metric providing a quantitive indicator of anonymity, the anonymity set size, is defined as the size of the set of subjects that a subject is not identifiable in.

Though the privacy-enhancing technologies described in Sect. 5 are theoretically secure, several factors inherent to the context can limit the provided unlinkability and anonymity. Firstly, the theoretical upper bound for the anonymity set size of the total number of vehicles is reduced by the information that is revealed on the application-layer. Static vehicle attributes, for instance, partition the anonymity set into subsets of vehicles with shared properties. Furthermore, other factors can limit the unlinkability of V2G instances. An aggregator can, e.g., use knowledge about a specific vehicle owner's habits and behaviour to improve his success with identifying vehicles and linking V2G instances. We will now show a concrete example of how the aggregator can exploit other constraints, such as physical ones, combined with information observed at charging stations, to improve his ability to link distinct V2G instances. More specifically, we will provide an adversary algorithm that exploits the fact that vehicles need a certain amount of time to travel from one location to another.

Adversary Formalisation. Let $V = \{v_1, \ldots, v_n\}$, $n > 1$ denote the vehicles in a city c and $L = \{l_1, \ldots, l_m\}$, $m \geq n$ denote the locations of the charging stations in c. The adversary divides time into a series of discrete steps and records his observations for each point in time. For the sake of simplicity, let us assume that at any time t, a vehicle $v_i \in V$ will either be driven through c or be parked at a location $l_j \in L$ but will never leave town. Let $pos_t(v_i) \in L \cup \{c\}$ be an oracle that returns the position of v_i for a point in time t. Furthermore, let $id_t(l_j) \in V \cup \{\epsilon\}$ denote an oracle returning the unique identity $v_i \in V$ of the vehicle parked at l_j at time t. If the charging station at l_j is not in use at time t then $id_t(l_j) = \epsilon$. Note that $pos_t(v_i) = l_j \rightarrow id_t(l_j) = v_i$ and vice versa for $l_j \neq c$ and $v_i \neq \epsilon$. Last but not least, the oracle $own(v_i) = \omega_z$ gives the unique identity $\omega_z \in \{\omega_1, \ldots, \omega_n\}$ of a vehicle's owner of a vehicle $v_i \in V$.

We can now formalise the aggregator's goals. First, he would like to determine the owner's identity of a vehicle parked at a location $l_j \in L$ at time t, meaning he wants to determine $own(id_t(l_j))$. The privacy-enhancing technologies used in Sect. 5 prevent this from being possible directly. Yet, as discussed before, there exists another way of learning a vehicle owner's identity. If an adversary can successfully link V2G instances, he can over time determine both a vehicle owner's home and his work location. This, in turn will reveal the latter's identity. In other words, the adversary can achieve his first goal by his second goal of linking distinct V2G instances. Here, he would like to know if $id_t(l_j) = id_{t'}(l_{j'})$ with $t \neq t'$ and $l_j, l_{j'} \in L$. Note that knowing the latter does neither imply knowing $id_t(l_j)$ nor knowing $id_{t'}(l_{j'})$. A vehicle identifier $v_i \in V$ is not of interest by itself to the aggregator. Instead, the aggregator is interested in recognising if a vehicle that is connected to the grid at a location l_j at time t is the same that is connected at location $l_{j'}$ at time t'. Since the aggregator can achieve both goals through the second one, we focus in the following on the latter goal.

Adversary Algorithm. Let us discuss aggregators that observe and analyse connect and disconnect events at their charging stations for a time frame $T = (t_0, \ldots, t_p)$. Formally, if and only if $pos_{t_{k-1}}(v_i) = c$ and $pos_{t_k}(v_i) = l_j$ with $l_j \in L$ then they observe a connect event at l_j. We denote such an event by $connect_{t_k}(l_j)$. Analogously, if and only if $pos_{t_{k-1}}(v_i) = l_j$ and $pos_{t_k}(v_i) = c$ with $l_j \in L$ then they observe a disconnect event at l_j, denoted by $disconnect_{t_k}(l_j)$. We denote the set of all connect and disconnect events observed by the aggregators during T by *events*. We assume that the aggregators have access to a function $dist(l_i, l_j)$ returning the expected travel times for tuples $(l_i, l_j) \in L \times L$ of charging station locations.[1] Furthermore, for simplicity, we assume that all vehicles are initially parked at charging locations at time t_0 meaning that for all $v_i \in V$ it holds that $pos(v_i) \in L$. In practice, the adversary could choose t_0 to be a point in time of low traffic (e.g., at night) to approximate this situation.

Let us now discuss, how the aggregators can improve their knowledge regarding their second goal. For this, they proceed as described by Algorithm 1. First, they create initial hypotheses sets for t_0 by assigning a unique identifier to each vehicle parked at their charging stations. In other words, they let $h_{t_0}(l_i) := \{v_i\}$ for all charging stations that are in use, meaning for all $l_i \in L$ with $id_{t_0}(l_i) \neq \epsilon$.

---

[1] They can, e.g., use a route planning software to determine such values.

For those not in use, they let $h_{t_0}(l_i) := \emptyset$. The city hypothesis set is initialised with the empty set. Then for each point in time $t_{i'}$ from t_1 to t_p, they check for each location if an event was observed.

Algorithm 1. Adversary relating events based on *dist*

Data: *events, dist*
Result: h
$h_{t_0}(c) := \emptyset;$ /* initially no vehicle in c */
foreach $l_i \in L$ **do**
    if $id_{t_0}(l_i) \neq \epsilon$ **then** $h_{t_0}(l_i) := \{v_i\};$ /* number all vehicles at t_0 */
    else $h_{t_0}(l_i) := \emptyset;$

for $t_{i'} \leftarrow t_1$ **to** t_p **do**   /* for every time step */
    $h_{t_{i'}}(c) := \emptyset;$ /* initialise c */
    foreach $l_{j'} \in L$ **do**   /* check for every location */
        if $connect_{t_{i'}}(l_{j'}) \in events$ **then**   /* if connect observed */
            /* then for prior disconnects with matching distance   */
            foreach $disconnect_{t_i}(l_j) \in events$ **with** $t_i = t_{i'} - dist(l_j, l_{j'})$ **do**
                $h_{t_{i'}}(l_{j'}) := h_{t_{i'}}(l_{j'}) \cup h_{t_{i-1}}(l_j);$ /* update hypothesis set */
                for $t_j \leftarrow t_i$ **to** $t_{i'-1}$ **do**
                    $h_{t_j}(c) := h_{t_j}(c) \cup h_{t_i}(l_j);$ /* in c between events */

        else if $disconnect_{t_{i'}}(l_{j'}) \in events$ **then** $h_{t_{i'}}(l_{j'}) := \emptyset;$
        else $h_{t_{i'}}(l_{j'}) := h_{t_{i'}}(l_{j'-1});$ /* if no event, no change */

If for a connect event at $t_{i'}$ at location $l_{j'}$ there exists a prior disconnect event at time t_i at location l_j with $dist(l_j, l_{j'}) = t_{i'} - t_i$ then they join the hypothesis set $h_{t_i}(l_j)$ to $h_{t_{i'}}(l_{j'})$. This means that one of the vehicles that was connected at l_j at time t_i has potentially moved on to $l_{j'}$. Between the two events, the aggregators expect the vehicles to have been in the city. Thus, they add them to the according hypotheses sets $h_{t_j}(c)$ for t_{i+1} to $t_{i'-1}$. If a disconnect event was observed then the hypothesis set for the location is equal to the empty set, since the vehicle has left the location. Last but not least, if no event was observed for the respective location, there is no change and thus the hypothesis set remains equal to that of the preceding point in time. As result, the algorithm returns the hypotheses set for each location for each point in time based on the time a vehicle needs to travel from one location to another. A vehicle's anonymity set size for a point in time t_i is therefore given by the number of hypotheses sets in which a vehicle is contained in for all elements of $l_j \in L \cup \{c\}$. Note that our use of *dist* corresponds to a worst case assumption for anonymity. In practice, a lower limit for the traveling time between two locations is given by physical limitations. Traffic conditions and detours can extend this time. Factors such as battery capacities, in turn, limit the range of vehicles. In the future, our model could be extended to consider such factors and probabilistic adversary knowledge. Yet, to limit complexity, we focus in this initial analysis on the deterministic case.

Let us now study the algorithm using a simple example and analyse how the adversary's knowledge can change. Connect and disconnect events can relate in different ways. The example shown in Tab. 1 describes how two vehicles v_1 and v_2 move between three charging station locations l_1, l_2, and l_3. In addition, the according hypotheses sets returned by the algorithm are given. The travel times between the locations are defined to be symmetrically with $dist(l_1, l_3) = 3$, $dist(l_1, l_2) = 6$, and $dist(l_2, l_3) = 9$.

Table 1. Example with events and adversary hypotheses sets

t	$pos_t(v_1)$	$pos_t(v_2)$	events for t	$h_t(l_1)$	$h_t(l_2)$	$h_t(l_3)$	$h_t(c)$
t_0	l_1	l_2	$\emptyset$	$\{v_1\}$	$\{v_2\}$	$\emptyset$	$\emptyset$
t_1	l_1	c	$disconnect_{t_1}(l_2)$	$\{v_1\}$	$\emptyset$	$\emptyset$	$\{v_2\}$
t_3	c	c	$disconnect_{t_3}(l_1)$	$\emptyset$	$\emptyset$	$\emptyset$	$\{v_1, v_2\}$
t_6	l_3	c	$connect_{t_6}(l_3)$	$\emptyset$	$\emptyset$	$\{v_1\}$	$\{v_2\}$
t_7	l_3	l_1	$connect_{t_7}(l_1)$	$\{v_2\}$	$\emptyset$	$\{v_1\}$	$\emptyset$
t_{10}	c	l_1	$disconnect_{t_{10}}(l_3)$	$\{v_2\}$	$\emptyset$	$\emptyset$	$\{v_1\}$
t_{13}	c	c	$disconnect_{t_{13}}(l_1)$	$\emptyset$	$\emptyset$	$\emptyset$	$\{v_1, v_2\}$
t_{16}	c	l_3	$connect_{t_{16}}(l_3)$	$\emptyset$	$\emptyset$	$\{v_2\}$	$\{v_1, v_2\}$
t_{19}	l_2	l_3	$connect_{t_{19}}(l_2)$	$\emptyset$	$\{v_1, v_2\}$	$\{v_2\}$	$\emptyset$

Figure 3 shows how the adversary knowledge develops. The vehicles interact in different ways influencing the aggregator's hypotheses sets accordingly. First, they behave in a way that excludes the possibility of confusing them. This can be because their disconnection events cannot match with each others prior connect events (see t_6 and t_7). If, however, either one of their connection events potentially matches with the other's disconnection event (see t_{19}) or there exists a match between both connection and disconnection events[2], the adversary algorithm cannot distinguish between the two vehicles.

Thus, certain conditions need to hold true for vehicles to be mixed with each other. This is also reflected by the anonymity set sizes. As described above, the hypotheses sets can be used to determine these set sizes for individual vehicles. Figure 4 gives both the number of vehicles in the city and the adversary's uncertainty about a vehicle's position. An important observation in these graphs is the difference in the two anonymity set sizes starting from t_{19}. While the anonymity set size for v_1 equals 1, for v_2 the anonymity set size is 2. The reason for this difference lies in the adversary's deductions from the observations. As shown in Fig. 3, at t_{16} respectively t_{19} the adversary observes a connection event at l_3 respectively l_2. For the first case, one matching disconnect event can be identified. For the latter, two possible matches exist.

In this example, the adversary can reduce the anonymity set for v_2 using logical deductions. Since there exists a one-to-one and onto mapping between parked vehicles and charging stations in use and there is only one possible location for

---

[2] Note that this case requires $m > 3$ and is thus not shown in Fig. 3.

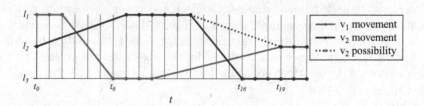

Fig. 3. Visualisation of vehicle movements and adversary knowledge

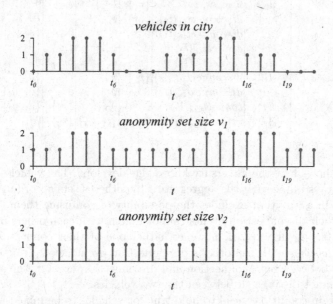

Fig. 4. Vehicles in city and anonymity set sizes for vehicles

v_1, v_2 cannot be at l_2. We will now investigate the general case of removing such spurious anonymity set entries in detail.

6.1   Optimisation

For every point in time $t \in T$, we can model the adversary's knowledge in form of a bipartite graph $G = (X, Y, E)$ with two sets of nodes containing vehicles and locations respectively and a set of edges describing possible relations between them. Based on the adversary's hypotheses sets, we can construct the graph as follows. Let the set X contain any vehicle $v \in V$ for which holds that $v \in h_t(l)$ for any $l \in L$. In other words, we choose X to contain all vehicles that the adversary suspects at any location. However, it does not contain those vehicles of which the adversary knows that they can only be in the city, meaning that $v \notin h_t(l)$ but $v \in h_t(c)$.

We then let set of nodes Y contain all locations $l \in L$ for which it holds that $h_t(l) \neq \emptyset$, meaning those locations of charging stations that are in use at time t. In addition, the set Y contains r additional nodes with r being equal to $|X| - |Y|$. These city nodes, which we denote by $c_1, \ldots, c_r$ intuitively can be understood as potential locations for those vehicles of X that could be in the city. We use them to make G a balanced bipartite graph with two node sets of an equal number of elements. In other words, for every vehicle there exists one location. This is an important property which we will exploit in our algorithm.

The edge set $E \subseteq X \times Y$ of G is then constructed in two steps. First, G contains an edge e between a $v \in X$ and a $l \in Y \cap L$ if and only if $v \in h_t(l)$. This means, every hypothesis of a vehicle being at a location is represented by an edge between the two respective nodes. In a second step, we add r edges for every $v \in X$ with $v \in h_t(c)$ from v to every $c_o \in \{c_1, \ldots, c_r\}$. These edges capture the hypotheses of vehicles being in the city. This completes the construction of our bipartite graph G that models the adversary's knowledge for t.[3]

Figure 5 depicts the example graph G modelling the adversary knowledge of the example from Sect. 6 for t_{19}. Here, the set of nodes X is equal to V and contains both v_1 and v_2, as both vehicles are suspected to be at a location. The respective locations, in turn, form the node set Y with the two nodes l_2 and l_3. The location l_1 is excluded from Y since it is not in use at t_{19} and its hypothesis set $h_t(l_1)$ is empty. As explained in Sect. 6, the adversary can logically deduce that the edge $\{v_1, l_2\}$ is spurious. We will now discuss which property of an edge in G is equivalent to this.

Aside from the explicitly excluded knowledge about which vehicles are in c at t, such a graph G captures the hypotheses sets of the adversary and describes the possible matchings of vehicles with locations. The graph possesses several properties in this context. For every point in time t, a vehicle is either parked at

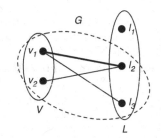

Fig. 5. Bipartite graph for t_{19} with the thick edge being spurious

---

[3] Note that G does not include vehicles that the adversary knows to be in the city. Though it is possible to add these vehicles, this is not needed for the removal of spurious entries and is therefore omitted here.

a location or driving through the city. Furthermore, charging stations can only be used by one vehicle at a time. Finally, due to our construction using city nodes, it holds that $|X| = |Y|$. Therefore, there exists a maximum matching between X and Y involving all nodes from X and Y that describes the true locations of the individual vehicles. However, due to the adversary's imperfect knowledge, G contains more than the solution describing the real situation.

Spurious edges, however, are not part of any solution. Thus, to eliminate the spurious entries, we can check for every edge $e \in E$ if it is part of a maximum matching for G that covers all nodes. To do this, for every e, we look at a subgraph $G' = (X, Y, E')$ of G. The edge set $E' \subseteq E$ contains every edge from E except those that connect to the same vehicle $v \in V$ as e. In other words, we check if there exists a solution if we would have to choose e as part of the solution. Thus, for G' we can now check if there still exists a maximum matching covering all nodes. Hopcroft and Karp's algorithm for finding maximum matchings in bipartite graphs constructs a maximum matching in $n^{5/2}$ steps [23]. Here n is equal to $|X|$. If the algorithm returns a maximum matching for all nodes, the edge is part of a maximum matching and is to be kept. If not, the edge is spurious and can be removed from G.

7   Conclusions

A common assumption in vehicle-to-grid communications is that vehicle owners trust aggregators and are willing to reveal their individual driving patterns to them. We discussed how current privacy-preserving technologies can be used to construct an architecture that reduces the need to reveal such sensitive information. Yet, we identified limitations to such an approach and demonstrated that an adversary can still use information inherent to the context to decrease vehicle owner privacy. As a concrete case, we showed how honest but curious aggregators can reduce the provided anonymity by using an adversary algorithm that aims at linking distinct vehicle-to-grid interaction instances based on vehicle travel times.

In the future, it would be interesting to extend our model to include further information and structures inherent to V2G scenarios such as battery management and information on a vehicle battery's SoC and how this can influence vehicle owner privacy. Furthermore, we intend to extend and particularise those architectural aspects on which we have not focused on in this work. In addition, an evaluation of the provided anonymity using real-world datasets could provide interesting insights. Simulation could be a first step if available datasets contain insufficient information.

Acknowledgements. We would like to thank Vinh Pham for participating in the discussions that led to this work.

References

1. Kempton, W., Letendre, S.E.: Electric vehicles as a new power source for electric utilities. Transportation Research Part D: Transport and Environment 2(3), 157–175 (1997)
2. Guille, C., Gross, G.: A conceptual framework for the vehicle-to-grid (V2G) implementation. Energy Policy 37(11), 4379–4390 (2009)
3. Tomic, J., Kempton, W.: Using fleets of electric-drive vehicles for grid support. Journal of Power Sources 168(2), 459–468 (2007)
4. Kempton, W., Tomic, J., Letendre, S., Brooks, A., Lipman, T.: Vehicle-to-grid power: Battery, hybrid, and fuel cell vehicles as resources for distributed electric power in california. Research Report UCD-ITS-RR-01-03, Institute of Transportation Studies, University of California (June 2001)
5. Guo, H., Yu, F., Wong, W.-C., Suhendra, V., Wu, Y.D.: Secure wireless communication platform for EV-to-Grid research. In: Helmy, A., Mueller, P., Zhang, Y. (eds.) IWCMC, pp. 21–25. ACM (2010)
6. Brooks, A.N.: Vehicle-to-Grid Demonstration Project: Grid Regulation Ancillary Service with a Battery Electric Vehicle. Technical Report 01, AC Propulsion, Inc. (2002)
7. Smart Grid Interoperability Panel - Cyber Security Working Group: Guidelines for Smart Grid Cyber Security: Vol. 2, Privacy and the Smart Grid. Technical Report NISTIR 7628, National Institute of Standards and Technology (August 2010)
8. Cavoukian, A., Polonetsky, J., Wolf, C.: SmartPrivacy for the Smart Grid: embedding privacy into the design of electricity conservation. Identity in the Information Society 3, 275–294 (2010), 10.1007/s12394-010-0046-y
9. Kempton, W., Tomic, J.: Vehicle-to-grid power implementation: From stabilizing the grid to supporting large-scale renewable energy. Journal of Power Sources 144(1), 280–294 (2005)
10. Sandels, C., Franke, U., Ingvar, N., Nordström, L., Hamrén, R.: Vehicle to Grid - Reference Architectures for the Control Markets in Sweden and Germany. In: Proceedings of the IEEE PES Conference on Innovative Smart Grid Technologies Europe. IEEE (October 2010)
11. Golle, P., Partridge, K.: On the Anonymity of Home/Work Location Pairs. In: Tokuda, H., Beigl, M., Friday, A., Brush, A.J.B., Tobe, Y. (eds.) Pervasive 2009. LNCS, vol. 5538, pp. 390–397. Springer, Heidelberg (2009)
12. McDaniel, P., McLaughlin, S.: Security and privacy challenges in the smart grid. IEEE Security and Privacy 7, 75–77 (2009)
13. Markel, T., Kuss, M., Denholm, P.: Communication and control of electric drive vehicles supporting renewables. In: IEEE Vehicle Power and Propulsion Conference, VPPC 2009, pp. 27–34. IEEE (September 2009)
14. den Bossche, P.V., Mulders, F.V., Mierlo, J.V., Timmermans, J.M.: The evolving standardization landscape for electrically propelled vehicles. The World Electric Vehicle Journal 2(4), 41–48 (2008)
15. Freudiger, J., Raya, M., Félegyházi, M., Papadimitratos, P., Hubaux, J.P.: Mix-Zones for Location Privacy in Vehicular Networks. In: ACM Workshop on Wireless Networking for Intelligent Transportation Systems (WiN-ITS). ACM, Vancouver (2007)
16. Papadimitratos, P., Buttyan, L., Holczer, T., Schoch, E., Freudiger, J., Raya, M., Ma, Z., Kargl, F., Kung, A., Hubaux, J.P.: Secure vehicular communication systems: design and architecture. IEEE Communications Magazine 46(11), 100–109 (2008)

17. Papadimitratos, P., Gligor, V., Hubaux, J.P.: Securing Vehicular Communications - Assumptions, Requirements, and Principles. In: Workshop on Embedded Security in Cars (ESCAR), pp. 5–14 (2006)
18. Dingledine, R., Mathewson, N., Syverson, P.: Tor: the second-generation onion router. In: Proceedings of the 13th Conference on USENIX Security Symposium, SSYM 2004, p. 21. USENIX Association, Berkeley (2004)
19. Security Team, IBM Research Zurich: Specification of the identity mixer cryptographic library. IBM Research Report 3730, IBM Research (April 2010)
20. Camenisch, J., Lysyanskaya, A.: An Efficient System for Non-transferable Anonymous Credentials with Optional Anonymity Revocation. In: Pfitzmann, B. (ed.) EUROCRYPT 2001. LNCS, vol. 2045, pp. 93–118. Springer, Heidelberg (2001)
21. Camenisch, J., Hohenberger, S., Lysyanskaya, A.: Compact E-Cash. In: Cramer, R. (ed.) EUROCRYPT 2005. LNCS, vol. 3494, pp. 302–321. Springer, Heidelberg (2005)
22. Pfitzmann, A., Hansen, M.: A terminology for talking about privacy by data minimization: Anonymity, unlinkability, undetectability, unobservability, pseudonymity, and identity management, v0.34 (August 2010),
http://dud.inf.tu-dresden.de/literatur/Anon_Terminology_v0.34.pdf
23. Hopcroft, J.E., Karp, R.M.: An $n^{5/2}$ algorithm for maximum matchings in bipartite graphs. SIAM Journal on Computing 2(4), 225–231 (1973)

Insider Attacks and Privacy of RFID Protocols

Ton van Deursen* and Saša Radomirović

University of Luxembourg

Abstract. We discuss insider attacks on RFID protocols with a focus on RFID tag privacy and demonstrate such attacks on published RFID protocols. In particular, we show attacks on a challenge-response protocol with IND-CCA1 encryption and on the randomized hashed GPS protocol.

We then show that IND-CCA2 encryption can be used to prevent insider attacks and present a protocol secure against insider attacks. The protocol is based solely on elliptic-curve operations.

1 Introduction

Radio frequency identification (RFID) tags are inexpensive devices that communicate wirelessly with RFID readers. Due to their low fabrication cost, their small size, and their ability to uniquely identify an item, RFID tags are found in a myriad of everyday objects. RFID tags can, for instance, be embedded in passports [1], electronic fare tickets [2], library books [3], and clothes [4]. They are often passively powered and respond to any query. Embedding such tags in items we always carry with us leads to privacy concerns. To protect the privacy of the RFID tag bearer while maintaining the tag's functionality, a vast number of cryptographic RFID protocols have been proposed.

Designing a secure and private RFID protocol is difficult for a number of reasons. Tags are computationally limited due to their small size and the absence of an active power source. Implementing full-fledged cryptography often makes tags too expensive or the communication with them too slow. Yet, attackers have a broad range of possibilities to attack an RFID system, from eavesdropping on communications to studying and tinkering with a tag's circuits.

Insider attacks. In this paper, we study insider attacks on RFID protocols. Insider attacks are a major source of security breaches of computer systems in general. Some estimates even show that the majority of breaches (70% - 90%) are caused by insiders [5]. One can think of various scenarios for insider attacks. For instance, a malicious merchant may want to cheat one of his customers, a disgruntled employee may want to inflict damage on his employer's assets, or a legitimate user of a system could be compromised and used in an attack against another user. The latter is the case when a computer system is infected with malware or Trojan horses and used to attack another, more important, system.

---

* Ton van Deursen was supported by the National Research Fund Luxembourg.

S. Petkova-Kikova, A. Pashalidis, G. Pernul (Eds.): EuroPKI 2011, LNCS 7163, pp. 91–105, 2012.

Common to all insider attacks is that the adversary abuses the credentials and knowledge of one compromised user to violate a particular security goal of *another* user.

Many cryptographic protocols achieve security in the absence of insider attackers, but fail to achieve their security goals when insider attackers are present. A well-known example is the Needham-Schroeder protocol [6], which was first proven to be secure [7], but later shown to be flawed in the presence of insider attackers [8]. It is therefore not surprising that standard frameworks for security protocol analysis assume that the adversary controls one or more malicious users in the system [9–11].

To perform an insider attack, the adversary needs the key material stored in one legitimate tag. Since RFID tags are often used as hardware tokens, the users of RFID tags usually have no access to the key material. However, one can think of several practical scenarios for the adversary to acquire the key material. For instance, RFID tags are often not sufficiently tamper resistant. If the adversary is a user of the RFID system he can reverse engineer and obtain the key material of one of his own tags. In an entirely different scenario, the adversary could compromise the manufacturer of RFID tags or influence the key generation process for a number of tags.

Our contribution. The main goal of this paper is to show the relevance of insider attacks on privacy of RFID protocols and designing a purely elliptic-curve-based protocol that resists insider attacks.

As a starting point, we take the widely used RFID adversary model originally proposed by Vaudenay [12]. We argue that none of the eight adversary classes proposed in the model faithfully represents insider attackers. We characterize the powers of insider attackers by restricting its oracle access. We then show insider attacks on a collection of protocols. More precisely, we show that the randomized hashed GPS protocol [13] does not resist insider attacks. Furthermore, we show that an IND-CCA1 secure encryption scheme is not sufficient to resist insider attacks.

We then design a purely elliptic-curve-based RFID protocol that withstands insider attacks. As a basis, we use a protocol proposed by Vaudenay and the hash-free public key encryption scheme of Cramer and Shoup. The construction of such a protocol is interesting for several reasons. Public key-based protocols aim to maintain privacy against strong attackers. In fact, it can be shown that public-key cryptography is necessary to achieve strong privacy [12]. Asymmetric protocols also enable efficient tag lookup procedures on the reader's side. These are important when there is a large number of tags in the system as well as to defend against timing attacks [14]. Damgård and Pedersen have shown that in a system with symmetric keys, either privacy, security, or efficiency has to be sacrificed [15]. The protocol we present is currently the only protocol based solely on elliptic-curve cryptography that resists insider attacks.

2 Preliminaries

2.1 RFID Privacy

We adopt the RFID privacy model by Hermans et al. [16] which is a refinement of the widely used privacy model by Vaudenay [12]. We give a minimal description of the model and refer the reader to the original paper [16] for full details. The model assumes a reader R and a set of tags $\mathcal{T}$. The adversary $\mathcal{A}$ can interact with the reader and the tags by means of querying oracles.

Tags may either be in the vicinity of the adversary (we call the tag *drawn*) or out of the vicinity of the adversary (*free*). If a tag is drawn, it gets a temporary identity *vtag* through which it can be addressed by the adversary. Initially, all tags are free tags.

The model defines a game-based definition of privacy. The experiment in which the adversary participates is as follows. The experiment chooses a bit b at random. The adversary is then allowed to interact with readers and tags by accessing oracles. At the end of the experiment, the adversary returns a guess for the value of b. If the guess is correct, the adversary wins the experiment.

The following eight oracles define the capabilities of the adversary.

- CREATETAG $\rightarrow T_i$: creates a new legitimate tag T_i.
- LAUNCH $\rightarrow \pi, m$: makes the reader launch a new protocol instance π and returns the first message m sent by the reader.
- DRAWTAG$(T_i, T_j) \rightarrow$ *vtag*: moves the tags T_i and T_j from the set of free tags to the set of drawn tags. A fresh identifier *vtag* is created and the tuple $(vtag, T_i, T_j)$ is stored. The identifier *vtag* can be used to address the tag T_b. If T_i or T_j is already drawn, then $\perp$ is returned.
- FREE$(vtag)$: removes the tuple $(vtag, T_i, T_j)$ and moves tags T_i and T_j to the set of free tags. The tag T_b is rest, that is, its volatile memory is erased.
- SENDTAG$(m, vtag)_b \rightarrow m'$: looks up the tuple $(vtag, T_i, T_j)$ and sends the message m to T_i (if $b = 0$) or T_j (if $b = 1$). The oracle call returns the tag response m'.
- SENDREADER$(m, \pi) \rightarrow m'$: Sends the message m to the reader's protocol instance π. If the message m corresponds to the message that the reader expected, he responds with message m'. If no active protocol instance π exists, $\perp$ is returned.
- RESULT$(\pi) \rightarrow x$: when the protocol instance with identifier π completed successfully, the oracle returns 1, otherwise 0. If no protocol instance π exists, $\perp$ is returned.
- CORRUPT$(T_i) \rightarrow S$: Returns the state S of the tag. The state contains the current values of the variables mentioned as initial knowledge of the tag. If the tag T_i is drawn, $\perp$ is returned.

Definition 1 (Privacy). *A protocol is said to be private if for all polynomial adversaries $\mathcal{A}$, the probability that $\mathcal{A}$ wins the experiment is smaller than $1/2 + \epsilon$ for ϵ negligible in the security parameter.*

The privacy model defines eight adversary classes by restricting access to the CORRUPT and RESULT oracle. The eight classes are obtained by separating four modes of access to the CORRUPT oracle and two modes of access to the RESULT oracle.

The corruption separation is based on the time in the game, at which the attacker may corrupt tags. A *strong* adversary can corrupt tags at any time. The same holds for a *destructive* adversary, with the restriction that he cannot query any other oracles on the corrupted tag. A *forward* adversary can corrupt tags only at the end of the game and a *weak* adversary cannot corrupt tags at all.

A second separation concerns the ability of the attacker to recognize whether a protocol execution between a reader and a tag was successful. In many practical situations this is a reasonable assumption. For instance, in an RFID system for electronic transport tickets, a reader flashing a green light indicates that authentication was successful while a red light indicates it failed. In the model, we call an adversary with access to the RESULT oracle *wide*, while an adversary with no access to the RESULT oracle is called *narrow*.

2.2 Elliptic Curves and Cramer-Shoup

Let $\mathbb{F}_{2^n}$ be a finite field with 2^n elements. Let $\mathcal{E}$ be the group of $\mathbb{F}_{2^n}$-rational points of an ordinary elliptic curve over $\mathbb{F}_{2^n}$. That is, $\mathcal{E}$ denotes the set of points which satisfy the equation $y^2 + xy = x^3 + ax^2 + b$, with $a, b \in \mathbb{F}_{2^n}$ being fixed parameters, together with $\mathcal{O}$, the "point at infinity", which serves as the group's neutral element. We will assume that the group $\mathcal{E}$ contains a subgroup $\mathcal{G}$ of large prime order p and small index in $\mathcal{E}$.

In the following, we recall the elliptic-curve version of the Cramer-Shoup public-key encryption scheme. In section 4.3 we will use and recall the hash-free variant of the scheme.

Cramer-Shoup public-key encryption scheme. Let $P_1 \in \mathcal{G}$, $P_1 \neq \mathcal{O}$ and $1 < w, c, d, z < p$ be randomly chosen, system-wide parameters and let h be a collision-resistant hash function. Set $P_2 = wP_1$, $C = cP_1$, $D = dP_1$, $H = zP_1$. The tuple (P_1, P_2, C, D, H) is the RFID reader's public key and (w, c, d, z) its secret key.

To encrypt a message $M \in \mathcal{G}$, we choose a random integer $1 < r \leqslant p$ and compute $U_1 = rP_1$, $U_2 = rP_2$, $E = rH + M$, $\alpha = h(U_1, U_2, E)$, and $V = rC + r\alpha D$. The ciphertext is (U_1, U_2, E, V).

To decrypt, correctness of V and U_2 needs to be verified first. For this, $\alpha = h(U_1, U_2, E)$ is computed, then V is compared to $cU_1 + \alpha dU_1$ and U_2 is compared to wU_1. If the terms are equal, then the plaintext is recovered via $M = E - zU_1$.

3 Insider Attacks

Insider attackers are a class of adversaries whose powers are not accurately represented by any of the eight classes of the privacy model [12, 16]. The four modes of corruption restrict the adversary with respect to *when* he corrupts tags, but not with respect to *which* tags he corrupts. *If* the adversary can corrupt tags he can corrupt *all* tags. We call this type of corruption *full corruption*. In this paper, we are interested in a weaker form of corruption, which we call *selective corruption*. We assume that the attacker can only corrupt his own tags. In particular, the adversary cannot corrupt tags with the purpose of tracing them. Therefore, we only allow corruption of freshly created tags and disallow any queries to corrupted tags. Selective corruption models the case in which an attacker corrupts a tag of his own, with the purpose of tracing some *other* tag in the system.

Although corruption of tags is one way to obtain the keys of a legitimate tag in an RFID system, it is certainly not the only way. Very often, the manufacturer of RFID systems is not the party that implements or deploys the system. In turn, the implementing party is not the same as the maintainer of the system. In practice, before an RFID system is in use, many parties will have possessed the system. All these parties have the possibility to insert tags into the system and later perform insider attacks. For another scenario, consider cell phones with near-field communication (NFC) chips. Nowadays, several cell phones contain NFC chips that can execute RFID protocols. To this end, they contain the key material of RFID tags. If the NFC chip (or possibly the operating system of the cell phone) is compromised, an attacker can obtain the key material of the RFID tags stored on the NFC chip. The key material can then be used in an insider attack. We emphasize that our notion of selective corruption covers both scenarios.

A second restriction we impose on insider attackers is in the way they access the RESULT oracle. We assume that insider attackers can *only* query the oracle on protocol executions in which no tag was involved. This faithfully models the case where an attacker does not have access to the RESULT oracle except for the protocol executions which involve only him and an RFID reader.

In the next sections, we demonstrate the relevancy of the class of insider attackers. We show that even under selective corruption and with restricted access to the RESULT oracle the privacy of several public-key RFID protocols can be broken.

3.1   The Randomized Hashed GPS Protocol

The randomized hashed GPS protocol [13] is a privacy-enhancing extension of the GPS identification scheme [17]. Both schemes employ interactive zero-knowledge identification and have been shown to provide strong authentication assuming that the discrete logarithm with short exponents problem is hard. The randomized hashed GPS scheme requires additionally that the decisional Diffie–Hellman problem is hard. The lightweight design of these schemes makes them interesting for low-cost smart cards and RFID tags.

The randomized hashed GPS scheme is based on a group G of prime order, an element $g \in G$, and three integers A, B, and S. The discrete logarithm with short exponents problem and decisional Diffie–Hellman problem are assumed to be hard in G for basis g. It further uses a collision and preimage resistant hash function h.

Tags have a secret exponent $s \in \mathbb{Z}_S$ and readers a secret exponent $v < 2^k$ (for a security parameter k). The public counterpart g^s is known to the reader and g^v is known to the tag. The protocol is initiated with the tag generating two random values $a, b \in \mathbb{Z}_A$. The tag sends $h(g^a, (g^v)^b)$ to the reader upon which it responds with a random challenge $c \in \mathbb{Z}_B$. The tag computes $y = a + b + sc$ and sends it, together with g^a and $(g^v)^b$ to the reader. The reader recovers g^s by computing

$$(g^{vy}(g^a)^{-v}((g^v)^b)^{-1})^{1/cv},$$

verifies that the first message equals $h(g^a, (g^v)^b)$, and verifies that $0 \le y \le 2A - 2 + (B-1)(S-1)$. The protocol is depicted in Figure 1.

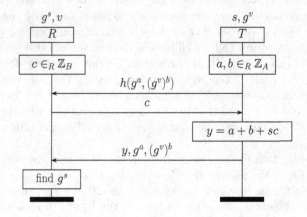

Fig. 1. Randomized hashed GPS protocol

The protocol was proven narrow-strong private, wide-forward private, and secure [13, Theorem 5]. We now show that the protocol is vulnerable to insider attacks.

Theorem 1. *The randomized hashed GPS protocol (Figure 1) is vulnerable to insider attacks.*

Proof. The attack strategy is as follows. The attacker queries two legitimate tags T and T'. He combines the tag responses and uses a protocol execution between an insider tag and the reader to verify whether $T = T'$.

We construct an adversary $\mathcal{A}$ that executes the protocol with two legitimate tags T and T'. The protocol transcripts for these executions are

$$(h(g^a, (g^v)^b), c, y, g^a, (g^v)^b)$$

and

$$(h(g^{a'}, (g^v)^{b'}), c', y', g^{a'}, (g^v)^{b'}).$$

By the protocol specification, y and y' are defined by $y = (a + b + sc)$ and $y' = (a' + b' + s'c')$. It is the attacker's goal to decide whether $T = T'$ which amounts to deciding whether $s = s'$.

The adversary computes α, β, and γ as follows:

$$\alpha = \frac{(g^a)^{c'}}{(g^{a'})^c} = g^{ac' - a'c}$$
$$\beta = \frac{((g^v)^b)^{c'}}{(g^v)^{b'})^c} = g^{vbc' - vb'c} \tag{1}$$
$$\gamma = c'y - cy' = (ac' - a'c) + (bc' - b'c) + cc'(s - s')$$

Terms α, β, and γ satisfy the following equation if and only if $s = s'$.

$$\alpha \cdot \beta^{1/v} = g^{\gamma} \tag{2}$$

Since the adversary has insider capabilities, he knows the secret s'' of one legitimate tag as well as g^v and g. To test whether Equation (2) holds, the adversary initiates a protocol execution with a reader. He sends $h(\alpha, \beta)$ upon which the reader challenges with c''. The adversary computes $y'' = \gamma + s'' \cdot c''$. If $0 \leq y'' \leq 2A - 2 + (B - 1)(S - 1)$, then the adversary sends y'', α, β to the reader. In this case, the reader accepts the adversary's insider tag if and only if $s = s'$. Therefore, if the reader accepts the insider tag, we know that $T = T'$, otherwise $T \neq T'$. The protocol flow between the reader and adversary is depicted in Figure 2. For the case that the inequality $0 \leq y'' \leq 2A - 2 + (B - 1)(S - 1)$ is not satisfied, the adversary simply restarts the protocol with the RFID reader. The adversary can avoid this case entirely, if he chooses $c = c' = 1$ and ensures that $\gamma \geq 0$ by swapping, if necessary, y and y' and all other terms from the two protocol transcripts.

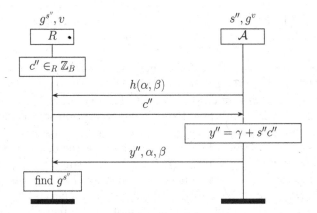

Fig. 2. Insider attack on the randomized hashed GPS protocol

Thus, the protocol is vulnerable to insider attacks.   □

Remark 1. The messages of the EC-RAC protocols [18–20], the randomized Schnorr protocol [21], and the recently proposed hierarchical ECC-based protocol [22] possess homomorphic properties similar to the randomized hashed GPS protocol. It is easy to see that the insider attack shown in the preceding proof can be adapted to all of these protocols and that consequently none of these protocols withstand insider attacks on privacy.

3.2 Protocols with IND-CCA1 Encryption

In this section, we show that IND-CCA1 encryption is not sufficient to prevent insider attacks. Consider Vaudenay's protocol [12, 16] depicted in Figure 3. The protocol assumes that every pair of reader and tag share a secret key[1] k. The reader starts the protocol by sending a random challenge c to the tag. The tag combines the challenge with k and responds with the encryption of c and k under the public key of the reader. The reader decrypts this message with its public key and identifies and authenticates the tag based on the plaintext of the encryption.

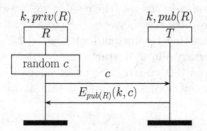

Fig. 3. RFID protocol with IND-CCA1 encryption

Hermans et al. [16] show that if the encryption scheme used in the protocol satisfies IND-CCA2, then the protocol is wide-strong private. Since a wide-strong attacker is stronger than insider attackers, it also resists insider attacks.

We show that if a homomorphic IND-CCA1 encryption scheme is used, then the protocol is vulnerable to insider attacks. An encryption scheme is said to be homomorphic if the elements of the plaintext set and the ciphertext set form a group with operators $\otimes$ and $\oplus$, respectively, so that for any encryption key k and for any messages m_1 and m_2 the encryption function $E_k(\cdot)$ satisfies $E_k(m_1) \oplus E_k(m_2) = E_k(m_1 \otimes m_2)$. Examples of homomorphic encryption schemes are ElGamal [23], DEG [24], and the "lite" version of the Cramer-Shoup scheme [25, Section 5.4]. The latter is an IND-CCA1 scheme which is obtained from the regular Cramer-Shoup scheme (see Section 2) by eliminating the point D and

---

[1] This key represents the identity (*ID*) and the key (*K*) of the original proposal [12, 16].

the hash function h. Thus, to encrypt a message $M \in \mathcal{G}$ with the *lite* Cramer-Shoup scheme, we choose a random $r \in \mathbb{Z}_p$ and compute $U_1 = rP_1$, $U_2 = rP_2$, $E = rH + M$, and $V = rC$. The ciphertext is (U_1, U_2, E, V). Before decrypting, the reader verifies $V = cU_1$ and $U_2 = wU_1$. One can easily see that the scheme is homomorphic if the group operation $+$ is used for each component of the encryption tuple.

Theorem 2. *Let $E_{pk}(m)$ denote a homomorphic IND-CCA1 encryption of message m under key pk. Then the protocol depicted in Figure 3 does not resist insider attacks.*

Proof. By homomorphy of the encryption scheme, we have

$$E_{pub(R)}(k, c) \oplus E_{pub(R)}(k', c') = E_{pub(R)}((k, c) \otimes (k', c')).$$

To attack the scheme, the adversary performs the following insider attack. Suppose tags T_1 and T_2 share secret keys k_1 and k_2 with the reader. Clearly, T_1 and T_2 are the same tag if $k_1 = k_2$. The attacker queries the two tags with the same challenge c. The tags return the ciphertexts $E_{pub(R)}(k_1, c)$ and $E_{pub(R)}(k_2, c)$, respectively.

By correctness of the protocol, the two observations concern the same tag if and only if $k_1 = k_2$. The adversary can test this by using his insider tag with key k_I and executing one protocol run with an RFID reader. Say, the reader's challenge is c''. The adversary encrypts $E_{pub(R)}(k_I, c'')$ and computes

$$E_{pub(R)}(k_1, c) \oplus E_{pub(R)}(k_2, c)^{-1} \oplus E_{pub(R)}(k_I, c'')$$
$$= E_{pub(R)}((k_1, c) \otimes (k_2, c)^{-1} \otimes (k_I, c'')).$$

The reader accepts the adversary's response if $k_1 = k_2$ and rejects it otherwise. If the reader accepts the response, the adversary knows that $T_1 = T_2$, otherwise he knows that $T_1 \neq T_2$. Thus, the protocol is not private against insider attacks. □

4   A Protocol Private against Insider Attacks

We present the first provably wide-strong and authenticating RFID protocol exclusively based on elliptic-curve and scalar operations. Since the insider adversary has a restricted access to oracles that the wide-strong adversary has full access to, it follows that a wide-strong private protocol is also private against insider attacks.

A wide-strong private scheme which only uses elliptic-curve group operations is interesting for two reasons. For one, like any public-key-based scheme, it permits scalable tag identification: As shown by Damgård and Pedersen [15], for symmetric schemes, RFID privacy can only be obtained at the cost of non-scalable tag lookup procedure for the RFID reader. For the other, the implementation of a typical IND-CCA2 public-key cryptosystem on an RFID tag is quite expensive. To achieve IND-CCA2 security, most cryptosystems rely on three components. An intractable number-theoretic problem, a symmetric block cipher, and a cryptographic hash function. The main cost in such a scheme is incurred by the large number of gates required to implement the number-theoretic operations on one side and an even larger number of gates to implement the cryptographic hash function on the other. Thus, there is interest in reusing the number-theoretic circuits to implement the same functionality provided by a hash function instead of implementing a separate hash function with additional primitives.

Our protocol is an implementation of Vaudenay's public-key protocol which has been proved to be authenticating in [12] and wide-strong private in [16]. The privacy proof requires the protocol to employ an IND-CCA2 public-key encryption scheme.

The encryption scheme we use in the protocol is the hash-free variant of the Cramer-Shoup scheme [25] shown in Section 2. It provides IND-CCA2 security assuming only the decisional Diffie–Hellman assumption.

The RFID protocol requires the RFID tags to encrypt one message for the system's RFID readers, thus one private-key / public-key pair needs to be generated. The RFID readers will store the private key, the RFID tags will be equipped with the public key. The message to be encrypted by the RFID tag consists of the RFID tag's ID and a challenge it receives from the RFID reader. This message needs to be a concatenation of ID and challenge (to avoid algebraic attacks [26]) as well as an element of the group $\mathcal{G}$. Thus we will represent ID and challenge as bit strings and map their concatenation into the group $\mathcal{G}$.

4.1 Mapping into the Elliptic Curve

To map the reader's challenge and the tag's identity into the elliptic curve, we use a simple try-and-increment method [27]. In the following, we identify elements in finite extensions of $\mathbb{F}_2$ with bit strings. Let k be a security parameter. The map $\phi : \mathbb{F}_{2^{n-k}} \to \mathcal{G} \cup \{\text{fail}\}$ is defined as follows. It assigns to $x \in \mathbb{F}_{2^{n-k}}$ an element $(x', y) \in \mathcal{G}$, where the $n - k$ most significant bits of $x' \in \mathbb{F}_{2^n}$ are equal to x and the remaining k bits are such that $(x', y) \in \mathcal{G}$. To find such a pair (x', y) we simply step through all 2^k possible bit strings. If no such bit string is found the map returns fail. Since the expected number of try-and-increment steps is 2 [27], the probability of failure is $1/2^{2^k}$. Thus the security parameter k can be fairly small. We refer to [27] for a discussion on how to implement the try-and-increment algorithm securely, that is, resistant to timing attacks.

Lemma 1. *If $\mathcal{E}$ has cardinality $2p$, p prime, then the map ϕ can be implemented with 2^{k+1} computations of the trace function of $\mathbb{F}_{2^n}$ over $\mathbb{F}_2$, and one square root computation over $\mathbb{F}_{2^n}$.*

Remark 2. There are several more sophisticated algorithms to map bit strings to points on an elliptic curve than the try-and-increment method we employ above. The most efficient, deterministic maps are Icart's $f_{a,b}$ function [27] and the SWU map [28–30]. However, special care needs to be taken in order to implement them securely. The $f_{a,b}$ function, for instance, can have up to four elements in the preimage of a point (x, y). For the case of characteristic 2, where the point satisfies the equation $y^2 + xy = x^3 + ax^2 + b$, with $a, b \in \mathbb{F}_{2^n}$ being fixed parameters, these four elements are the solutions of the quartic polynomial $u^4 + u^2 + xu + (y + a)$ over $\mathbb{F}_{2^n}$. If Icart's function is used in the way our ϕ function is used above, an adversary might be able to launch a man-in-the-middle insider attack. The attacker's goal would be that the victim's answer is accepted by the reader if and only if the quartic polynomial contains the adversary's solution as well as the victim's which would identify the victim to the adversary.

4.2   The Basic Protocol

For simplicity, we first demonstrate how to use the regular Cramer-Shoup scheme to implement the protocol. In the next section we will replace the cryptographic hash function by elliptic-curve point operations to obtain a purely elliptic-curve-based protocol.

Let ID_T be a tag T's identity, encoded as a randomly chosen bit string of length $\frac{1}{2}(n-k)$, where k is the security parameter associated with the ϕ function. The basic protocol now runs as follows. The reader challenges the tag with a randomly generated bit string N of length $\frac{1}{2}(n-k)$. The tag concatenates its identity ID_T with the challenge string N and applies the ϕ function to obtain the point $M = \phi(ID_T, N)$ on the elliptic curve. Thus, the tag sends $rP_1, rP_2, rH + \phi(ID_T, N), rC + r\alpha D$ to the reader. The reader accepts the tag if the response verifies correctly. The protocol is depicted in Figure 4 (left).

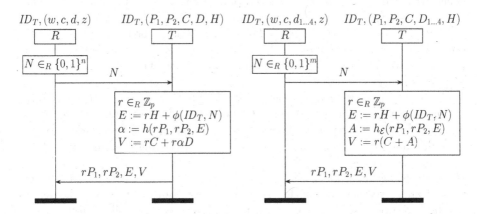

Fig. 4. Elliptic-curve-based protocol with a cryptographic hash function (left) and with an elliptic-curve-based hash function (right)

Correctness, security, and privacy. Correctness of the scheme follows immediately from correctness of the Cramer-Shoup encryption scheme [25]. Privacy and security follow Vaudenay [12] and Hermans et al. [16] and the IND-CCA2 security of the Cramer-Shoup encryption scheme.

4.3   A Purely Elliptic-Curve-Based Solution

We now use the hash-free variant of the Cramer-Shoup scheme [25, Section 5.3] to implement a purely elliptic-curve-based protocol. Recall that $\mathcal{E}$ is an elliptic curve over a finite field $\mathbb{F}_{2^n}$ such that it contains a subgroup $\mathcal{G}$ of order p, where p is a large prime.

Let $P \in \mathcal{G}$ and $c, d_1, \ldots, d_4, w, z \in \mathbb{Z}_p$ be randomly chosen, system-wide parameters. Set $C = cP$, $D_i = d_i P$ for $1 \leq i \leq 4$, and $H = zP_1$. Then the reader's public key is $(P_1, P_2, C, D_1, \ldots, D_4, H)$ and its secret key is $(c, d_1, \ldots, d_4, w, z)$. Encryption and decryption are as in the regular scheme, shown in Section 2, but the value αD is replaced by $A = h_{\mathcal{E}}(U_1, U_2, E)$, where $h_{\mathcal{E}}$ is a function whose range is a subset of the elliptic curve $\mathcal{E}$. It remains to define the function $h_{\mathcal{E}}$.

The hash function $h_{\mathcal{E}}$. The hash function in the encryption scheme needs to hash three points on the elliptic curve onto a single point in a collision-resistant manner. Let $x(Q)$ be the x-coordinate of a point Q and $y(Q)$ be its y-coordinate. Since $\mathcal{E}$ is a an ordinary elliptic curve over $\mathbb{F}_{2^n}$, a pair $(x(P), y(P))$ is a point on the curve if and only if $(x(P), x(P) + y(P))$ is. Thus for each point on the curve, given its x-coordinate, there are only two possible y-coordinates. Therefore, only one bit is needed to encode the y-coordinate. Furthermore, by Seroussi [31] the x-coordinate can be represented within $n - 1$ bits, since $\mathcal{G}$ has odd order. We will henceforth refer to this as the n-bit encoding of the coordinates. For the point at infinity, we fix an n-bit representation.

Define $h_{\mathcal{E}}(X_1, X_2, X_3)$ as follows. For $i = 1, 2, 3$, let s_i be the n-bit strings obtained from the n-bit encoding of the points $X_1, \ldots, X_3$. We then split the string s_1, s_2, s_3 into the four $\lfloor \log_2 p \rfloor$-bit strings $a_1, \ldots, a_4$. Then $h_{\mathcal{E}}(X_1, X_2, X_3) = \sum_{i=1}^{4} a_i D_i$.

Let ID_T be a bit string of length $\frac{1}{2}(n-k)$. The hash-free variant of the protocol is depicted in Figure 4 (right). The protocol can be implemented on an RFID tag with 8 point multiplications, 5 point additions, 2^{k+1} computations of the trace function of $\mathbb{F}_{2^n}$ over $\mathbb{F}_2$, and one square root computation over $\mathbb{F}_{2^n}$.

Correctness, security, and privacy. Correctness of the scheme follows immediately from correctness of the hash-free Cramer-Shoup encryption scheme. As for the basic version of the protocol, privacy and security follow from Vaudenay [12] and Hermans et al. [16] and the IND-CCA2 security of the hash-free Cramer-Shoup encryption scheme. The latter follows by observing that the $h_{\mathcal{E}}$ function matches the hash function replacement in the hash-free variant of the Cramer-Shoup scheme [25, Section 5.3].

4.4 Practicality and Different Approaches

The protocol presented in the preceding section cannot be considered practical for most applications. There are several aspects to our approach that could be attempted in a different manner. Our current solution employs four elliptic curve point multiplications to implement the "hash-free" collision resistant function suggested by Cramer and Shoup [25]. The main reason for using a purely elliptic-curve based function is that existing circuits can be reused.

If we allow for hybrid encryption approaches, then a particularly efficient solution would be the OTP-PSEC-3 encryption scheme [32]. This scheme uses two elliptic curve point multiplications and two hash function applications. The scheme has been shown to be IND-CCA2 secure in the random oracle model and based on the elliptic curve gap Diffie–Hellman assumption. One of the two hash functions takes as input a random bitstring, the other takes two bitstrings and two points on the elliptic curve. Using the methods above to produce a purely elliptic-curve based solution, it can be easily seen that the number of point multiplications is at least as large as in our solution.

Finally, a simple way to reduce the complexity of our protocol, albeit at the cost of a rigorous proof of security, is to modify the ϕ map as follows. Let N be a scalar and ID_T be a point on the elliptic curve, representing a randomly generated challenge and a tag T's identity, respectively. Then let $\phi(ID_T, N) = N ID_T$. The remaining notation and protocol flow are as in Section 4.3 and Figure 4 (on the right). This modification replaces the trace and square root computations of the original ϕ map (Lemma 1) by a point multiplication.

5 Conclusion

In this paper, we have studied insider attacks on public-key RFID protocols. We have defined insider attackers by restricting the oracle access of a wide-strong adversary in the privacy model by Hermans et al. [16] and Vaudenay [12]. Insider attackers are allowed to corrupt their own tags, but not other tags. Furthermore, insider attackers can only find out whether a protocol execution was successful if it did not involve any legitimate (non-corrupt) tag.

We have shown that insider attacks are a threat to privacy of RFID protocols and we have supported that claim by presenting insider attacks on a number of protocols. Firstly, we have shown an insider attack on the randomized hashed GPS protocol [13]. This attack is more widely applicable and can be performed on other protocols [18–22] as well. Secondly, we have shown that IND-CCA1 cryptosystems are not sufficient to prevent insider attacks. To this end, we used a protocol proposed by Vaudenay which is wide-strong private if an IND-CCA2 secure encryption scheme is used. We have shown an insider attack on the protocol instantiated with an IND-CCA1 secure encryption scheme.

At present, there exists no RFID protocol based solely on elliptic curve cryptography that withstands insider attacks. Motivated by this fact, we have designed the first wide-strong RFID protocol based solely on elliptic curve operations. Since wide-strong attackers are stronger than insider attackers, our

protocol resists insider attacks. Although our solution may be too computationally expensive in practice, we stress that it is provably secure, and can therefore
serve as a starting point for further research.

Insider attacks are a plausible and important class of attacks, relevant for
wide adversaries. In current privacy models, insider attacks are not naturally
represented, but can be modeled by assuming a wide-destructive or wide-strong
adversary. This is, however, an unreasonable over-approximation of the powers of
an insider attacker who cannot corrupt the tags he wants to trace, but only some
of his own tags. In the future, we would like to design more efficient protocols
that resist insider attacks, but which are not necessarily wide-strong private.

Acknowledgments. We thank the anonymous reviewers for valuable comments
that helped improve this work. We appreciate in particular a reviewer's reference
to the randomized hashed GPS protocol.

References

1. Juels, A., Molnar, D., Wagner, D.: Security and privacy issues in e-passports. In:
   IEEE Conference on Security and Privacy for Emerging Areas in Communication
   Networks – SecureComm (2005)
2. Sadeghi, A.R., Visconti, I., Wachsmann, C.: User privacy in transport systems
   based on RFID e-tickets. In: PiLBA (2008)
3. Molnar, D., Wagner, D.: Privacy and security in library RFID: issues, practices, and
   architectures. In: ACM Conference on Computer and Communications Security
   (2004)
4. Quartararo, P.: Permanent RFID garment tracking system (US Patent
   005785181A) (1998)
5. Gollmann, D.: Insider fraud (position paper). In: Security Protocols Workshop,
   pp. 213–219 (1998)
6. Needham, R.M., Schroeder, M.D.: Using encryption for authentication in large
   networks of computers. Commun. ACM 21(12), 993–999 (1978)
7. Burrows, M., Abadi, M., Needham, R.: A logic of authentication. SIGOPS Oper.
   Syst. Rev. 23(5), 1–13 (1989)
8. Lowe, G.: Breaking and Fixing the Needham-Schroeder Public-Key Protocol using
   FDR. In: Margaria, T., Steffen, B. (eds.) TACAS 1996. LNCS, vol. 1055, pp. 147–
   166. Springer, Heidelberg (1996)
9. Lowe, G.: Casper: a compiler for the analysis of security protocols. J. Comput.
   Secur. 6(1-2), 53–84 (1998)
10. Blanchet, B.: An efficient cryptographic protocol verifier based on Prolog rules. In:
    14th IEEE Computer Security Foundations Workshop (CSFW), pp. 82–96. IEEE
    Computer Society (2001)
11. Cremers, C.: Scyther - Semantics and Verification of Security Protocols. Ph.D.
    dissertation, Eindhoven University of Technology (2006)
12. Vaudenay, S.: On Privacy Models for RFID. In: Kurosawa, K. (ed.) ASIACRYPT
    2007. LNCS, vol. 4833, pp. 68–87. Springer, Heidelberg (2007)
13. Bringer, J., Chabanne, H., Icart, T.: Efficient zero-knowledge identification schemes
    which respect privacy. In: ASIACCS, pp. 195–205 (2009)

14. Erguler, I., Anarim, E.: Scalability and security conflict for RFID authentication protocols. Cryptology ePrint Archive, Report 2010/018 (2010), http://eprint.iacr.org/
15. Damgård, I., Pedersen, M.Ø.: RFID Security: Tradeoffs between Security and Efficiency. In: Malkin, T. (ed.) CT-RSA 2008. LNCS, vol. 4964, pp. 318–332. Springer, Heidelberg (2008)
16. Hermans, J., Pashalidis, A., Vercauteren, F., Preneel, B.: A New RFID Privacy Model. In: Atluri, V., Diaz, C. (eds.) ESORICS 2011. LNCS, vol. 6879, pp. 568–587. Springer, Heidelberg (2011)
17. Girault, M., Poupard, G., Stern, J.: On the fly authentication and signature schemes based on groups of unknown order. J. Cryptology 19(4), 463–487 (2006)
18. Lee, Y.K., Batina, L., Singelée, D., Verbauwhede, I.: Low-cost untraceable authentication protocols for RFID. In: 3rd ACM Conference on Wireless Network Security – WiSec 2010 (2010)
19. Lee, Y., Batina, L., Verbauwhede, I.: Untraceable RFID authentication protocols: Revision of EC-RAC. In: IEEE International Conference on RFID – RFID 2009, Orlando, Florida, USA, pp. 178–185 (April 2009)
20. Lee, Y.K., Batina, L., Singelée, D., Verbauwhede, I.: Wide–Weak Privacy–Preserving RFID Authentication Protocols. In: Chatzimisios, P., Verikoukis, C., Santamaría, I., Laddomada, M., Hoffmann, O. (eds.) MOBILIGHT 2010. LNICST, vol. 45, pp. 254–267. Springer, Heidelberg (2010)
21. Bringer, J., Chabanne, H., Icart, T.: Cryptanalysis of EC-RAC, a RFID Identification Protocol. In: Franklin, M.K., Hui, L.C.K., Wong, D.S. (eds.) CANS 2008. LNCS, vol. 5339, pp. 149–161. Springer, Heidelberg (2008)
22. Batina, L., Seys, S., Singelee, D., Verbauwhede, I.: Hierarchical ECC-based RFID authentication protocol. In: Workshop on RFID Security – RFIDSec 2011 (to appear, 2011)
23. Gamal, T.E.: A public key cryptosystem and a signature scheme based on discrete logarithms. IEEE Transactions on Information Theory 31(4), 469–472 (1985)
24. Damgård, I.: Towards Practical Public Key Systems Secure against Chosen Ciphertext Attacks. In: Feigenbaum, J. (ed.) CRYPTO 1991. LNCS, vol. 576, pp. 445–456. Springer, Heidelberg (1992)
25. Cramer, R., Shoup, V.: A Practical Public Key Cryptosystem Provably Secure against Adaptive Chosen Ciphertext Attack. In: Krawczyk, H. (ed.) CRYPTO 1998. LNCS, vol. 1462, pp. 13–25. Springer, Heidelberg (1998)
26. van Deursen, T., Radomirović, S.: Algebraic Attacks on RFID Protocols. In: Markowitch, O., Bilas, A., Hoepman, J.-H., Mitchell, C.J., Quisquater, J.-J. (eds.) WISTP 2009. LNCS, vol. 5746, pp. 38–51. Springer, Heidelberg (2009)
27. Icart, T.: How to Hash into Elliptic Curves. In: Halevi, S. (ed.) CRYPTO 2009. LNCS, vol. 5677, pp. 303–316. Springer, Heidelberg (2009)
28. Coron, J.S., Icart, T.: An indifferentiable hash function into elliptic curves. Cryptology ePrint Archive, Report 2009/340 (2009), http://eprint.iacr.org/
29. Shallue, A., van de Woestijne, C.: Construction of Rational Points on Elliptic Curves over Finite Fields. In: Hess, F., Pauli, S., Pohst, M. (eds.) ANTS 2006. LNCS, vol. 4076, pp. 510–524. Springer, Heidelberg (2006)
30. Ulas, M.: Rational points on certain hyperelliptic curves over finite fields. Bull. Pol. Acad. Sci. Math. 55(2), 97–104 (2007)
31. Seroussi, G.: Compact representation of elliptic curve points over $\mathbb{F}_{2^n}$. Technical report, Research Contribution to IEEE P1363 (1998)
32. Okamoto, T., Pointcheval, D.: PSEC-3: Provably secure elliptic curve encryption scheme - V3 (Submission to P1363a). In: IEEE P1363a (2000)

Cell-Based Roadpricing

Flavio D. Garcia[1], Eric R. Verheul[1,2], and Bart Jacobs[1]

[1] Institute for Computing and Information Sciences,
Radboud University Nijmegen,
P.O. Box 9010, NL-6500 GL Nijmegen, The Netherlands
{flaviog,Eric.Verheul,bart}@cs.ru.nl
[2] PwC Advisory
P.O. Box 22735, 1100 DE Amsterdam, The Netherlands
eric.verheul@nl.pwc.com

Abstract. This paper proposes a new approach to electronic roadpricing, based on a division of the roadpricing area into cells, each with their own fee. Some of the cells are secretly marked as check cells. On board equipment contains a secure element that is made aware of these check cells and helps the pricing authorities to monitor the user. This approach is not only original but it also improves upon earlier approaches since it solves issues regarding positioning accuracy, collusion between different users, and the required level of interaction.

1 Introduction

Roadpricing, also known as Electronic Traffic Pricing (ETP), refers to a location-based charge for road use. It exists in several forms, for instance via charges for entering the city center (London) or for particular motorways (France or Italy), or for lorries (Germany). Here we consider satellite-based systems, using GPS or Galileo, for personal vehicles. Such approaches have been elaborated to some extent in the Netherlands, as part of earlier, now abandoned, government plans. However, at the European level this form of roadpricing is still on the political agenda (based on the framework [1,2]). The main reasons for replacing a flat road tax by a location-based approach are: (1) fairness of charges, since one only pays for actual road use, and (2) the possibility to steer the traffic supply via a flexible pricing policy (*e.g.* making busy roads expensive during rush hours).

Location-based roadpricing for personal vehicles is a highly privacy sensitive matter since it requires detailed location information of individual vehicles. Public support depends on proper privacy protection via an architecture guaranteeing data minimalisation focused on the goal of roadpricing itself, and not on secondary goals (like speed limit enforcement). The topic has been picked up in the computer security research community, see [3,7,6], and several different protocols have been proposed. This paper contributes with a novel protocol, that uses cells (covering the roadpricing area) both for fee calculation and for fraud detection (via a secure element, like a smart card, embedded in the car's toll device). Our approach addresses some problems with fraud detection in earlier

S. Petkova-Kikova, A. Pashalidis, G. Pernul (Eds.): EuroPKI 2011, LNCS 7163, pp. 106–122, 2012.

protocols, like time-dependence, collusion, GPS-precision and required level of interaction. The paper does not introduce any new cryptographic primitives and makes use of existing techniques. Its value lies in adapting these techniques in an original manner to a context of considerable societal relevance.

2   Preliminaries

We adopt the main building blocks of the Electronic Toll Pricing (ETP) architecture proposed by the European Union [1]. It distinguishes the following five components/parties of the system:

- an ETP subscriber;
- a toll charger TC;
- a toll service provider TSP;
- an on board unit OBU, in every (personal) vehicle;
- a secure element SE incorporated in the OBU.

An ETP subscriber is the party that uses the road of the toll charger and for this subscribes to a toll service provider. The main information security objectives of the subscriber are twofold. The first objective is that he gets to pay the correct amount for road usage and that he can validate that. The second objective is that the subscriber's privacy can sufficiently protected in the scheme. This obviously includes more than protection of the subscriber's road movements but we concentrate on this aspect in this paper. With *sufficient protection* we mean that the subscriber accepts the privacy protection design of the toll service provider system and has assurance that the actual implementation adheres to the design ('public trust').

Preferably, the privacy protection the scheme provides should be parameterizable and the subscriber should be able to validate the privacy protection himself without having to rely on a (trusted) third party. The toll charger TC is the party that collects a toll fee for the usage of the roads and defines the prices and conditions of use. Typically national or regional authorities are TCs, but also commercial parties 'owning' the roads, can be a TC.

The toll service provider TSP is the party that provides the ETP service. It periodically determines the fee to be paid by each subscriber (vehicle) for his road usage. In this paper we are often not very explicit about the difference between the TC and TSP, since the distinction is not so relevant for the protocol.

An important information security objective shared by the TC and TSP is that subscribers are correctly charged for the road usage and can detect fraud. A specific security objective of the TC is that he should be able to validate that usage of its roads is correctly reflected in the payments of the TSP.

The on board unit OBU is a satellite (GPS or Galileo) enabled device that will be attached to every vehicle subscribed to the ETP service. We assume that this device stores a pricing function $\mathcal{P}$ that takes as input a location l and a time t and it outputs a price p which corresponds the toll price of the corresponding road at time t. Furthermore, the OBU must have a timing device which is reasonably in sync with the local time. It should also be able to occasionally communicate with the TSP in order to report usage and to update the pricing function (and a list of checkpoints that corresponds with the location of surveillance cameras, see below).

Although the OBU should be reliable it is untrusted, from a systems perspective: subscribers may try to manipulate it, for instance via the power supply or via the satellite signals (shielding the device or feeding it false signals), in order to reduce the fee they need to pay.

The secure element SE is a tamper resistant device, like a smartcard, which has a modest amount of non-volatile memory and processing power. This processing power must be enough to perform basic (public key) cryptographic operations. Typically, the secure element does not have its own power or clock. It is comparable to a SIM card in a mobile phone albeit with more cryptographic capabilities.

2.1 Thin and Fat OBU's

Before going into the technicalities, we briefly describe the setting and the main idea underlying the protocol that is proposed in this paper.

In all satellite-based roadpricing systems vehicles have an on board unit OBU that can at least determine the location of the vehicle and communicate with the back-office. In [7] a distinction is made between *thin* and *fat* OBU's. A thin OBU just collects location information and passes it on the back-office where the appropriate fee is calculated. This is a simple but extremely privacy-unfriendly approach, since the sensitive location information is stored outside the direct control of the individual involved, in a large database that is vulnerable in various ways. A fat OBU on the other hand is capable of calculating the price itself, via a pricing function that is executed in a secure environment. At the end of a reporting period the OBU sends the cumulative fee to the TSP.

The fat approach is privacy friendly but has two big disadvantages:

1. A fat OBU is more complex than a thin one, and thus more expensive and more vulnerable;
2. Fraud detection is more complex with fat OBU's in comparison with thin ones.

One way to handle the first point is to reduce the trusted computing base (TCB) of an OBU to a minimum and to place this TCB on a tamper-resistant secure element SE such as a smart card. This separation makes it easier to add additional (commercial) services to the OBU, or alternatively, to add roadpricing functionality to existing in-car equipment (such as satellite navigation) by adding the secure element[1].

The second point is a serious issue. First, fraud detection with thin OBU's is easy: a TC/TSP just places roadside camera's at random places and check

---

[1] The secure element is bound to a particular individual, and can via this separation be transferred from one vehicle to another.

if the vehicles that pass by report the location where they are spotted. If not, the car owners will be fined. One sensitive point in this approach is that camera locations must remain secret, throughout the reporting period. If they become known, drivers may simply switch off their OBU and take a different route, avoiding cameras. With a fat OBU one way of fraud detection is to have the TC/TSP communicate briefly from a roadside detection point with the (secure element in the) OBU of each passing car in order to check if the last few locations used by the pricing function are consistent with the check locations. We remark that the ETP architecture [1] actually suggests the usage of 5.8 GHz Dedicated Short-Range Communications (DSRC) for this. However, since such checks are active, involving two-way communication, they will be noticed very quickly by passing cars. The check locations will thus become publicly known, negatively affecting the efficacy of the checks.

Another fraud detection approach is to let the OBU (or its secure element) commit itself to each step of the fee calculation, for instance via a simple hash function [7] or via a more complex non-interactive commitment scheme [3] (using homomorphic encryption and zero-knowledge proofs to exclude negative sub-fees). After receiving a (cumulative) fee report, the TC/TSP may ask the OBU to "open" certain commitments, corresponding to roadside camera locations, in order to check details of the cumulative report. Auditing thus involves interaction with the user, even in the case where everything turns out to be fine. In contrast, with the approach proposed here there will only be interaction with the user in case fraud is detected.

A crucial problem with the commitment approach is its vulnerability to collusion, exploiting time dependence. During such commitment checks the locations of the road-side camera's become known. If checks are performed immediately, like in [3], people may collude, where one of them (who drives a lot) reports first and learns about the check locations and the other ones subsequently delete commitments for non-check locations in their fee reports (thus reducing their fee).

Hence such checks can only be performed well after the reporting period, when all OBU's have sent in their fee report. But such timing dependency may introduce other vulnerabilities. What should happen if you are on holiday at the end of the reporting period, outside the roadpricing area, and outside reach of the TSP? If you are allowed to send in your report with a delay, when you return, you could adapt your fee report based on knowledge of the checkpoints. Such manipulations can exploit the fact that secure elements do not have their own (secure) clock and so you can feed them false timing information. One way of addressing this "absence" problem is forcing OBU's to report their fee as soon as they leave the roadpricing area. This naturally leads to the idea of carving up the area into cells (where border cells play a special role). Another problem with the commitment approach is that it requires communication with the OBU after fee reporting allowing fraudsters to claim their OBU is broken or stolen.

We finally note the scheme described in [8]. It has a *thin* OBU in the sense that it is based on a vehicle transponder that constantly sends time-location tuples to the TSP. However these tuples are not associated with vehicles but with commitments to random tags constructed by the subscribers in a registration phase and transferred to their vehicle transponder. During the reconciliation phase the fee is calculated based on secure multiparty computation involving the TSP and the subscriber through a web application. Enforcement is also based on spot checks; in a zero knowledge fashion the subscriber needs to prove he generated a time-location consistent with the spot check. This scheme not only requires substantial subscriber interaction but also allows the subscriber to claim his tag information being lost.

2.2 Current Protocol Idea

We now assume that the roadpricing area (country, region, or continent) is covered by square, non-overlapping cells of a relatively small size (*e.g.* a square kilometer). When you enter a cell you will have to pay a certain amount, depending on the cell (and possibly the time of day). These payment details are incorporated in a payment function $\mathcal{P}$ that will be left unspecified. As long as you stay within one cell, there is no further charge. But there will be a new charge as soon as you enter the next cell. In Subsection 2.3 we elaborate a bit more on the organization of these cells.

A certain subset of cells are marked as "check cells" or "checkpoints" and contain (hidden) roadside cameras connected with Automated Number Plate Recognition (ANPR) equipment. These markings are chosen by the TSP and the TC and change every billing period (of, say, one or three months). The secrecy of these markings is crucial for the protocol. Another crucial aspect is that the secure element in the OBU gets to know these checkpoint markings, via a secure connection with the TSP, but the subscriber or its (untrusted) OBU should not learn any information about the current checkpoints. This confidential transfer of checkpoints happens before the beginning of each new billing period.

Upon entering a new cell, the OBU reports— or 'declares', as we shall say below—this transition to its SE. The SE replies with a "ticket". The ticket is a (randomized) encryption of fixed data, e.g. 'OK' or '0' with some padding if the new cell is *not* a checkpoint. But if the cell is a checkpoint—which is known to the SE but not to the OBU—the ticket will be meaningful for fraud detection later on. The encryptions should be such that one cannot determine which tickets are for checkpoint cells and which are for non-checkpoint cells. In this way the trusted element works against its owner, in the interest of the TC and TSP: it secretly monitors the user. Thus, the SE is the TC and TSP's ambassador (or spy, if you like), see also [4].

Driving around *without* a proper, up-to-date list of check cells is dangerous, because without it your SE cannot produce appropriate tickets when you happen to enter a check cell (leading to subsequent fines, when audited). Hence it is in the own interest of users to have their system up-to-date. Whenever the SE does not have—for whatever reasons—an up-to-date list of check cells, it should report so via an alarm signal to the user. There should be procedures in place for malfunction, for instance by pushing a 'reset' button (including an implicit notification to the TSP) or by going quickly to some service station. Alternatively, one could consider to let the SE resort to treat all cells as check cells when it is not equipped with a proper, up-to-date list of check cells. This implies that the scheme provides no privacy when subscribers do not properly update their OBU (Jeroen Prins is thanked for this suggestion).

From a system perspective the secure element is trusted and inaccessible to malicious users. In contrast, the OBU is untrusted. When the trusted element ever gets compromised, the system breaks down. This is usually the case with a TCB: if a SIM gets compromised identities can be stolen and phone bills will probably end up with the wrong person. But having this tamper resistant SE as TCB also simplifies matters a lot: the SE is trusted so it can simply accumulate the fees per cell, store the result in its non-volatile memory, and report the cumulative fee, appropriately authenticated, to the TSP at the end of the reporting period. Because we have such a clearly separated TCB we do not need to use the homomorphic encryptions and proofs as in [3].

Both the TC and TSP trust the accumulation of fees reported by the SE, but they do not trust that the SE has been notified appropriately by the OBU at every cell transition. The TC and TSP thus check these notifications via the tickets. As part of the fee reporting—or possibly only on request of the TSP— the OBU sends all tickets of the reporting period to the TSP. The TSP can then open the tickets for the checkpoint cells where the vehicle has been spotted and see if the content is appropriate. The TSP can also communicate this evidence to the TC. Details are given below, in Section 3.

2.3   Cells and Roads

One thing that is new in our approach is the reliance on cells, and not on road segments or distance, as basis for payment. It deserves some more explanation. One basic idea in roadpricing is that certain roads (*e.g.* busy motorways) or bridges/tunnels are more expensive than for instance quiet country roads. Simply making all cells in which an expensive motorway occurs expensive is too crude, since there may be multiple roads in a particular cell. What we propose is that the price of a cell with multiple roads corresponds to the price of the cheapest road

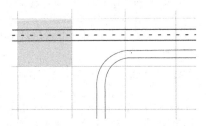

Fig. 1. An expensive cell exclusively covering a motorway segment, in between two exits, surrounded by inexpensive cells

(in that cell). In order to charge the appropriate fee for an expensive road one cell is made very expensive that only contains this road and cannot be avoided. Such a cell can for instance be found on a stretch of motorway in between two exits, as illustrated in Figure 1. Of course, such a cell is a prime candidate to be (regularly) a check cell.

One (more) advantage of using cells over road segments is that substantial margins can be allowed in the accuracy of the location provided by the positioning system, see Figure 2. This is a great benefit, since in practice the positioning accuracy is influenced for instance by atmospheric disturbances or by reflections of satellite signals in urban areas. Such lack of accuracy may be a problem for a road-segment based approach, when there are adjacent, parallel roads with different prices. In contrast, our cell-based approach is more robust. Also, the system is independent of the (often proprietary) mechanisms for transforming satellite signals into road segments, on which other roadpricing approaches rely. Hence it can be realized more easily via open (international) standards.

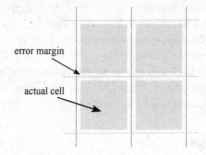

Fig. 2. Positioning system error margin around cells

An interesting question is what the ideal size of cells is. We think this is a topic of its own that requires a systematic quantative analysis. At this stage we only provide intuitive argumentation why small cells are good for privacy.

The privacy sensitive event at stake is when your position becomes known to the system. There are two occasions when this may happen:

1. When your car is photographed by a road-side camera; necessarily, the cell in which this camera is located is a check cell;
2. When you pass through a check cell and you report this passage—assuming that you follow the protocol.

It is best for privacy if these occasions coincide. Concretely, this means that in every check cell you should be photographed. Or, formulated differently, you do not pass through a check cell without being photographed. Thus, a cell needs to be small in order to guarantee that you will be photographed when it contains a camera.

More concretely, assume a city like Nijmegen has 5 cameras. If the city is covered by 9 cells and we assume the cameras are in different cells, there is a chance of $\frac{5}{9}$ that you will report your presence in Nijmegen to the back office, independent of whether you are photographed or not. However, if Nijmegen is covered by 50.000 cells (in the order of 100×100 meters), there is a chance of only $\frac{5}{50.000}$ that you reveal your presence.

Hence smaller cells means less unnecessary reporting of presence and thus better privacy protection. In Section 6 we use 100×100 meter as cell size in a sample calculation.

2.4 Timing

As we argued above, the timing of fee reporting, auditing, and feedback is a sensitive matter in road pricing. In our approach, fee reporting takes place:

1. At the end of the reporting period;
2. When a vehicle leaves the road pricing area (*e.g.* the country);
3. When a vehicle is sold or taken out of service.

The last point is rather special. It can be handled by giving an OBU a special 'report now' button; after pushing it the embedded SE should be removed.

The passage of a border will be detected by the OBU and should lead to an (automatic) fee report. It may create some administrative overhead for people who frequently cross borders, but since fee reporting is automatic this should not be such a problem.

It is a more serious problem if the fee report is suppressed by a malicious user upon leaving the road pricing area. In this way a vehicle may disappear from the grid. However, upon re-entering there are two options.

- This re-entering happens 'soon', still within the same reporting period as the departure; then the vehicle can in principle continue to drive around in the roadpricing area, using the (still valid) list of check cells in its SE. The OBU/SE will have to report normally, at the end of this period.
- Re-entering happens 'late', in a subsequent reporting period. There is now a window for fraud, because the check locations from the reporting period of departure must be assumed to be publicly known. However, the vehicle will need an (updated) list of check cells before it can drive around after re-entering without any risk. It is at this point that it has to communicate with the TSP, to request the new list, and the TSP notices the missing report (from the period of departure); the TSP will impose a (hefty) penalty.

The first, ordinary way of reporting happens at the end of the reporting period, say once a month. Vehicles will be forced to report, because only after reporting they will receive the new list of check cells. Since there is some time in between entering one cell and entering the next one, the fee reporting need not interfere with the ordinary declaring.

After (some time after) receiving the fee reports and distributing the new lists of check cells, the TSP goes into the auditing phase: tickets for check cells will be decrypted and inspected, possibly leading to penalties. Notice that this auditing does not require any interaction with the user—assuming appropriate tickets for check cells are submitted.

(There is one practical issue related to performance. If all vehicles submit their fee report at 24:00 hours of the last day of the month, communication channels will be overloaded. Hence one may wish to allocate different reporting times to different vehicles, in order to balance the load. This involves some additional administration, including management of check cells lists and delay of auditing, but it does not change the system fundamentally.)

3   The Protocol

This section describes our new, privacy-friendly ETP protocol. This protocol is a triple $< \mathcal{S}, \mathcal{U}, \mathcal{D} >$ of polynomial-time interactive protocols. The Setup Protocol $\mathcal{S}$ is a two party protocol involving the TSP and the SE. This protocol is run when a new SE is added to the system. The Update protocol $\mathcal{U}$ is a three party protocol involving the SE, the TSP and the OBU. This protocol runs periodically, at the end/begining of a billing period, *e.g.* monthly. The protocol Declare Segment $\mathcal{D}$ is a two party protocol involving the SE and the OBU. This protocol runs every time that the vehicle enters a new cell.

Notation: We write $\{ m \}_{\mathrm{pk}}$ to denote the encryption of message m with public key pk, while $[m]_{\mathrm{sk}}$ denotes message m followed by a signature on m with private key sk.

System Setup $\mathcal{S}$. When the system is initialized,

- The TSP creates a public key pair $(\mathrm{pk}_{\mathrm{TSP}}, \mathrm{sk}_{\mathrm{TSP}})$ and together with the TC partitions the map of the country (or region under consideration) in small cells, forming a grid that overlaps the relevant area. Let $\mathcal{C}$ be a mapping from GPS coordinates $(lat, long)$ to a cell number c. These cells must be small enough to provide the desired granularity level for road pricing. The function $\mathcal{P}$ assigns to each cell c and time t the corresponding road price p.
- The OBU stores a ticket list T which is initialized to the empty list.
- The SE of a vehicle generates its own public key pair $(\mathrm{pk}, \mathrm{sk})$. The public key is registered by the TSP and the public key $\mathrm{pk}_{\mathrm{TSP}}$ of the TSP is stored in the SE and in the OBU. The SE also has a counter *balance* which is initialized to zero.

Update $\mathcal{U}$. The purpose of the update protocol is threefold:

- For the TSP to get the toll charge for the last billing period;
- For the SE to get the updated checkpoint list for the next billing period;
- To perform fraud detection.

At the beginning of each billing period, the TC creates a list CHECKPOINTS of checkpoint cells. The checkpoint cells are those cells where the TC will have a surveillance camera for the next billing period. These checkpoint cells will be used later on for fraud detection. To prevent abuse from the TC/TSP, the maximum size of the CHECKPOINTS list N_{chk} must be enforced by the SE to be a small fraction of the total number of cells in the map N_{cells}. This prevent TC or TSP to set too many cells in the system as checkpoints thus hampering privacy.

At the end of of each billing period, the TSP, OBU and SE execute the following protocol.

1. OBU $\rightarrow$ TSP : update vehicle v
2. SE $\rightarrow$ OBU : $[balance, ts]_{sk_{SE}}$
3. OBU $\rightarrow$ TSP : $\{[balance, ts]_{sk_{SE}}, T\}_{pk_{TSP}}$
4. TSP $\rightarrow$ OBU : $\{[CHECKPOINTS_{new}, ts]_{sk_{TSP}}\}_{pk_{SE}}$
5. OBU $\rightarrow$ SE : $\{[CHECKPOINTS_{new}, ts]_{sk_{TSP}}\}_{pk_{SE}}$

The OBU initiates the update protocol identifying the vehicle. Then, the SE sends the current balance $balance$ and the time stamp ts signed with its private key sk_{SE}. The OBU sends this last message, together with the ticket list of tickets T, encrypted to the TSP in step (3). In step (4) the TSP sends the checkpoint list for the next billing period CHECKPOINTS$_{new}$ signed together with a timestamp ts. This list is encrypted with the public key pk_{SE} of the SE. In step (5) of the protocol, the OBU simply forwards this message to the SE. The SE validates that the time stamp ts is in the future with respect of its notion of time i.e., $ts > time$ and sets $time = ts$ and updates its checkpoint list.

When the TSP performs fraud detection, it is assumed that the TC provided TSP with evidence that the vehicle v has been at cell c at time t. Then the TSP will decrypt each entry in the transcript list T provided by v (see Section 6 for optimizations), ignoring those entries that decrypt to zero. One of these entries must be of the form $< c_{pre}, c_{cur}, ts, p >$ with $c = c_{cur}$ and $ts \approx t$. If that is not the case it means that this vehicle has committed fraud.

The signature over the new checkpoint list on steps (4) and (5) is there to prevent an adversary from being able to send a corrupt (potentially empty) checkpoint list to the SE which would result on fines, or other kind of damage, for the affected vehicles. Note that these signatures are not required for the security of the protocol as defined in Section 4.

Declare Segment $\mathcal{D}$. Every time that the vehicle enters a new cell c_{cur}, the OBU and the SE run the following protocol

1. OBU $\rightarrow$ SE : c_{pre}, c_{cur}, ts, p
2. SE $\rightarrow$ OBU : $ticket$

where c_{pre} is the previous cell, c_{cur} is the current cell $\mathcal{C}(lat, long)$, ts is the local time and p is the toll price $\mathcal{P}(c_{cur}, ts)$. Upon receival of message (1), the secure element verifies that the cell c_{pre} correspond to the c_{cur} of the previous Declare Segment protocol run. The SE validates that the time stamp ts is in the future with respect of its notion of time *i.e.*, $ts > time$ and checks that $p > 0$. Then the SE adapts it local time, by setting $time = ts$, and increases the counter *balance* by p, and subsequently it returns a ticket. If the cell $c_{cur} \in$ CHECKPOINTS then the SE sets $ticket := \{\, [c_{pre}, c_{cur}, ts, p]_{SE} \,\}_{pk_{TSP}}$. Otherwise it sets $ticket := \{\, 0 \,\}_{pk_{TSP}}$. The OBU stores the ticket from message (2) in the ticket list T, until the next update protocol execution.

We remark that the subscriber's OBU can, independently of the SE, store all declarations in plaintext and keep its own balance register allowing the subscriber to validate the charges sent to the TSP during the update protocol. We also remark that one can easily let the cell numbers support a notion of adjacency allowing the SE to determine that the previous and current cell are not adjacent allowing an additional form of fraud detection.

4   Security Notions

This section introduces different security notions. Most of it is standard and it is taken from the literature. It first recalls the notion of indistinguishability under chosen ciphertext attacks for an encryption scheme and the notion of strong existential unforgeability under chosen message attacks for a signature scheme. Then we propose a new security definition for ETP protocols that capture realistic threats that have not been considered in previous security definitions from the literature.

Definition 4.1. *An encryption scheme is a triple $\Gamma = (\mathcal{K}, \mathcal{E}, \mathcal{D})$ of probabilistic polynomial-time algorithms. $\mathcal{K}$ takes as input the security parameter 1^η and produces a key pair (pk, sk) where pk is the public encryption key and sk is the private decryption key. $\mathcal{E}$ takes as input a public key pk and a plaintext m and outputs a ciphertext. $\mathcal{D}$ takes as input a private key sk and a ciphertext and outputs a plaintext or $\bot$. It is required that $\mathbb{P}[(pk, sk) \leftarrow \mathcal{K}(1^\eta); c \leftarrow \mathcal{E}(pk, m); m' \leftarrow \mathcal{D}(sk, c) : m = m'] = 1$. We write $\{\, m \,\}_{pk}$ to denote $\mathcal{E}(pk, m)$.*

Definition 4.2 (IND-CCA-Game)

> ***IND-CCA-Game***$_{\Gamma, \mathcal{A}}(\eta)$:
> $(sk, pk) \leftarrow \mathcal{K}(1^\eta)$
> $p_0, p_1 \leftarrow \mathcal{A}_0^{\mathcal{D}}(pk)$
> $b \leftarrow \{0, 1\}$
> $b' \leftarrow \mathcal{A}_1^{\mathcal{D}}(\{\, p_b \,\}_{pk})$
> ***win** if $b = b'$.*

Adversaries implicitly pass state i.e., from $\mathcal{A}_0$ to $\mathcal{A}_1$.

Definition 4.3 (IND-CCA). *An encryption scheme Γ is said to be* IND-CCA *secure if for all probabilistic polynomial-time adversaries $\mathcal{A} = (\mathcal{A}_0, \mathcal{A}_1)$*

$$\mathbb{P}[\textit{IND-CCA-Game}_{\Gamma,\mathcal{A}}(\eta)] - 1/2$$

is a negligible function of η. This adversary has access to a decryption oracle $\mathcal{D}$ that on input a bitstring c' outputs $\mathcal{D}(sk, c)$ with the only restriction that c is not equal to the challenge ciphertext $\{p_b\}_{pk}$.

We recall the definition of signature scheme and the notion of strong existential unforgeability under chosen message attacks.

Definition 4.4. *A signature scheme is a triple* (Gen, Sign, Vrfy) *of probabilistic polynomial-time algorithms.* Gen *takes as input the security parameter 1^η and produces a key pair (vk, sk) where vk is the signature verification key and sk is the secret signing key.* Sign *takes as input sk and a message m and produces a signature s of m.* Vrfy *takes as input vk, a message m and a signature s and outputs whether or not s is a valid signature of m.*

$$\boxed{\begin{array}{l} \mathbf{SEU}_\Sigma(A)\colon \\ (vk, sk) \leftarrow \mathrm{Gen}(1^\eta) \\ m, \sigma \leftarrow A^{\mathcal{S}_{sk}}(vk) \\ \mathbf{winif}\ \mathrm{Vrfy}(vk, (m, \sigma)) \end{array}}$$

We recall the standard notion of strong existential unforgeability under chosen message attacks [5].

Definition 4.5 (Strong existential unforgeability). *A signature scheme $\Sigma = $* (Gen, Sign, Vrfy) *is a* strong, existential unforgeable *if the success probability of any probabilistic polynomial-time adversary A in the game $\mathbf{SEU}_{\Sigma,\mathcal{A}}(\eta)$ is negligible in the security parameter η.*

Next we introduce a new security notion for ETP protocols. Here an adversary is able to navigate a number of vehicles at will and it is also able to communicate with a number of secure elements and with the TSP. The adversary wins the game if it is able to get a toll fee reduction for any vehicle and manages to do so with low probability of being detected. Low probability here means lower probability than that of simply driving by through a random cell without declaring it. Such an adversary models, for instance, the situation where a number of users collude in order to avoid toll charges. This threat has not been considered by Balasch et al [3].

Definition 4.6 (Security-Game)

$$
\boxed{
\begin{aligned}
&\textbf{\textit{Security-Game}}_{\Pi,\mathcal{A}}(\eta)\ : \\
&\quad params \leftarrow Setup(1^{\eta}) \\
&\quad v \leftarrow \mathcal{A}^{\mathcal{O},\mathcal{D}}(params) \\
&\quad (\boldsymbol{l},\boldsymbol{t}) \leftarrow Trajectory(v) \\
&\quad p,b \leftarrow Result(v) \\
&\quad \textbf{\textit{winif}}\ if\ b = 1\ and\ p < \mathcal{P}((\boldsymbol{l},\boldsymbol{t}))
\end{aligned}
}
$$

were the adversary $\mathcal{A}$ has access to an oracle $\mathcal{D}$ which on input a vehicle identifier v and a GPS coordinate g, models the (physical) movement of vehicle v from the current location to GPS coordinates g. If g corresponds to a cell $c \in$ CHECKPOINTS then the oracle provides the corresponding evidence to the TSP. $\mathcal{A}$ has also access to an oracle $\mathcal{O}$ which allows her to communicate to the other parties (in this case the SE and the TSP) in the ETP protocol Π. The function Trajectory, on input a vehicle identifier v returns a vector of pairs Location $\times$ Time, corresponding to the trajectory of vehicle v that has been submitted to the oracle $\mathcal{D}$ during the previous billing period. The function Result, on input a vehicle identifier v returns the toll charge p which v has to pay as a result of the last Update protocol run, together with a bit b which equals one when no fraud has been detected for vehicle v. The function $\mathcal{P}$ is overloaded in the definition to vectors of Location $\times$ Time pairs and computes the correct price of this trajectory.

Definition 4.7 (Security). *An ETP protocol $\Pi =< \mathcal{S},\mathcal{U},\mathcal{D} >$ is said to be secure if for all probabilistic polynomial-time adversaries $\mathcal{A}$*

$$\mathbb{P}[\textbf{\textit{Security-Game}}_{\Pi,\mathcal{A}}(\eta)] < N_{chk}/N_{cells} + negl(\eta)$$

where negl is a negligible function on its input η.

5   Security and Privacy of the Protocol

Theorem 5.1 (Security). *If the encryption scheme Γ is IND-CCA secure and the signature scheme Σ is strong, existential unforgeable then the protocol proposed in Section 3 is secure with respect to Definition 4.7.*

Proof. Assume by the contrary that there is an adversary $\mathcal{A}$ that wins the **Security-Game** with probability significantly larger than N_{chk}/N_{cells}. In order for $\mathcal{A}$ to be able to win the Security-Game, it must be able to drive a vehicle through a cell without declaring it or do so but with a lower price. In order to win with probability significantly higher than N_{chk}/N_{cells}, it must either be able to construct valid tickets for the checkpoint cells or be able to avoid checkpoint cells with non-negligible advantage. In the first case case we build the following adversary $\mathcal{B}$ against the IND-CCA security of the encryption scheme. In the second we build the following adversary C against the strong unforgeability of the signature scheme.

The adversary B will first simulate the environment for A, this is, it will proceed as in System Setup, creating all public key pairs by itself, except for pk_{SE} of a randomly chosen vehicle v. For this key B will use the challenge key from the IND-CCA game to A. Then, B creates a checkpoint list containing one single cell c and sets the challenge plaintext $p_0 = \{c\}$ and sets p_1 equal to the empty checkpoint list. B receives then a challenge ciphertext $\{p_b\}_{pk_{SE}}$ which it uses in step 4 of the Update protocol for v. At some point A stops and outputs a vehicle identifier v'. If $v \neq v'$ then B stops and outputs a random bit b'. Otherwise B picks a random cell c' and compare how many times the vehicle v drives through c and c'. If v drives through c' more than through c then B stops and outputs zero. By the contrary, if v drives through c more (or equally) often than through c' then it outputs one.

Next we construct an adversary C against the strong unforgeability of the signature scheme. Just as before, C will simulate the environment for A, creating all public key pairs by herself, except for pk_{SE} of a randomly chosen vehicle v. For this key C will use the challenge key from the SEU game. Whenever C needs a signature using sk_{SE} it will simply invoke the signing oracle S_{sk}. At some point A stops and outputs a vehicle identifier v'. If $v \neq v'$ then C stops as well and outputs $\perp$. If $v = v'$ then C will analyze the transcript of the Update protocol for vehicle v submitted by A to the oracle O, in particular to message 5. C decrypts this message (since it has possession of sk_{TSP}) and all tickets in the ticket list T. As a result C obtains a number of signatures (ignoring those tickets that decrypt to zero). From these signatures C ignores those that it has submitted to the signing oracle S_{sk}. From the remaining signatures it chooses one at random and stops. In case that there is no such a signature, then it outputs $\perp$.

Theorem 5.2 (Privacy). *If the checkpoint list matches the actual positioning of surveillance cameras, then the scheme proposed in Section 3 does not leak any extra location information about the vehicles.*

Proof. It is straightforward to see that whenever the current position of a vehicle is not a checkpoint cell, then the only information received by the TSP is an encryption of zero.

6   Practical Considerations and Extensions

This section elaborates on practical issues concerning getting public trust in the SE, regarding memory, communication and computational complexity of the protocol and it discusses possible optimizations.

With respect to getting public trust in the SE we suggest that it is certified against an appropriate common criteria profile and that its source code (*e.g.* JavaCard applet) is disclosed. In addition, we suggest that after a certain period of time the checkpoint lists are also disclosed and that subscribers can get access to cryptographic keys through the TSP allowing them to inspect the actual tickets sent in the update protocol. To further convince subscribers that they are not sent checkpoints specifically tailored for them one could sent the checkpoints in through broadcast (e.g., through the Radio Data System (RDS) which is commonly used for dissemination of road traffic information). Using RDS would also allow for regular checkpoint updates without the need for the subscriber to be connected to a two way communication network such as GSM, GPRS or UMTS that also allow for pinpointing the subscriber's location. Actually, it might also be cheaper to use RDS broadcasts than point-to-point communication. To avoid usage of a static cryptographic key shared by all SEs in this context, we suggest a common temporary session key is negotiated with all (non-revoked) SEs as part of the update protocol.

If we consider cells of 100 by 100 meters, then in a European context 32 bit cell numbers will be sufficient. The protocol described in Section 3 generates a ticket list of approximately 1 MB per 1000 km. Given that the average car usage in Europe is in the order of 15000 km per year, this accounts for 15 MB of data per car per year, which is manageable but it can be improved.

It is possible to reduce the computational and bit complexity of the protocol by a small modification in the Declare Segment protocol $\mathcal{D}$. This modification consists of accumulating a number of tickets at the SE and issuing only one ticket every N cells. This ticket contains the same information as the earlier N tickets, but it requires only one signature and one encryption. This modification does not affect the security of the scheme as long as the resulting ticket is of constant size, $i.e$, padding should be used for those tickets that are just zero. For $N = 10$ this optimization reduces the size of the transcript file to just 200 KB per 1000 km which accounts to roughly 3Mb of data per year for an average user. If we consider monthly reports, the transcript file that needs to be sent will be on average of size 300 KB.

If this modest communication complexity is considered unacceptable, it can further be reduced by only auditing a small random set of users. In Step (3) in the Update protocol $\mathcal{U}$ the vehicle can first commit to a certain balance and then the TSP decides probabilistically whether it will request the ticket list T or not. This comes of course as a trade off for security but it can be a viable option when the sanctions for fraud are severe enough.

Both optimizations reduce the amount of data that needs to be transmitted and the computational complexity of the protocol. This is also important for the TSP. In order to search for the ticket for a particular spot check, the TSP needs to perform a number of decryptions. The timestamp in the tickets can be used to search through the ticket list in (probabilistic) logarithmic time.

We remark that the scheme can obviously support more than one balance register corresponding with cell cost categories instead of actual monetary values. In this way the OBU does not need to be updated with actual cost information; the transformation from cell cost categories to actual cost can be done by the TSP. Also the scheme can support various checkpoint lists varying from more locally oriented lists to list for subscribers who have been caught on actual fraud and get larger checkpoint list as a penalty. We also remark that the scheme trivially supports toll roads by just letting toll road segments correspond to cells. We finally remark that the system can also support parking fee payment, by introducing a status to cells, e.g "driving" and "parking". The transition from one status to another would give rise to the Declare protocol. In a parking environment this would give rise to two declarations: one from driving to parking and one from parking to driving, which can be associated with a parking fee. Of course, the OBU would somehow need to know how the status of the vehicle; for parking this could be induced by turning of the vehicle ignition key. If the parking cell is in the checklist then - as before - both declarations will be submitted to the TSP, allowing for inspection.

7   Conclusions

We have proposed a novel protocol for Electronic Traffic Pricing. This protocol has fairly relaxed accuracy requirements for positioning hardware, making it easier to implement in practice, in an open manner. The protocol is resilient to colluding adversaries where the positioning of the checkpoints remain secret, even after the reporting of road usage to the TSP. In contrast to other systems from the literature, this reporting procedure does not require user interaction which would drastically improve its acceptability. Additionally, the current approach only involves interaction with the user when fraud is detected, and not during honest usage.

Acknowledgements. We want to thank Gert Maneschijn, corporate security officer of the Dutch vehicle authority RDW for many stimulating discussions on road-pricing and its security and privacy concerns. The present scheme can be considered as an enhancement of a scheme developed by him and Eric Verheul in 2008.

References

1. Directive 200452EC of the European Parliament and of the Council of 29 april 2004 on the interoperability of electronic road toll systems in the Community (2004)
2. Commission decission of 6 october 2009 on the definition of the European Electronic Toll Service and its technical elements (2009)
3. Balasch, J., Rial, A., Troncoso, C., Geuens, C., Preneel, B., Verbauwhede, I.: PrETP: Privacy-preserving electronic toll pricing. In: USENIX Security (2010)
4. Chaum, D., Pedersen, T.: Wallet Databases with Observers. In: Brickell, E.F. (ed.) CRYPTO 1992. LNCS, vol. 740, pp. 89–105. Springer, Heidelberg (1993)
5. Goldwasser, S., Micali, S., Rivest, R.L.: A digital signature scheme secure against adaptive chosen-message attacks. SIAM Journal on Computing 17, 281–308 (1988)
6. Hoepman, J.-H., Huitema, G.: Privacy Enhanced Fraud Resistant Road Pricing. In: Berleur, J., Hercheui, M.D., Hilty, L.M. (eds.) HCC9/CIP 2010. IFIP AICT, vol. 328, pp. 202–213. Springer, Heidelberg (2010)

7. de Jonge, W., Jacobs, B.: Privacy-Friendly Electronic Traffic Pricing via Commits. In: Degano, P., Guttman, J., Martinelli, F. (eds.) FAST 2008. LNCS, vol. 5491, pp. 143–161. Springer, Heidelberg (2009)
8. Popa, R.A., Balakrishnan, H., Blumberg, A.: VPriv: Protecting Privacy in Location-Based Vehicular Services. In: 18th USENIX Security Symposium, Montreal, Canada (August 2009)

Ballot Aggregation and Mixnet Based Open-Audit Elections
(Extended Abstract)

Olivier Pereira*

Université catholique de Louvain
ICTEAM – Crypto Group
B-1348 Louvain-la-Neuve, Belgium

1 Introduction

Two main families of cryptographic techniques have been proposed for realizing open-audit remote elections on adversarially controlled networks: one is based on the homomorphic aggregation of encrypted ballots, while the other anonymizes ballots by transferring them through a network of mixes.

During the last three years, we organized several real-stake browser-based open-audit elections, involving more than 25000 voters in several cases, using each of the two cryptographic approaches mentioned above. We discuss the lessons we learned when adopting each of these approaches. In particular, our perspective on their relative advantages and disadvantages was strongly influenced by our experiments. Running these elections also motivated new research challenges which, if solved, would help simplifying the organization of open-audit elections in the future.

2 Two Approaches of Open-Audit Tally

2.1 Tallying by Ballot Aggregation

A first approach of open-audit elections, pioneered in the works of Cohen and Fischer [5], follows the following general outline, common to many protocols (see [6,3,7] for instance).

First, a set of trustees generate keys for a threshold homomorphic encryption scheme. The resulting public key is then published, together with the rest of the election setup (election questions, ballot filling rules, submission time and place, ...).

Voters then encrypt their choices and compute a zero-knowledge proof that the resulting ciphertexts correspond to a valid ballot. As individual ballots will never be decrypted, this proof is crucial in order to prevent a voter from submitting a ballot that would give 1000 votes to one candidate for instance.

---

* Olivier Pereira is a Research Associate of the Belgian Funds for Scientific Research F.R.S.-FNRS.

S. Petkova-Kikova, A. Pashalidis, G. Pernul (Eds.): EuroPKI 2011, LNCS 7163, pp. 123–127, 2012.

All submitted ballots are published on a bulletin board: this enables every voter to check that his/her vote was recorded properly, and to check that the other displayed ballots correspond to valid votes.

At the end of the voting phase, an encryption of the election outcome is built by aggregating all submitted ciphertexts. This operation does not require the knowledge of any secret, thanks to the homomorphic properties of the encryption scheme, and it can therefore be verified by anyone.

Eventually, the trustees jointly decrypt the election outcome, and provide a zero-knowledge proof of the validity of this decryption. Everyone then becomes able to verify that the tally was computed properly from all ballots displayed on the bulletin board.

2.2   Tallying Using Mixnets

A second approach of open-audit elections, pioneered by Sako and Kilian [13], and developed in numerous subsequent works (see [11,8,9,14] for instance), follows the following general outline.

First, a key generation and election setup procedure is executed, as in the previous approach.

Then, voters encrypt their choices, but without needing to prove anything about them, excepted the independence of the ciphertext their submit with respect to other votes, which is considerably simpler. Those ballots are then displayed on a bulletin board for verification by the voters, who can verify whether their vote was recorded properly, but not the validity of the published votes (at this stage, at least).

When the ballot submission phase is complete, all ballots go through a series of mix servers, which all shuffle and rerandomize all encrypted votes, and publish the result of this operation together with a proof of its validity. By going through those mixes, the encrypted votes are separated from the identity of the person who submitted them.

Eventually, when the mixing is complete, all ciphertexts are decrypted individually, and the decrypted votes are published together with proofs of correct decryption. The validity of the votes can now be verified by everyone, and the election outcome is computed publicly.

3   Running Open-Audit Elections

We adapted the Helios voting system [1] in various ways in order to run elections based on the two approaches described above. The specific protocols and algorithmic choices we made are described elsewhere [2,4], and we focus here on our observations while running those elections.

Table 1 summarizes observations on the ballot aggregation and mixnet-based tallying procedures, which we discuss now.

Table 1. Comparative benefits of ballot aggregation and mixnet-based tallying

	Ballot aggregation		Mixnet-based tallying
	ZK proofs of ballot validity:		Validity checked after decryption:
-	– heavy computation;	+	– no validity proof needed;
-	– need changes depending on elec-tion bylaws;	+	– universal ballot format;
+	– validity can be checked at sub-mission time.	-	– invalid ballots are hard to trace.
+	Public aggregation of ballots into election outcome.	-	Trustees anonymise ballots.
	Trustees decrypt outcome only:		Trustees decrypt all shuffled bal-lots:
+	– little information revealed;	-	– more information revealed;
+	– little computation needed.	-	– computation grows with number of voters.

Ballot preparation. The computational power of the platforms used by voters to prepare their ballot is usually fairly low. In particular, when using a web browser, the JavaScript engine is used, which strongly limits the amount of computation that can be performed. This becomes even more clear if one would like to allow voters to use their smartphone to vote. As a result, the cost of the cryptographic operations is of crucial importance for the usability of a ballot preparation system. With this respect, the mixnet-based approach offers a big advantage, since no ballot validity proof needs to be computed, which is the essential part of the ballot preparation cost in the ballot aggregation approach.

The cost of these proof is not only computational: as soon as ballot filling rules change (from one election to one other), the validity proofs need to be modified as well, requiring to touch sensitive and technical parts of the code. The mixnet-based approach is then more versatile in this respect.

The absence of submission of ballot validity proof however brings an important inconvenience: invalid ballots will only be discovered after decryption, that is, when ballots are anonymous. This strongly complicates any investigation that election officers may by willing to make on the origin of invalid ballots: they may have been produced deliberatelly by a voter, but they also may be the result of a technical failure or of a malware. While none of the ballots we received showed to be invalid, this problem already appeared in other contexts, such as during the 2011 Estonia parliamentary elections [12].

Tallying procedure. Trustees need to accomplish very sensitive tasks, manipulating secret data. However, for the needs of the elections, one will typically not desire to make the confidentiality of the votes rest on the shoulders of IT experts. Therefore, it is of crucial importance to make the task of the trustees as simple as possible, especially during the parts that require manipulating secret data.

Here, the ballot aggregation approach brings important benefits. The ballot aggregation procedure is a public operation that is typically cheap from a computational point of view. On the other hand, running mixnets requires heavy computation by the trustees, typically performed in a sequential way, and requiring to manipulate secret permutations and reencryption factors. Furthermore, at the end of these anonymization procedures, the ballot aggregation approach requires to only decrypt the election outcome, a task that is usually even cheaper than preparing a ballot. But if mixnets are used, the trustees need to decrypt all ballots individually, which is a much more challenging task as soon as the number of voters grows. As a result, while the tallying procedure can typically remain browser-based when ballot aggregation is used, the computational cost of the mixing and decryption operations require more efficient computational platforms (we used Python scripts).

Another aspect of these tallying procedures is that much more information on the votes is usually disclosed when using mixnets than when ballots are aggregated: in the first case, all individual ballots become public while, in the second, only the election outcome is available. This loss of confidentiality may, when ciphertexts encrypt complex choices, open the way to various attacks related to the detection of specific patterns in the decrypted ballots (Italian attack, . . .). Aggregation may also enable levels of privacy that would not have been possible otherwise. For instance, during the UCL university president election [2], the votes of voters with a different status in the university (students, faculty, . . .) received different weights, but it was desired that nobody should know whether the elected university president received more support from one category of voters rather than from another. This has been implemented by weighting the votes in the encrypted domain during ballot aggregation, but could not have been accomplished using mixnets or traditional paper-based voting: those approaches would have required to perform separate tallies for the different categories of voters and to weight the corresponding results in the clear.

4   Conclusions

Comparatively, the ballot aggregation approach brings most of the efforts on software programmers (who need to adapt ZK ballot validity proofs) and voters (who might receive a fairly large computational load), while the mixnet-based approach brings most of the efforts on the trustees (who need to shuffle and decrypt all ballots) and on the election organizers (who need to orchestrate a more complex tallying procedure at the end of which they might need to investigate cases of invalid ballots).

Our experiences stressed the importance of having a tallying procedure as smooth and simple as possible, keeping the private data manipulation and need for investigation to its strict minimum. These aspects, which became more and more clear to us after each election we organized, support the adoption of the ballot aggregation approach is all cases where it is feasible.

We however had to face elections where we had to adopt the mixnet-based approach, due to a very large number of election candidates (> 250) and complex ballot filling rules that required a computational load that was too heavy to bear by the voters.

As a result, we look forward to further research results that would allow reducing the computational load during the ballot preparation in the ballot aggregation approach. One way to accomplish this is to improve the performances of cryptographic operations in JavaScript [10]. Another way would be to find more efficient ballot encoding and validity proof techniques, that could be adapted to different kind of elections with minimal burden.

References

1. Adida, B.: Helios: web-based open-audit voting. In: Sec 2008: Proceedings of the 17th Conference on Security Symposium, pp. 335–348. USENIX Association, Berkeley (2008)
2. Adida, B., de Marneffe, O., Pereira, O., Quisquater, J.J.: Electing a University President Using Open-Audit Voting: Analysis of Real-World Use of Helios. In: Jefferson, D., Hall, J.L., Moran, T. (eds.) Electronic Voting Technology Workshop/Workshop on Trustworthy Elections. Usenix (August 2009)
3. Baudron, O., Fouque, P.A., Pointcheval, D., Stern, J., Poupard, G.: Practical multicandidate election system. In: Symposium on Principles of Distributed Computing, pp. 274–283. ACM (2001)
4. Bulens, P., Giry, D., Pereira, O.: Running mixnet-based elections with Helios. In: Shacham, H., Teague, V. (eds.) Electronic Voting Technology Workshop/Workshop on Trustworthy Elections. Usenix (2011)
5. Cohen, J.D., Fischer, M.J.: A robust and verifiable cryptographically secure election scheme (extended abstract). In: 26th Annual Symposium on Foundations of Computer Science, pp. 372–382. IEEE (1985)
6. Cramer, R., Gennaro, R., Schoenmakers, B.: A Secure and Optimally Efficient Multi-authority Election Scheme. In: Fumy, W. (ed.) EUROCRYPT 1997. LNCS, vol. 1233, pp. 103–118. Springer, Heidelberg (1997)
7. Damgård, I., Jurik, M.: A Generalisation, a Simplification and Some Applications of Paillier's Probabilistic Public-Key System. In: Kim, K. (ed.) PKC 2001. LNCS, vol. 1992, pp. 119–136. Springer, Heidelberg (2001)
8. Furukawa, J., Sako, K.: An Efficient Scheme for Proving a Shuffle. In: Kilian, J. (ed.) CRYPTO 2001. LNCS, vol. 2139, pp. 368–387. Springer, Heidelberg (2001)
9. Groth, J.: A Verifiable Secret Shuffle of Homomorphic Encryptions. In: Desmedt, Y.G. (ed.) PKC 2003. LNCS, vol. 2567, pp. 145–160. Springer, Heidelberg (2002)
10. Haustenne, L., De Neyer, Q., Pereira, O.: Elliptic curve cryptography in javascript. In: ECRYPT Workshop on Lightweight Cryptography (2011)
11. Neff, C.A.: A verifiable secret shuffle and its application to e-voting. In: Proceedings of the 8th ACM Conference on Computer and Communications Security, pp. 116–125. ACM (2001)
12. OSCE/ODIHR: Estonia parliamentary elections, 6 march 2011 – OSCE/ODIHR election assessment mission report (May 2011), http://www.osce.org/odihr/77557
13. Sako, K., Kilian, J.: Receipt-Free Mix-Type Voting Scheme - a Practical Solution to the Implementation of a Voting Booth. In: Guillou, L.C., Quisquater, J.-J. (eds.) EUROCRYPT 1995. LNCS, vol. 921, pp. 393–403. Springer, Heidelberg (1995)
14. Wikström, D.: A Universally Composable Mix-Net. In: Naor, M. (ed.) TCC 2004. LNCS, vol. 2951, pp. 317–335. Springer, Heidelberg (2004)

PKI as Part of an Integrated
Risk Management Strategy for Web Security

Peter Gutmann

University of Auckland, Auckland, New Zealand
pgut001@cs.auckland.ac.nz

Abstract. In the real world, risk is never binary but always comes in shades of grey. When security systems treat risk as a purely boolean process, they're prone to failure because the quantisation that's required in order to produce a boolean result has to over- or under-estimate the actual risk. What's worse, if an all-or-nothing system like this fails, it fails completely, with no fallback position available to catch errors. Drawing on four decades of experience with security design for the built environment (buildings and houses) known as crime prevention through environmental design (CPTED), this paper looks at how CPTED is applied in practice and, using browser PKI as the best-known example of large-scale certificate use, examines certificates as part of a CPTED-style risk-mitigation system that isn't prone to all-or-nothing failures and that neatly integrates concepts like EV vs. DV vs. OV and OCSP vs. non-checked certificates into the risk-assessment process, as well as dealing with the too-big-to-fail problem of trusted browser CAs.

Keywords: PKI, risk management, crime prevention through environmental design.

1   Introduction

When we go on holiday, most of us don't just lock the door on the way out and leave it at that. We set the alarm, tell the neighbours to keep an eye on the place, arrange to have someone clear the mailbox, and set a timer for the lights in the evening to make it appear like someone's home. All of these measures can be defeated (locks can be picked, alarms bypassed, the neighbours aren't present around the clock, and so on), but the combination of defences present a fairly formidable obstacle for an attacker to overcome. By diversifying our defences, we can ensure that a failure in one of them won't result in a total loss of security. Furthermore, with this diversification the attacker can never be entirely sure that there aren't additional security measures present that'll foil their attack. This reverses the usual defender's conundrum where the defender has to defend everywhere but the attacker only has to succeed once, so that now the attacker has to attack everywhere, including locations that they may not be able to identify as being critical to the success of their attack.

Security through diversity differs somewhat from the defence-in-depth strategy that's often applied as a security mechanism in that it isn't a set of layered defences

S. Petkova-Kikova, A. Pashalidis, G. Pernul (Eds.): EuroPKI 2011, LNCS 7163, pp. 128–146, 2012.

that an attacker has to knock out one after the other but a diversification of defences for risk management purposes where each individual defensive feature may only make a tiny contribution to the overall strategy but the combination of all of these features makes an attacker's task much more challenging. The goal of risk management has been best summed up by Bankers Trust risk manager Dan Borge as "risk management means taking deliberate action to shift the odds in your favour — increasing the odds of good outcomes and reducing the odds of bad outcomes" [1].

2   Crime Prevention through Environmental Design

Diversification for risk management purposes has been a standard aspect of physical security systems since time immemorial, and in recent times has been formalised in methods like crime prevention through environmental design (CPTED, pronounced "sep-ted") [2][3][4][5]. CPTED takes ideas from behavioural theory and community organisational theory and uses them to analyse the intended use of an area and how it can be arranged to minimise crime, with the idea being that "certain kinds of space and spatial layout favor the clandestine activities of criminals. An architect, armed with some understanding of the structure of criminal encounter, can simply avoid providing the space which supports it" [3]. More succinctly it "reduces the propensity of the physical environment to support criminal behaviour" [5]

CPTED includes not only standard security measures that are traditionally applied to the built environment like providing adequate lighting (but see the discussion further down for more on this) and minimising dense shrubs and trees that provide cover for miscreants but extends to a whole host of less immediately-obvious ones as well.   One frequently-advocated (but less frequently-applied) measure involves positioning windows for so-called passive surveillance of outside public spaces, based on the "eyes on the street" concept of influential urban activist Jane Jacobs [6], with the intended goal being that "abnormal users [of the environment] will feel at greater risk of detection" [5]. Designing for passive surveillance includes measures like locating a car park in front of an office building so that the cars are in direct view of office workers rather than around the side of the building out of sight or, for schools, placing bike racks in front of classroom windows.

More generally it involves placing potential crime targets in easily-observed locations for surveillance, for example placing ATMs out on the street in full view of passers-by (if you've ever wondered why they always seem to be positioned with no regard to privacy so that anyone can observe the people using them, they're put where they are precisely so that anyone who walks up to them can be observed) and having front entrances of buildings face directly onto the street so that passing pedestrians and motorists can observe any unusual happenings. Further variations include using glazed-in balconies for residential buildings which encourages the occupants to sit in them and provide (as a side-effect of using them) surveillance of the area outside the building, and orienting houses in a cul-de-sac at 45 degrees to the main street entrance to the cul-de-sac rather than the more conventional right-angle arrangement so that they provide natural surveillance of anyone entering the cul-de-sac.

Other measures can include using slippery paints for columns and supports to prevent them from being scaled, planting climbing plants along walls subject to graffiti (a so-called "living wall") and thorny plants to discourage people from entering certain areas, or where a living wall isn't feasible for combating graffiti, using textured or boldly patterned coloured surfaces to the same effect (there's a whole science built around just this aspect of CPTED alone), eliminating architectural features that provide easy access to roofs, painting areas around night-time lighting with white, reflective paint to increase the illumination being provided, and so on. Some of these security measures like the choice of paint used are extremely trivial and all can be bypassed, but in combination they add up to make a considerable integrated defensive system for attackers to overcome.

As with computer security, security for the built environment is rarely a case of blindly following a fixed set of rules. For example trying to bolt on security through the simple expedient of adding CCTV cameras doesn't work in schools because "many of the kids committing school crimes are trying to have their moment of fame on video. CCTV gives the kids their chance to be famous" [7]. Similarly, a blanket application of the "provide adequate lighting" principle that was mentioned earlier isn't always a good thing because in some cases darkness can be a legitimate lighting strategy for CPTED. Staying on the theme of school security, lighting up the school sports grounds at night is an invitation for unauthorised use, with the accompanying risk of vandalism or burglary to adjacent facilities. What's worse, it provides a perfect excuse for trespassers to be on the school grounds after dark, with police unlikely to want to prosecute a couple of teenagers for (apparently) wanting to kick a ball around.

Similarly, having buildings brightly lit aids intruders because they don't have to provide their own lighting. Providing only the minimal lighting required by building codes, typically lit emergency exit signs, means that intruders either have to turn on the lights (which can be wired to an alarm) or use flashlights. As urban explorers have repeatedly found out, there are few things more attention-grabbing for police and security guards than a torch flashing around inside a dark, supposedly empty building. So this usage reverses the conventional thinking about using illumination for security and makes darkness a part of the security instead.

3   Risk Diversification in Browsers

Moving from security for the built environment back to security for the virtual one, one commonly-encountered situation where you can effectively apply security through diversity is to secure web browsers, or more specifically the people who use them. Although this and the following few sections focus on web browsers, they're just used because they're a representative platform that everyone's familiar with, and the general principles for risk diversification that are presented here can be applied to many other applications beyond web browsers.

A nice thing about the Internet as it's used for web browsing is that it has a great deal of what economists term diversifiable risk. This means that instead of having to rely on one single defence mechanism to try and cope with all risk, and thus risk total failure when the sole mechanism that you're relying on doesn't work, you can diversify the mechanisms that you use so that a failure of one of them may increase your overall risk but won't lead to a total failure of security.

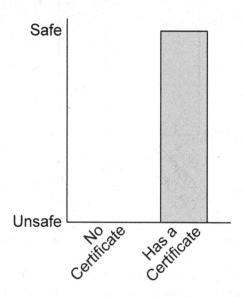

Fig. 1. Silver bullet-based assessment of site security

Web browsers currently rely almost exclusively on browser PKI to protect users from dubious and malicious web sites, and since this has little to no effect as a defence mechanism the end result is that users end up more or less unprotected, leading to the multi-billion dollar cybercrime industry that we enjoy today. The current silver-bullet approach to web browsing security is shown in Fig.1. If a web site doesn't have a certificate then it's unsafe even if it belongs to a reputable store that's been doing business at the same online location for over a decade, and if it has a certificate then it's safe even if it's run by the Russian Business Network.

What's shown in Fig.1 is the theory anyway, in practice as implemented by browsers today the situation is more like what's depicted in Fig.2. In contrast to this silver bullet-based assessment mechanism, a risk-based security assessment mechanism treats online risk as a sliding scale that goes from "probably safe" down to "probably unsafe". Just as some web browsers allow users to choose different levels of site privacy settings (mostly based around specifying the handling of different types of cookies in mind-numbing detail) and permissiveness for content on sites (this time based around the mind-numbing details of unsigned, signed, and scriptable plugins and extensions), so they could also allow the user to choose their level of risk aversion, preferably in consultation with interaction designers in order to avoid introducing any mind-numbing detail into this option as well.

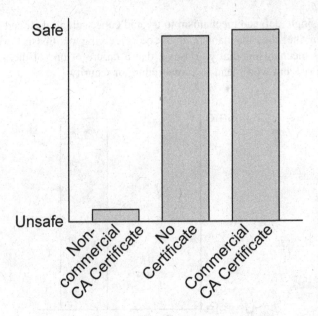

Fig. 2. Silver-bullet site security assessment in reality

With this capability users could choose their level of risk aversion, ranging from highly risk-averse (a site has to pass some fairly stringent checks in order to be regarded as safe) through to highly permissive (few checks are performed before the site is regarded as safe, the current default for all browsers). Over time, as the risk assessment measures used by browsers mature and become more robust, the default setting can be moved progressively from the current totally permissive level to more restrictive settings, and obviously users can choose to voluntarily apply the more restrictive settings themselves before they become the browser default.

The browser can also choose to automatically apply changes in risk tolerance in a situation-specific manner. For example if your laptop normally connects to the Internet through a home wireless network but is now connected through an unrecognised network (corresponding to the Internet cafe that you're currently sitting in) then the browser can increase the risk-aversion factor so that extra checking is applied to sites before they're regarded as being safe.

3.1   Risk Diversification for Internet Applications

In terms of managing risk through diversification we don't have any magic list of silver-bullet measures that will always work. What we do have though is a series of measures that we know tend to make things better, and ones that we know tend to make things worse. For example in the case of CPTED we know (now) that high-rise multi-unit housing for low income-earners ("public housing", "housing projects", or "housing estates" depending on where you're from) with a high proportion of young family members (to see the problem here, think of them as "youths" rather than "children") with shared communal entrances and elevators feeding double-hung corridors (hotel-style corridors with doors to the left and right), the type of construction famously described by urbanist William Whyte as being created by people who "dislike the city's variety and concentration, it's tension, it's hustle and bustle. The new redevelopment projects [are] physically in the city but in spirit they deny it", with the result being "anti-cities" [8], is more or less doomed to failure. Conversely, we have entire books on design patterns for effective CPTED that have been shown, through both research and real-world experience, to reduce crime and vandalism [4][5].

Let's look at some of the risk-diversification measures that you can apply to the previous example of web browsers. The aim here isn't to try and come up with some silver bullet to give you a definitely OK/definitely bad result but to create a risk-based analysis of a site's trustworthiness. What this risk-based analysis will give you is an indication that a site is probably OK or probably dubious, along with indications as to why it is or isn't OK and a general measure of the overall level of risk or non-risk.

One of the more obvious risk-based security assessment mechanisms that you can apply is the use of key continuity. Since key continuity will be upset once a year as certificates change when the CA's renewal fee is due, a variation on this checks whether the key in the certificate is the same even if the certificate as a whole isn't (sites typically re-certify the same key year in, year out rather than generating a fresh key for each certificate). You can also check whether the new certificate was issued by the same CA as the previous one (sites tend to stick with the same CA over time), and whether the combination of CA and site location make sense. For example if a CA in Brazil has issued a certificate for a site in France then there's something a bit odd going on, and if the site was previously certified by a European CA then the combination is highly suspicious.

Alongside these checks you can still use the fact that a CA sold someone a certificate as a risk-mitigation measure, as long as you remember that all it does is move the risk balance somewhat further towards "less risky" rather than being a boolean pass/fail measure. The overall level of risk reduction is defined not only by the type of the certificate (in the form of standard vs. EV certificates) but also by who issued it, with a more trustworthy CA being rated more highly than a negligent one (there are actually CAs out there who take their job very seriously, but under the current one-size-misfits-all model used by browsers they're treated no differently to the most negligent CA.

This also deals with the CA too-big-to-fail problem, since a CA can now be downgraded to a high-risk category in the same way that risky financial ventures will have their ratings downgraded by ratings agencies. This type of downgrading has been a standard feature of the finance industry since credit ratings agencies first appeared more than a century ago, and apart from recent issues during the 2008 financial crisis the ratings that they provided have been a pretty good indicator of a particular venture's credit risk.

So rather than the current pass/fail measure that rewards negligent CAs (the less checking that the CA does, the lower its operating costs), a risk-evaluation based system rewards diligent CAs by assigning them a lower risk rating than less diligent ones. This won't necessarily work on smaller CAs that have issued an insignificant number of certificates so that there are no good statistics available on how negligent (or diligent) they've been, but it doesn't matter in their case because, as in the case of the Diginotar CA, they're not too big to fail. If a CA has been active enough, and issued a large enough number of certificates, to become too big to fail then they'll also have a sufficiently visible track record that they can be rated on it.

Another aspect of key continuity is to use the user's history of interaction with a site over time as a risk assessment measure. The browser can now change its behaviour depending on whether this is a user's first visit to a site, an infrequent visit, or a frequent visit. For example if the user frequently visits `https://www.paypal.com` but is now visiting `https://www.paypai.com` for the first time then the browser would increase the risk level associated with the site since it's one that the user doesn't normally visit (just this basic measure alone has been shown to significantly increase a user's ability to detect spoofed web sites [9]).

Fig. 3. Checking a site via its AS data

A risk-based approach to browser security isn't limited purely to certificate use though (the browsers' exclusive focus on something that's entirely outside their control as a silver bullet for security makes it more a part of the problem set than the solution set). There are far more ways of estimating a site's legitimacy than just "is there a certificate present". For example many larger and better-known sites (the ones that are typically targeted for phishing attacks) are hosted and run by network operators that run their own Internet autonomous systems (ASes). Taking one example of a site hosted within a particular AS, the web site of the Société Générale (a large French bank) is hosted within an AS named "SOCIETE GENERALE", located in the EU, and allocated in 1995, as shown by the browser plugin depicted in Fig.3. This positive result moves the risk assessment some way towards "safe". On the other hand if the AS was located in eastern Europe, or had been allocated yesterday, then it'd move the assessment some way towards "unsafe". In some cases it's even easier than that. A number of ASes are known to host no legitimate content, in which case they can simply be blocked completely [10].

Since it's relatively easy to geolocate servers, an additional check would be to verify that the server is located at a matching location for the AS that it's associated with. In practice this is mostly a no-op check, but it does add a small amount of confidence to the overall risk assessment. A more useful check is the time-to-live (TTL) for the DNS A and NS records, with short TTLs typically being a sign of a fast-flux botnet. One slight complicating factor here is that some content-distribution networks (CDNs) can also use very short TTLS, for example Akamai uses an extremely low TTL in order to force clients to re-request often so that Akamai can use the data to do path optimisation to clients. This is relatively rare though, and when it does occur it can be handled through whitelisting of the CDNs that do it.

A second item to check is the domain's registration date via a whois lookup, serving the same purpose as checking the registration date for the AS that was mentioned earlier. Another check that you can make using DNS records is whether the A, MX, and/or NS records share the same IP prefix or AS, typically reflecting a web site and mail server hosted in the same data centre rather than being scattered across machines in different locations as they might be for a malicious site designed to be takedown-resistant.

Another risk-based assessment technique that you can use is to check the operating system that the remote site is running via network stack fingerprinting (since you're already communicating with the remote system's network stack, this isn't too hard to do). In order to make phishing sites resilient and hard to detect, they're often hosted on botnets via reverse proxies and other tricks, so if your (purported) e-commerce site is hosted on a machine running Windows 7 Home Premium then that's a good sign that something's wrong. Finding a site hosted in an IP address block assigned to, or AS administered by, a DSL or cable modem provider is another fairly sure sign of a problem.

Something else that you might check for, although it's pretty rare, is the use of non-ASCII characters in what would otherwise be ordinary .com or similar domains. For example if an obviously non-Russian site has a Cyrillic 'r' (U+0440, which looks like an ASCII 'p') or a Cyrillic 's' (U+0441, which looks like an ASCII 'c') in the middle of the URL then this could be an attempt to disguise the URL as one for a different site.

3.2   Risk Diversification through Content Analysis

As is already being done for spam filtering, there are statistical classification techniques that you can apply to web sites to try and detect potential phishing sites. One rather straightforward one uses text-mining feature extraction from the suspect web page to create a list of keywords (a so-called lexical signature) to submit to Google as a search query. If the domain hosting the site matches the first few Google search results then it's regarded as probably OK. If it doesn't match, for example a page with the characteristics of the eBay login page hosted in the Ukraine (or at least hosted somewhere that doesn't match an immediate Google search result), then it's regarded as suspicious. In evaluations of a sample of 100 phishing and 100 legitimate pages, this detected 97% of phishing pages with a 10% false positive rate [11] (malware already uses Google search APIs to find targets for attacks [12], so there's no reason why the defenders shouldn't take advantage of the same service).

A variation of this might be to use the Wayback Machine to see how a particular site looked a few months ago and whether there's at least a general similarity to what's there now (the downside to this is that Wayback Machine lookups can be rather slow, the Google cache is faster but doesn't provide the same level of control over date ranges that Wayback does).

A more sophisticated approach is used in a scheme called Prophiler that was originally developed as a front-end filter for web crawlers that try and detect malicious web pages. The standard way of doing this involves processing the suspect page in an emulated browser or even a real browser running in a VM. Since this is rather slow, Prophiler provides a fast filter that doesn't require rendering the web page or running any scripts on it [13]. The results achieved by Prophiler are quite impressive. When run on a set of 19 million pages crawled over a two-month period, it exhibited a mis-classification rate (malicious sites classed as benign) close to zero, with a false positive rather of 14%. Remember that, with the risk-diversification process that we're using here, a false positive only moves a site slightly further into the "risky" category, it's not a purely boolean decision that automatically marks it as bad. In any case if it's really a concern then you can move the classification threshold down a bit, trading off a lower false positive rate for a slight increase in the mis-classification rate. This was the approach used in one Javascript-based web site classifier, which achieved a false positive rate of zero at the cost of a slightly higher mis-classification rate [14]. Another classifier exhibited a false positive rate of 0.0003% while processing Javascript at over a megabyte a second [15].

There are quite a number of web page features that you can check quickly and efficiently that contribute towards providing a good estimate of whether a site is suspicious or not [16][17][18]. Some of the features that have been found to be effective in practice include the number of elements like div, iframe, and object with small areas (used to hide web bugs and carry out drive-by downloads and other malicious activities), the number of elements with suspicious content like potential shellcode, the number of overtly suspicious items such as object tags containing the classids of exploitable ActiveX controls, the number of objects pulled in from other locations via script, iframe, frame, embed, form, or object tags, the number of out-of-place elements (typically caused by using XSS to inject scripts or iframes into odd locations), the presence of double documents (ones with multiple html, head, title or body elements, a side-effect of certain types of web-site compromise), the presence of known malicious patterns like a meta refresh pointing to an exploit server, and finally various known malicious patterns like swfNode.php and pdfNode.php that are commonly used by exploit toolkits (explicit checks for these will eventually be evaded by the toolkit authors but it doesn't hurt to check anyway).

The features listed above have all been fairly obvious ones obtained through human analysis, but they can be augmented with others that are less obvious to human observers that have been obtained through machine-learning techniques. For example one analysis using Bayesian classifiers and support vector machines (a classifier for high-dimensional data) discovered non-obvious indicators like the presence of the string members in the URL, triggered by the presence of phishing and malware sites on free hosting services like members.aol.com and members.tripod.com. Another example of an indicator discovered through machine learning was the fact that sites with DNS NS records pointing at IP ranges owned by major registrars like RIPE (the European regional Internet registry) were far less likely to be malicious than ones pointing at IP ranges assigned to GoDaddy. This type of machine-learning approach is quite beneficial because it can automatically extract new, non-obvious features that go beyond the more obvious ones that humans can come up with [19].

Checking Javascript in web pages is particularly effective because if it directly performs a malicious action then it's fairly easy to detect using simple signature-based checking and if it's obfuscated and packed in order to evade detection then it ends up looking like no normal Javascript [14]. Some of the checks that you can apply to Javascript on web pages include the keyword-to-word ratio (in most exploits the number of keywords like var, for, while, and others is limited in comparison to other operations like instantiation, arithmetic operations, and function calls), the number of long strings and their entropy (typically used to obscure payloads) alongside various other characteristics that indicate the likely presence of obfuscated payloads, the presence of classes of function calls like eval(),substring(), and fromCharCode() that are widely used for de-obfuscation and decryption, the length of strings passed to functions like eval() (another de-obfuscation indicator), the number of string assignments (de-obfuscation and decryption procedures tend to have unusually large numbers of string assignments), the number of bytes allocated through string operations like assignments, concat(), and substring() (used for heap exploits and heap spraying), the number of DOM-modifying functions (operations like document.write and document.createElement, typically used to instantiate vulnerable components or create page elements that are used to load scripts and exploit pages), the values of attributes and parameters in method calls (long strings are typically used for buffer-overflow attacks), the number of event attachments like page load triggers that are used for drive-by downloads, and the presence of iframe-injection code or code to inject other objects or scripts into a page.

In the anti-virus field there's been an ongoing arms race between the creators of malware and the anti-virus industry, with the best malware being promoted as fully undetectable (FUD) by the malware industry. This is traditionally done using a scan from the VirusTotal service that runs (potential) malware through all commonly-used malware scanners, so that a clean VirusTotal report serves as a type of certification of undetectability [20]. In the case of malicious web sites the process isn't quite as straightforward for the bad guys. For example attackers don't have complete control over the output of an XSS, SQL injection, or similar injection attack, resulting in malformed strings, repeated or out-of-place tags, and other patterns that indicate that something untoward is going on.

Similarly, while it's relatively easy to obfuscate Javascript in order to disguise obviously malicious code, the artefacts of the obfuscation are rather harder to disguise because it results in page content that's nothing like what would be present on a legitimate web site. So while attackers can try and evade detection in the manner of traditional malware authors, the anti-detection mechanisms themselves then increase their detectability (recall that many of the suspicious-Javascript triggers mentioned above were for de-obfuscation artefacts). The Prophiler tool that was discussed earlier takes the additional step of submitting a small fraction of supposedly-benign pages to a back-end for more heavy-duty analysis in order to track evasion trends, in the same way that most anti-virus packages submit samples to their vendors for further analysis.

Another malware anti-detection artefact that you can try and detect is the fact that some malware sites try to hide their presence from site-scanners by returning different content depending on who's asking. So if you visit the site with Google/Googlebot as your user agent or using an open-source Javascript engine (typically used for site-scanning) then you'll get benign content, but if you visit it with MSIE as your user agent or using Microsoft's Javascript engine then you'll get malicious content. You'll have to be a bit careful here because some sites change their content slightly for Google indexability, but it's not nearly as severe as the switch from benign to malicious content.

In addition to these checks there are additional checks that you might one day be able to perform that depend on the emergence of additional support infrastructure outside of what exists today. One of these pieces of additional infrastructure moves certificate-related policy into the DNS, so that when you perform a DNS lookup for a site you can also retrieve information that can be used to help verify the site's certificate. Unfortunately the folks working on this decided to hitch their work to the DNSSEC bandwagon, which means that the efforts are progressing at the slower of the combined rates of DNSSEC deployment and deployment of the various certificate-policy-in-DNS mechanisms.

Recall from the earlier discussion of the concept of risk diversification that the use of DNSSEC is mostly redundant in this case, since the value that's being provided is a diversification of security-verification channels so that an attacker now has to go beyond simply setting up a phishing site and waiting for victims to scurry in to performing an active attack on every (potential) victim's DNS. Adding DNSSEC to the equation is at best a distraction and more probably a liability, since deployment of this additional checking now hinges on the successful global deployment of DNSSEC to end-user systems.

3.3   Applying Risk Diversification

Combining all of these risk-based factors for our sample site gives us the security assessment shown in Figure 4. None of the factors that are given are a clear indicator that the site is sound, but all of them help build confidence in the site to a point where you can declare it safe with a high degree of probability. In fact with this many factors speaking in its favour the site's rating would be well over 100%. This illustrates the fault-tolerant nature of the risk assessment mechanism in which even if some of the indicators aren't available you can still be reasonably confident that the site is safe to use. In the field of reliability engineering this is called de-rating, running a device at less than its rated maximum level in order to provide a safety margin for operations.

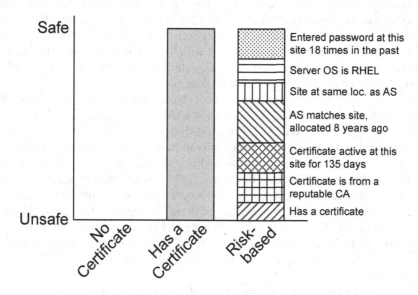

Fig. 4. Risk-based assessment of site security

These sorts of risk assessment-based techniques have already been in use for some years by email applications in the form of greylisting. Greylisting takes advantage of the fact that software designed for spamming exhibits quite different behaviour patterns than those exhibited by legitimate email applications. This arises from a combination of two factors, the first being that spam behaviour patterns are naturally quite different from normal email patterns, and the second being that spam-optimised mail software is often noticeably different from, and incompatible with, standard mailer behaviour. For example mailers that "talk too fast", not going through the proper SMTP handshake but sending data as soon as they connect in order to maximise the amount of spam that they can pump out, are a good indication that you're talking to a spambot. This can be combined with other heuristics that go beyond the traditional whitelisting, blacklisting, and statistical classification of message contents through to more advanced techniques like tracking which hosts a message has passed through via its Received headers [21] and TCP fingerprinting of the sending OS [22], including risk-assessment techniques that get updated as botnets and spammer techniques evolve over time [23]. The effects of email greylisting techniques can be quite impressive [24], and virtually all widely-used mailers already implement various forms of this type of filtering [25].

At the time of writing there's just one single mechanism, present in only one browser, that does anything like this, the SmartScreen filter that Microsoft introduced in Internet Explorer 9 in 2011 to help protect users from malicious downloads. Instead of blindly warning for every download, SmartScreen only warns for applications without a good "reputation", where "reputation" is somewhat vaguely defined by Microsoft but includes matching an existing known-good application, being signed, and possibly other measures [26][27]. The intent of SmartScreen is to reduce warnings from the generic, and effectively useless "This type of file may harm your computer" to one that only occurs with files without a "reputation", which hopefully includes malware, so that according to Microsoft's figures 90% of downloads no longer display (pointless) warnings.

Because this defence mechanism isn't based on blacklists, it takes effect immediately without the delay inherent in blacklist-based approaches. In one actual attack, SmartScreen blocked 99% of downloads of a particular piece of malware from the moment that it was released. Infection rates peaked 4-5 hours later, and another 6-7 hours after that, when infection rates had already decayed back to almost nothing, the first blacklist-based blocking (anti-virus signatures and browser blacklists) finally began to kick in [28]. Unfortunately there hasn't been any independent evaluation of the effectiveness of this reputation-based filtering (an approach that simply blocks all downloads could claim to be 100% effective in blocking malware, as long as you ignore the fact that it's also blocking 100% of non-malware), although it certainly seems to significantly improve on what other browsers are doing [29], which is nothing at all.

In order to test the resilience of your overall risk-assessment mechanism in the face of failure of one or more of the individual mechanisms, you can run automated tests that inject failures while visiting a representative sample like the top 1,000 Alexa sites in order to see how the overall assessment of risk functions when measures for some individual risks aren't available.

This type of automated fault-tolerance testing is often used in the computer industry to verify that things are working as they should, and to identify problem areas that need further attention. For example in the 1990s telecoms was a huge growth industry and telcos were having problems keeping up with billing for their services, something that was euphemistically termed "revenue assurance". In practice this meant that they often had little to no idea how much they were supposed to be billing their customers. One way of dealing with this was to use automated calling boxes that would make millions of calls at varying times and of varying durations and then compare the call logs to the telcos' billing records [30].

A far simpler technique for evaluating overall performance in the case of failures of individual components is used by Netflix, who use a system called the Chaos Monkey whose "job is to randomly kill instances and services within our architecture" [31]. As a result of engineering their systems to cope with the failure of individual components, when their hosting provider (Amazon Web Services) experienced a major outage in early 2011, Netflix wasn't affected [32][33]. You can use a similar type of Chaos Monkey to evaluate your risk-assessment mechanisms, removing some of them at random in order to see how this affects various sites' availability due to risk management.

Now that you've got some basic risk-assessment mechanisms laid out, you can combine them into a more unified site-assessment process. For example when going to a site that claims to be Gmail you might note that the user has a password for Gmail stored AND this new site has a name that's fairly close to Gmail's (there are any number of fuzzy/approximate string-matching algorithms out there, pick your favourite one from a textbook) AND the domain was registered a day ago, therefore we'd better take defensive action against a phishing attack.

There are many different variations of this process that you can apply. For example if the user goes to a new site that they haven't entered a password for before and the site asks for a password and what the user enters matches something that they've used at another site then you could notify them that they've already used this password for another site and ask whether they're sure that they're at the right site, a measure that conveniently also provides a gentle hint against password reuse.

One common argument that's been raised against this form of risk-assessment strategy when it's applied to secure browser users has been the fear expressed by vendors that applying the extra safety checks will causes users to switch to browsers that don't apply them. We don't have any evidence to support this claim, but in a related field, that of ISP walled gardens for which exactly the same objections have been raised, the result of ISPs applying the extra safety checks was that it increased rather than decreased user confidence in and loyalty to the ISPs that did it. So the sole evidence that we have in this area is that it increases, rather than decreases, user satisfaction in a product or service.

A notable factor of these checks is that they're all incredibly tedious to perform, but that's exactly why we have computers. In the real world no-one would, before entering a bank branch, go to the local records office and look up how long the bank has been at that location, check with the banking regulators to verify that the bank actually exists and is currently solvent, contact whatever local authorities oversee construction issues and verify that the building plans are on file and that it is indeed a bank, and so on. Instead they rely on proxies, "it looks like a bank so it must be a bank", because no (normal) person has the time or energy to perform that amount of checking.

Computers, however, are specifically designed to perform boring, repetitive operations over and over again. Running a series of checks on a site is effectively free as far as the user is concerned, to the point where it's downright negligent not to do so.

Obviously these checks are overkill if they're used on all sites. Here again, you can use risk-assessment heuristics to help decide which sites require extra checking. The most obvious heuristic is "is the site asking for user credentials (typically a password)?". A related indicator is the presence of certain strings like login, signin, secure, bank and account in the page URL, alongside situation-specific ones like webscr (for PayPal) and ebayisapi (for eBay) [16]. Since the goal of phishing is to acquire the user's credentials for a particular site, any site that tries to obtain these credentials should automatically be subject to extended checking.

Another heuristic is to check the page contents for keywords or other indicators that it represents a high-value site. Impersonating (for phishing purposes) a bank is more or less impossible without including a large number of banking-related keywords on the site (go to your bank's home page to see an example of this in action). If the phishers try and disguise this by using image text then a site that consists mostly of images and asks for a password would be another indicator that extra checking is required. Consulting a database of common phishing targets to identify the need for extra checking should also be a standard security check that browsers apply. The bad guys have been using extensive databases of financial institutions for their trojans to target for years so it's about time the defenders caught up, perhaps by using a target list from a banking trojan as a starting point, since the attackers have already done all of the necessary groundwork.

Another thing that some malware authors who create man-in-the-browser trojans (MITBs) have done is implement heuristics to detect potential phishing sites. This leads to the oxymoronic situation in which the MITB malware will recognise phishing sites and ignore them for the purposes of harvesting user credentials while the browser itself will happily let the user hand them over to the phishers. In the same way that malware vendors sometimes remove competing malware from a computer that they're infecting, the next logical step for the MITB developers would be to have it prevent users from entering their credentials at phishing sites on the basis that it reduces the value of the credentials if too many parties other than the MITB's clients get their hands on them.

Diversifying security mechanisms so that a failure of one won't lead to a total failure of security can apply to the CA side of browser PKI as well. Using the case of the CA failures that occurred in early 2011 (or at least one of the failures, specifically the one involving the compromised Comodo reseller), any one of a number of extremely rudimentary checks would have caught the problem long before it actually became a real problem. Certificates for well-known, high-profile US sites were being requested by someone in Iran (or, in the case of the reseller that they were being channelled through, by a small-scale reseller in Europe), in some cases EV certificates were being replaced by non-EV certificates, and in all of the cases certificates issued by completely different CAs were now being replaced by Comodo ones.

All of these anomalies should have triggered pretty much every alarm that it's possible to trigger with a CA. Apart from the obvious reactive checks, even a simple proactive check like opening an HTTPS connection to each site for which a certificate was being issued would have revealed that they already had certificates issued by other CAs, that the certificates were nowhere near the due date for their CA renewal fees (which is the usual reason for re-issuing a certificate), and that some of the certificates were EV certificates that were now being replaced by non-EV ones. As with the browser-based risk assessment, this combination should have moved the overall risk level to the high-risk end of the scale, triggering manual review and a requirement for more comprehensive authentication of the requester and verification that they controlled the sites that they were requesting the certificates for before the certificates were actually issued.

An additional safety measure in this case would have been to email the domain holder for a chance to object, an automatic process that doesn't require any manual intervention.   In risk-management terminology these measures are called self-generating risk controls, where one control for a particular risk situation can dynamically generate new controls to handle particular special-case conditions.

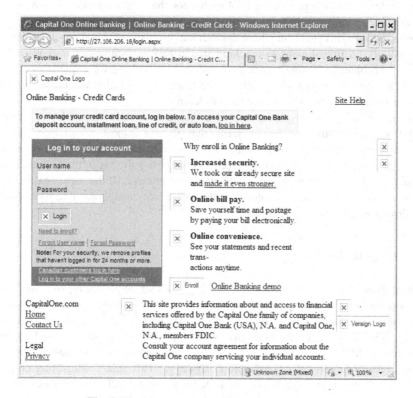

Fig. 5. Would you enter your password at this site?

The final step in providing security through diversity for browser users is the question of how to notify them that there's a problem. For this we can take advantage of something that at first glance appears to be a flaw, the fact that for users a site's appearance will override security indicators and browser-supplied phishing warnings. By changing a site's appearance if it registers as being high-risk we can turn the fact that its visual appearance overrides any other security indicators [34][35] to our advantage. Disabling Javascript and plugins (which is in any case a wise precaution when visiting a high-risk site, in the case of major US banks most of their sites don't function without Javascript and some simply display blank home pages if Javascript is disabled), blocking images (another good precaution given the number of attacks that exploit malformed image data), and rendering the site in the default font (no boldface headings, different fonts and font sizes, and so on) should be enough to override the standard "it looks OK so it must be OK" test that's applied by users. An example of a bank phishing site with most decorations stripped in this manner so that the result looks nothing like what the user would be expecting from the real site is shown in Fig.5. This example still has some minimal formatting and decorations allowed, if it turns out that this is still sufficient to convince some users that the site is genuine then you can remove that too.

By making this change you've now really got the user's attention so you should provide further information to explain why the site looks the way that it does. This reverses the standard situation where the user can see their goal and anything that you do is simply an impediment to reaching it. In this case they can instead see that there's a problem in getting to the goal and they're looking for explanations. This creates a scenario for providing just-in-time learning, exploiting the fact that people learn best when they have a specific need to learn.

In some cases sites may be evaluated as being extremely high-risk. A site may exhibit so many obvious danger signs that there's almost no chance that it's legitimate, but a very high chance that it's a direct threat to the user and/or their PC if they even visit the site. In situations like this the best policy is to treat an attempt to connect in the same way as a standard network server error. If the user is expecting to talk to a safe site and the indicators are that it's a very dangerous one then that's a fatal error and not a one-click speed-bump.

4   Conclusion

Current browsers (and by extension numerous other applications that deal with security) treat risk as a purely boolean process, an all-or-nothing system that, when it fails, fails completely. By taking advantage of the principle of risk diversification that's employed to secure the built environment (buildings and houses) and applying it to browser PKI, we can eliminate this single point of failure and make the PKI an integral part of an overall risk-mitigation strategy. This neatly integrating concepts like EV vs. DV vs. OV certificates and OCSP vs. non-checked certificates into the risk-assessment process, as well as dealing with the too-big-to-fail problem of trusted browser CAs.

References

[1] Borge, D.: The Book of Risk. John Wiley and Sons (2001)
[2] Jeffery, C.: Crime Prevention Through Environmental Design. Sage Publications (1971)
[3] Defensible Space: Crime Prevention Through Urban Design. Oscar Newman, Macmillan (1973)
[4] Poyner, B.: Design Against Crime: Beyond Defensible Space, Butterworth (1983)
[5] Crowe, T.: Crime Prevention Through Environmental Design. Butterworth-Heinemann (1991)
[6] Jacobs, J.: The Death and Life of Great American Cities. Random House (1961)

[7]   Atlas, R., Schneider, R.: Creating Safe and Secure Environments for Schools and Colleges. In: 21st Century Security and CPTED, p. 279. CRC Press (2008)

[8]   Whyte, W.: The Exploding Metropolis. Doubleday/Anchor (1958)

[9]   Biancuzzi, F.: Phishing with Rachna Dhamija (June 19, 2006), http://www.securityfocus.com/columnists/407

[10] Abu-Nimeh, S., Chen, T., Alzubi, O.: Malicious and Spam Posts in Online Social Networks. IEEE Computer 44(9), 23 (2011)

[11] Zhang, Y., Hong, J., Cranor, L.: CANTINA: A Content-Based Approach to Detecting Phishing Web Sites. In: Proceedings of the 16th International World Wide Web Conference (WWW 2007), p. 639 (May 2007)

[12] Shin, Y., Gupta, M., Myers, S.: The Nuts and Bolts of a Forum Spam Automator. In: Proceedings of the 4th Workshop on Large-Scale Exploits and Emergent Threats, LEET 2011 (March 2011), http://www.usenix.org/-event/leet11/tech/full_papers/Shin.pdf

[13] Canali, D., Cova, M., Vigna, G., Kruegel, C.: Prophiler: A Fast Filter for the Large-Scale Detection of Malicious Web Pages. In: Proceedings of the 20th International World Wide Web Conference (WWW 2011), p. 197 (March 2011)

[14] Cova, M., Kruegel, C., Vigna, G.: Detection and Analysis of Drive-by-Download Attacks and Malicious JavaScript Code. In: Proceedings of the 19th World Wide Web Conference (WWW 2010), p. 281 (April 2010)

[15] Curtsinger, C., Livshits, B., Zorn, B., Seifert, C.: ZOZZLE: Fast and Precise In-Browser JavaScript Malware Detection. In: Proceedings of the 20th Usenix Security Symposium (Security 2011), p. 33 (August 2011)

[16] Doshi, S., Provos, N., Chew, M., Rubin, A.: A Framework for Detection and Measurement of Phishing Attacks. In: Proceedings of the ACM Workshop on Rapid Malcode (WORM 2007), p. 1 (November 2007)

[17] Seifert, C., Welch, I., Komisarczuk, P.: Identification of Malicious Web Pages with Static Heuristics. In: Proceedings of the Australasian Telecommunication Networks and Applications Conference (ATNAC 2008), p. 91 (December 2008)

[18] Ma, J., Saul, L., Savage, S., Voelker, G.: Identifying Suspicious URLs: An Application of Large-Scale Online Learning. In: Proceedings of the 26th International Conference on Machine Learning (ICML 2009), p. 681 (June 2009)

[19] Ma, J., Saul, L., Savage, S., Voelker, G.: Beyond Blacklists: Learning to Detect Malicious Web Sites from Suspicious URLs. In: Proceedings of the 15th Conference on Knowledge Discovery and Data Mining (KDD 2009), p. 1245 (June 2009)

[20] Gutmann, P.: The Commercial Malware Industry, talk at Defcon (August 15, 2007), https://www.defcon.org/images/defcon-15/dc15-presentations/dc-15-gutmann.pdf, updated version at http://www.cs.auckland.ac.nz/-pgut001/pubs/malware_biz.pdf

[21] Leiba, B., Ossher, J., Rajan, V., Segal, R., Wegman, M.: SMTP Path Analysis. In: Proceedings of the 2nd Conference on Email and Anti-Spam, CEAS 2005 (July 2005), http://ceas.cc/2005/papers/176.pdf

[22] Esquivel, H., Mori, T., Akella, A.: Router-Level Spam Filtering Using TCP Fingerprints: Architecture and Measurement-Based Evaluation. In: Proceedings of the 6th Conference on Email and Anti-Spam, CEAS 2009 (July 2009), http://ceas.cc/2009/papers/ceas2009-paper-10.pdf

[23] Venema, W.: Postfix: Past, Present, and Future. In: Invited Talk at the 24th Large Installation System Administration Conference, LISA 2010 (November 2010)

[24] Levine, J.: Experiences with Greylisting. In: Proceedings of the 2nd Conference on Email and Anti-Spam, CEAS 2005 (July 2005),
http://ceas.cc/2005/-papers/120.pdf

[25] Lundgren, B.: Greylisting implementations (2011),
http://www.greylisting.org/implementations/

[26] Colvin, R.: Stranger Danger' — Introducing SmartScreen Application Reputation, October 13 (2010), http://blogs.msdn.com/b/ie/-archive/2010/10/13/
stranger-danger-introducing-smartscreen-application-
reputation.aspx

[27] Colvin, R.: SmartScreen Application Reputation — Building Reputation, March 22 (2011), http://blogs.msdn.com/b/ie/archive/2011/03/
22/-smartscreen-174-application-reputation-building-
reputation.aspx

[28] Haber, J.: SmartScreen Application Reputation in IE9, May 17 (2011),
http://blogs.msdn.com/b/ie/archive/2011/05/17/
smartscreen-174-application-reputation-in-ie9.aspx

[29] Web Browser Group Test Socially-Engineered Malware — Europe Q2 2011, NSS Labs (May 2011), http://www.nsslabs.com/assets/noreg-reports/2011/
nss%20labs_q2_2011_browsersem_FINAL.pdf

[30] Leitch, M.: Intelligent Internal Control and Risk Management. Gower Publishing (2008)

[31] Ciancutti, J.: 5 Lessons We've Learned Using AWS, December 16 (2010),
http://techblog.netflix.com/2010/12/
5-lessons-weve-learned-using-aws.html

[32] 'timf', Some quotes regarding how Netflix handled this without interruptions, April 21 (2011), http://news.ycombinator.com/item?id=2470773

[33] Hicks, C., Orzell, G.: Lessons Netflix Learned from the AWS Outage, Adrian Cockroft (April 29, 2011), http://techblog.netflix.com/-2011/04/lessons-
netflix-learned-from-aws-outage.html

[34] Turner, C., Zavod, M., Yurcik, W.: Factors that Affect the Perception of Security and Privacy of E-Commerce Web Sites. In: Proceedings of the 4th International Conference on Electronic Commerce Research, p. 628 (November 2001)

[35] Egelman, S., Cranor, L., Hong, J.: You've Been Warned: An Empirical Study of the Effectiveness of Web Browser Phishing Warnings. In: Proceedings of the 2008 Conference on Human Factors in Computing Systems (CHI 2008), p. 1065 (April 2008)

A PKI-Based Mobile Banking Demonstrator

Gauthier Van Damme, Nicolas Luyckx, and Karel Wouters

K.U. Leuven ESAT/SCD-COSIC and IBBT,
Kasteelpark Arenberg 10, B-3001 Leuven-Heverlee, Belgium
firstname.lastname@esat.kuleuven.be

Abstract. This paper presents the implementation of a home banking solution for mobile phones, using a secure micro-SD card. This card is used to implement a strong online authentication with the bank server, based on a public key infrastructure, providing a flexible way to add entities – users as well as banks – to the ecosystem. The implemented system is running on Android mobile phones, taking into account the possible weaknesses at operating system level. The microSD card is running Java Card 2.2.1. Different security features are discussed that considerably improve upon existing mobile banking systems and allow for seamless integration of our system in the current smart phone context.

1 Introduction

Very soon after mobile phones were launched throughout the world, system developers thought of offering a banking application on users' cell phones that would allow them to manage their bank account any time, any place. With mobile phones not having the computing power they have today, these systems were quite rudimentary and their security flexibility was based on the SIM Toolkit which allows for secret key sharing between the bank and the phone's SIM card [8, 2]. As mobile phones today can be considered complete computing devices, more complex and thus useful mobile banking applications can be developed that can lead to larger user acceptance. This is facilitated by the growing number of smart phones and the increasing penetration of mobile Internet access. In Belgium, some deployed advanced mobile banking applications in 2009-2010 which indicates that mobile banking is becoming a common service in the banking world. This phenomena will only grow, and we expect it to be part of the standard daily banking package within a couple of years.

2 Existing Mobile Banking Products

Dispite the deployment mobile banking solutions, their security remains debatable, as was also the case with Internet banking in its early days. The technology still has to mature, and some emerging solutions are therefore actually based on the Internet banking security solutions, involving separate security tokens, card readers etc. Although useful, mobile users need more compact and integrated

S. Petkova-Kikova, A. Pashalidis, G. Pernul (Eds.): EuroPKI 2011, LNCS 7163, pp. 147–158, 2012.
© Springer-Verlag Berlin Heidelberg 2012

solutions, in which the complete functionality is embedded in the mobile phone. However, it remains an open question whether or not the current solutions can be as secure as their non-mobile counterparts used in a more closed desktop environment. In this section we will briefly discuss two existing mobile banking systems while the next section will describe our own, fully integrated design.

In Belgium, at least two banks currently offer a mobile banking system: BNP Paribas Fortis [3] and Keytrade Bank [9]. Both banks provide a mobile banking site accessible via a smart phone's browser. The connection is secured by the HTTPS protocol. The authentication to the mobile banking server is a two-factor authentication, based on what the user knows, namely passwords/PINs and on what the user has, in this case a second communication or information channel (SMS, card reader, secure token). In Keytrade Mobile Banking, a RSA SecurID token [15] (what the user *has*) is combined with a password (what the user *knows*). This RSA secure token is a piece of hardware that generates an One-Time Password (OTP) at fixed time intervals (usually 30 or 60 seconds) using a built-in clock and a factory-encoded random key (known as the *seed*). The seed is different for each token, and is loaded into the corresponding RSA SecurID server as the tokens are purchased. The bank's server can then verify the OTP generated by the user's token by querying the correct RSA SecurID server entry. In Fortis Mobile Banking, a One-Time Password (OTP) is sent to the user by SMS during the authentication phase. This OTP, coupled to the mobile phone number, constitutes a first authentication factor (what the user *has*). As for the Keytrade application, the password of the user is the second factor used (what the user *knows*). The alternative in Fortis Mobile Banking, is using a card reader and the debit card of the user, the equivalence of the ordinary Internet banking.

Similar to PC-based solutions, mobile banking products are vulnerable to phishing and man-in-the-middle attacks: because of the fact that a standard browser is used, the user can be diverted to a fake man-in-the-middle website, using a phishing SMS or email. The OTP generated by the RSA secure token or the OTP, sent by SMS can also be recovered this way. Another disadvantage, in case secure tokens or card readers are used, is that the user must always carry around this device together with his phone. In case the OTP is sent by SMS, this might also involve additional costs for the user; for BNP Paribas Fortis Mobile Banking, one free SMS per day is offered, but additional OTP request come at premium SMS rates. Another potential risk in using SMS is the communication channel: not only does this require a trust relation with the Mobile Network Operator (MNO), but also depends on the security properties of the used mobile network. In Belgium, mobile phone communications are encrypted using the A5/1 standard. This standard presents several serious weaknesses [6]. In 2010, researchers Karsten Nohl and Sylvain Munaut gave a live demonstration of their GSM attack at the 27th annual Chaos Communication Congress in Berlin [4]. The whole process takes about 20 seconds, enabling phone conversations and SMS messages to be recorded and decrypted [7]. Finally, even the secure hardware tokens (RSA SecurID) seem to have their weaknesses. A recent hack of the backend systems of RSA[1], apparently revealed enough information to attack one of their customers using SecurID, Lockheed Martin. Breaches like these, were the token's seed are revealed, bring back these system's security to just one authentication factor (the user's password), which has been shown to be rather insecure.

To counter these problems, the solution proposed in this paper is based on public key cryptography and with this, a root of trust is constructed using a Public Key Infrastructure (PKI) with dedicated certificates. Of course, more general solutions based on a PKI and certificates have been proposed recently as well [12], but none of them provides for sufficient security against some long known and widespread problems. As these systems rely on the security of the OS of the mobile devices for storing their critical cryptographic data, they are vulnerable to malware and viruses, just as PC-based solutions are.

On the other hand, a fully integrated mobile system as presented in these papers and in the next section obviously lack the duality of two separate information sources or factors (namely the phone and some external token or channel) used in the previously presented applications. As will be explained in section 5, the proposed system therefor implements different security features to compensate this. The PKI based mobile banking system presented will then not only provide for the encryption and integrity of the transactions and non-revocation by the user, but will also avoid as much as possible that a compromised OS can affect it.

3 System Overview

Building mobile banking application based on shared secrets always implies some major risks and is often based on trust in third parties (MNO, RSA, etc.). For this reason an alternative way to the existing mobile banking systems is proposed, based on a PKI, built around what is called a secure element (SE) inside the mobile phone. Another obvious advantage of this approach is the absence of additional devices and tokens such as a card reader or a secure token.

The main feature of an SE is that it is considered secure against known hardware and software attacks. It typically consists of secure memory, a processor and one or more cryptographic co-processors. These characteristics allow developers to use SEs for storing cryptographic keys or other critical data and to securely deploy cryptographic functions in their applications.

Different types of SEs exist, although most of them today are so-called Java Cards [13]. These Java Cards are SEs on which a very limited subset of the Java Virtual Machine (JVM) is running, with a reasonable range of security functions available. Another aspect to SEs is that they come in different form factors. The SE can either be embedded into the phone, stored inside a removable microSD card or sit on the phone's SIM card. In our application we used a microSD card that supports Java Card version 2.2.1.

---

[1] Open letter to RSA customers, http://www.rsa.com/node.aspx?id=3872

Secure microSD cards are produced by several manufacturers; we used a card developed by the German company Giesecke & Devrient [5]. The card architecture is shown in Figure 1. A smart card chip is contained inside the micro-SD card. One accesses it via the flash controller which acts as a proxy, similar to a smart card reader. The APDUs[2], used to address the smart card are tunnelled via specific SD read/write commands. Towards the developer the smart card is presented as a classic Java Card, allowing a quick take-up and easy portability of the developed application to other types of SEs.

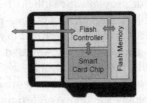

Fig. 1. Mobile Security Card Architecture

The banking application has been developed as a stand-alone application on a smart phone running the open Android OS containing this microSD card. The bank server has been simulated by a pseudo banking application running on Apache Tomcat [16], using Java Servlet technology. A comprehensive overview of our solutions, including a symmetric key version of our application, can be found in [10].

Summarised, the components in the system, depicted in Fig 2, are the following:

- The secure microSD card (further referred to as 'the card'): this is used as the root of trust at the user's side. It holds cryptographic key material that never leaves the card. The Java Card program on the card, is referred to as the applet.
- The mobile phone, with a dedicated application for mobile banking. The application implements the communication gateway between the secure microSD card and the mobile banking server. It also provides the GUI to the user.
- The mobile bank server, providing the interface to the bank's back-end systems.

4   The Mobile Banking Application

Our solution features a small Public Key Infrastructure (PKI). Both the card and the server have their own X.509 public certificate and associated private key, as shown in Figure 3. The card's certificate and private key are stored inside the

---

[2] APDU – Application Protocol Data Unit – is the communication format used to communicate with a smart card.

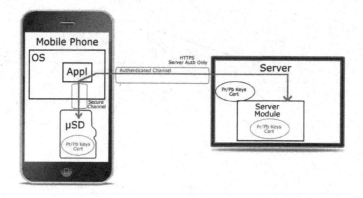

Fig. 2. Diagram of the proposed mobile banking setup

card's applet. This private key is actually generated inside the card at the card's personalisation stage, preventing the private key to ever leave the card, solving issues previously mentioned regarding shared secrets. The X.509 certificates, used in the communication with the mobile banking server, are parsed and analysed directly in the smart card. The reason for this is that we have designed the applet in the card to be independent of the bank. This way, we can decouple the issuing of the card and its private key from an individual bank. While it remains possible for a bank to deploy and manage its own secure microSD card, such a secure element is typically governed by a independent third party, such as a mobile network operator or a Trusted Service Manager (TSM, e.g. Venyon). Our generic card applet therefore allows for the bank to focus on the android application for branding and differentiation, while the trusted third party takes care of the secure applet deployment. This way, the complex ecosystem of deploying secure applets on mobile phones [1] gets simplified and customers can use the same applet for different mobile banking applications on their phone.

Unfortunately, the dependence on PKI certificates presented a complication: there is no Java class in the Java Card 2.2.1 specification to handle X.509 certificates. The existing proprietary implementations were not freely available to us, so we implemented our own X.509 certificate parser.

In what follows, we describes our application in more detail. After presenting the general authentication and key establishment methods used, more specific security features are described, protecting against certain dedicated attacks. A last subsection gives an overview of a mobile banking transaction as it is executed within our application.

4.1   Authentication and Key Establishment

The protocol, used for mutual authentication and (symmetric) key agreement between the card and the mobile banking server, is based on the "X.509 strong

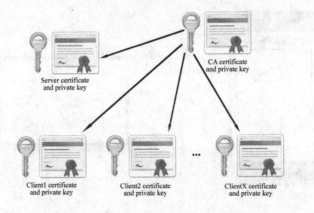

Fig. 3. PKI structure of the implementation

three-way authentication" protocol [11]. In our protocol, the micro-SD card and the server exchange X.509 certificates and signatures in order to prove their identity. The symmetric session keys are generated by the bank server and sent to the card, encrypted by the card's public key. The session keys are then used for the subsequent communication. One major advantage of asymmetric mobile banking is that the server must not store the client's keys anymore. Furthermore, this private key now resides in the user's hardware (card) only. Another advantage is the facility of deploying the system. The distribution of the public key certificates can be done independent of the server setup. As already mentioned, the cards generate their own keypair, and send a Certificate Signing Request (CSR) to the applet's manager (e.g., a TSM like Venyon), using a dedicated, bank-independent application. Upon successful verification of such a CSR, the TSM will issue and send a certificate for the card's public key that will be loaded into the applet.

Below, we describe the protocol's details.

Notation

SUMMARY: The card A and server B exchange 4 messages, after the user I has introduced his PIN code to confirm his authenticity to the card.
RESULT: Mutual entity authentication and session keys transport with key authentication.

- $P_X(y)$ denotes the result of applying X's encryption public key to data y.
- $S_X(y)$ denotes the result of applying X's signature private key to data y.
- r_A, r_B are freshly generated random numbers (to detect replay and impersonation).
- $cert_X$ is a certificate, binding party X to a public key suitable for both encryption and signature verification.

System Setup

(a) Each party has its public key pair for signing and encryption.
(b) A must acquire (and authenticate) the public key of B a priori.

Protocol messages

$$A \leftarrow I : PIN \tag{1}$$
$$A \rightarrow B \text{ (via I)} : B, cert_A, r_A \tag{2}$$
$$A \leftarrow B \text{ (via I)} : A, cert_B, r_B \tag{3}$$
$$A \rightarrow B \text{ (via I)} : S_A(r_A, r_B, B) \tag{4}$$
$$A \leftarrow B \text{ (via I)} : P_A(W_1, W_2), S_B(r_A, r_B, A, P_A(W_1, W_2)) \tag{5}$$

Protocol actions

- The user enters his PIN code. Upon successful verification by the card, the card is unlocked. A sends B's identifier (for example the subject common name of $cert_B$: www.nameofthebank.com), its own certificate $cert_A$ and a fresh random number r_A.
- The server verifies that the identifier in the previous message is correct. It verifies the certificate $cert_A$ and stores the challenge r_A. It then sends the identifier of the client A (which can also be the common name of $cert_A$) together with its own certificate $cert_B$ and a new challenge r_B.
- The card verifies B's certificate $cert_B$, verifies that the identifier is correct and stores the challenge r_B. Upon successful verification, the card sends a signature of both challenges and B's identifier using the client's private key.
- The server B verifies the signature using A's public key, thereby verifying that r_A, r_B and B (transmitted earlier in the previous messages) are indeed consistent.
- The server then randomly generates a session key W_1 and a MAC key W_2 that will be used as symmetric keys for subsequent communications. These keys are encrypted with A's public key. The server also sends a signature of r_A, r_B, B and $P_A(W_1, W_2)$ using its private key.
- A decrypts the session key W_1 and the MAC key W_2 using its private key, and verifies the signature using B's public key.

Limitations

One major limitation of this setup is the processing power of the secure microSD card. The authentication time is about 6 seconds with the material used, and this is mainly due to the signature generation and verification and the session key decryption in the card.

4.2   Two-Layered Security

On top of the previously discussed key establishment between the card and the backend server our implementation makes use of an TLS/SSL connection between the phone's application and the backend. The reason we added this extra layer of security is twofold. The first reason is to ensure data confidentiality and integrity already at the application level. This way, basic application level data transfer and authentication can be specifically implemented according to the bank's policy and vision. It allows for direct backend to user communication as shown in Figure 2, without passing by the slower secure card. This connection should nevertheless only be used for less critical data exchange, especially as the SSL protocol is executed without strong client authentication. In our implementation this is for example used for retrieving the user's account balance and history, but does not allow for setting up a money transfer. The other reason for this second layer of security is to prevent the user's personal applet certificate used during the applet level authentication protocol and other transaction information to be sent in the clear to the backend, thereby increasing the user's privacy.

The user authentication and key establishment described in the previous section should be used for the most critical transactions and is independent of the TLS/SSL tunnel through which it runs. This way, we obtain a two layered security architecture that allows for a robust mobile banking application that provides for confidentiality, integrity, secure client authentication and secure client authorisation.

In our implementation, the microSD card (and hence two layers of security) is used when initially authenticating to the mobile banking server, and for every money transfer. Of course, it is ultimately up to the banks to decide which features to put at which layer.

4.3   Securing the OS to Card Communication

As can be seen in Figure 2, another authenticated channel is set up inside the mobile phone, between the application running inside the Android operating system and the applet contained in the secure element. This is necessary because the Android banking application has now become the weakest link in the chain: it has to run in the Android OS, which can be compromised easily, as recent research has shown[3] or can at least easily be fooled to let users install malicious applications. The reason we thus need to set up yet another secure channel between the genuine application and the secure card is to prevent these malicious applications or code but also other unauthorised users or the user himself to abuse the secure card's critical applets. These applets are usually very sensitive and often protected by a limited number of PIN tries. Abusing these PIN tries can block the applet and therefore allows for an easily implemented denial of service attack.

---

[3] The Register – Toxic Plankton feeds on Android Market for two months; http://www.theregister.co.uk/2011/06/13/android_market_still_insecure/

Our implementation of such a secure channel as described by the Global Platform consortium [14] prevents that any external application can communicate with the card's applet, even when the PIN code is known. Secondly, it ensures that attackers with eavesdropping or modification abilities on the communication channel between the application and the applet can't influence the system's security.

During the installation of the applet on the secure microSD card, the client will enter a activation code, to be used in the mobile banking card applet installation application (at OS level). Using this application code, a long-term symmetric key is set up between the banking application and the applet in the card. This allows the application to authenticate to the applet later on, each time setting up a new encryption key S_1 and MAC key S_2 for the encrypted tunnel between application and applet. Note that this still allows for some attacks if the long-term symmetric key is recovered by an attacker. Securing this long-term key can be done using several existing (but not implemented) technologies, including:

- Obfuscation and steganography: the long-term key can be hidden in memory using classical obfuscation and steganographic techniques. In storage, a password-based encryption, combined with steganography and the classic access control features of Android, will be the best we can do.
- Another possibility, is the use of so-called white-box cryptography, in which the long-term symmetric key is hidden in the implementation of the application. The authors have not seen white-box cryptography in mobile phones at the time of writing, but it appears that the technology is ready to be used in this setting.

4.4   Avoiding Automated Attacks

Finally, to further avoid attacks on the OS level, a captcha[4] system was implemented. Each time the user would make a transfer, a captcha is presented, that represents a simple human-only-readable challenge, depending on the data in the transaction.

Our captcha is therefore not a classic captcha with random letters but is adapted to the mobile banking system, as shown in Fig 4(b). The idea is that the user receives, after each transfer, a summary of his transfer in the form of an image. Furthermore, a part of the image contains random letters generated by the bank server, the amount of the transaction inserted randomly among the letters and finally a box in which the user must make a calculation, based on digits issued from the recipient's account number. This way, the user can also verify his transaction data one more time before confirming it.

Involving such a captcha ensures that a human must be present during a transaction. For each transaction, an attacker will need to get involved to solve

---

[4] captcha – completely automated public Turing-test to tell computers and humans apart, http://www.captcha.net

the captcha, and this complicates the design of an automated and distributed attack. Moreover, injecting/replacing other beneficiary account numbers in a transaction in construction, and having this signed by the user is harder: the response of the server will show the wrong captcha and the user can be watchful for abnormal behaviour of his application.

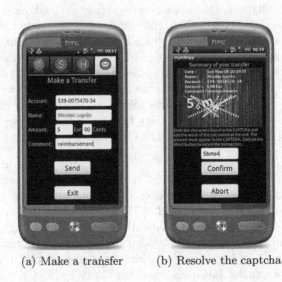

(a) Make a transfer   (b) Resolve the captcha

Fig. 4. Screen captures of the implemented Android application

4.5 Overview of a Money Transfer

For actual money transfers, the secure microSD card is used to authenticate the transaction. The protocol is shown in Figure 5. The money transfer including the amount and the recipient's account number is first sent to the secure element via the authenticated channel using the session keys S_1 (encryption key) and S_2 (MAC key) coming from the unilateral authentication between the card and the application. The card decrypts the message and encrypts it again using the session keys W_1 (encryption key) and W_2 (MAC key) shared between the card and the bank server. The encrypted message is sent, over the application, through the SSL connection, to the server. The server then responds it has received the transfer. The application then connects again to the bank server and receives an image containing the summary of the transaction and a captcha. The user has to solve the captcha, forming a confirmation code. This code is sent to the card, in the same way as the original transfer. The result is then sent to the server which verifies the confirmation code. If it is not correct, the protocol is repeated a limited number of times.

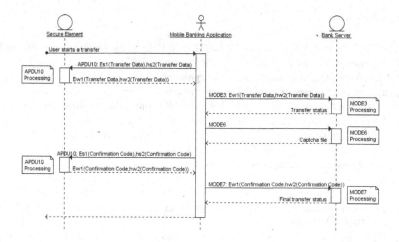

Fig. 5. UML sequence diagram for sending a transfer

5   Conclusion and Outlook

In this paper, we proposed a implementation of a PKI-based alternative for
existing mobile banking systems, using a secure micro-SD card inside a smart
phone. It makes mobile banking truly mobile, without the need of additional
hardware. The proposed application is less sensitive to attacks than other mobile
banking solutions, that are typically using any browser that the mobile phone OS
supports. The price for such an integrated system is that it cannot be switched off
easily: the microSD card is continuously accessible for attacks, and a considerable
amount of mobile phones is always online. However, this will be the case for
all mobile banking implementations, especially if no additional, non-networked
dedicated hardware is used. However, one big advantage of our system is that
every money transfer will necessarily go through the secure microSD card. The
necessary credentials to authorise these transfers cannot be extracted from the
card without breaking its strong security features.

Future work includes the implementation of the protection mechanisms
(obfuscation, steganography and white-box cryptography) for the long-term symmetric key that protects the link between application and applet. Another security improvement (but speed drawback) would be to include another public
key pair dedicated to signing money transfers, and to improve the speed of the
public key operations in the card. A possible way to achieve this is to migrate
to Elliptic Curve Cryptography. Speed improvements are also necessary to allow
for user testing, which was clearly out-of-scope for the prototype that we developed. Finally, as more and more mobile phones come without microSD card
slot, it would be interesting to port this work to a suitable SIM card or other
embedded secure elements as on the recent Google/Samsung Nexus S phone and
to implement the banking application on other OSs as well.

References

[1] The Smart Card Alliance, Proximity Mobile Payments: Leveraging NFC and the Contactless Financial Payments Infrastructure (2007),
http://www.smartcardalliance.org/pages/
publications-payments-mobile-payments-nfc

[2] Atos Worldline S.A./N.V., Banksys mobile banking application: m-banxafe (2008), http://www.atosworldline.be/landing-banxafe.html

[3] BNP Paribas Fortis (2011), https://www.bnpparibasfortis.be

[4] CCC, 27th Chaos Communication Congress (2010),
http://events.ccc.de/congress/2010/wiki/Main_Page

[5] Giesecke & Devrient (2011), http://www.gi-de.com/en/index.jsp

[6] Gold, S.: Cracking GSM. Network Security 2011(4), 12–15 (2011) ISSN: 1353-4858,
http://www.sciencedirect.com/science/article/pii/S1353485811700393,
doi:10.1016/S1353-4858(11)70039-3

[7] GSM Phones Now Vulnerable To Eavesdropping with Cheap Off-the-shelf Equipment (2011),
http://www.livehacking.com/2011/01/04/gsm-phones-
now-vulnerable-to-eavesdropping-with-cheap-off-the-shelf-equipment/

[8] Guthery, S.B., Cronin, M.J.: Mobile application development with SMS and the SIM toolkit. McGraw-Hill telecom professional. McGraw-Hill (2002) ISBN: 9780071375405

[9] Keytrade Bank (2011), https://www.keytradebank.com

[10] Luyckx, N.: Secure Mobile Banking. MA thesis. Katholieke Universiteit Leuven (2011)

[11] Menezes, A.J., Vanstone, S.A., Van Oorschot, P.C.: Handbook of Applied Cryptography, 1st edn. CRC Press, Inc., Boca Raton (1996) ISBN: 0849385237

[12] Narendiran, C., Albert, R.S., Rajendran, N.: Public key infrastructure for mobile banking security. In: Global Mobile Congress 2009, p. 6. IEEE (2009)

[13] Oracle, Java Card Technology (2011),
http://www.oracle.com/technetwork/java/javacard

[14] Global Platform, Secure Channel Protocol 2003 (2009),
http://www.globalplatform.org/specifications/card/
GPC_2%202_D-SecureChannelProtocol03-2nd-public_review.pdf

[15] RSA, RSA secureID (2011), http://www.rsa.com/node.aspx?id=1156

[16] The Apache Software Foundation, Apache Tomcat (2011),
http://tomcat.apache.org/index.html

Certification Validation: Back to the Past

Moez Ben MBarka and Julien P. Stern

Cryptolog International,
6 Rue Basfroi, 75011 Paris - France
{moez.benmbarka,julien.stern}@cryptolog.com
http://www.cryptolog.com

Abstract. Asymmetric cryptography based on public-private key pairs is nowadays used in many applications, notably for authentication and digital signature. It is very frequently used together with digital certificates which link public keys to real-world identities. In a system using digital certificates, one core issue is the question of whether a certificate is valid. This issue has been treated extensively in the literature. In this paper, we are interested in an issue which has received less attention: the question of whether a certificate *was* valid. This question is of particular importance for digitally signed documents which have to be verified a long time after their signature. We present and analyze a new algorithm to validate certificates "in the past", with the goals of it being simple to present, simple to implement and to fall back on standard algorithms with current time settings.

Keywords: certificate validation, signature validation, validation in the past.

1 Introduction

Asymmetric cryptography based on public-private key pairs is nowadays used in many applications, notably for authentication and digital signature. In practical contexts, it is customary to rely on a Public Key Infrastructure (PKI) in order to ascertain the identity of a key-pair owner, and among the different architectures, X.509 [1, 2] is one of the most widely used. X.509 defines "certificates", which from a high level standpoint can be viewed as signed bindings between entity names and public keys, as well as "revocation information" which allows to express the termination of some of these bindings. It also defines a "certification validation algorithm", in order to verify that a claimed binding is indeed legitimate. This algorithm essentially boils down to building a chain of certificates up to a known public key (usually called a trust anchor), verifying that the signatures are correct and verifying that none of the certificates in the chain is revoked. Details can be found in [1, 2].

However, the algorithms defined in these standards as well as in common literature, are primarily suited for *authentication*. Indeed, they provide an answer to the question: "is this certificate currently legitimate?". In the context of *digital*

S. Petkova-Kikova, A. Pashalidis, G. Pernul (Eds.): EuroPKI 2011, LNCS 7163, pp. 159–175, 2012.
© Springer-Verlag Berlin Heidelberg 2012

signature, the question that often needs to be asked is rather: "was this certificate legitimate when the signature was produced?".

While going from the first question to the second does not seem extremely complicated, it is not totally straightforward, and as we will show later the "naive" approach of applying the standard algorithm by simply tweaking the time is prone to failure. Furthermore, a formal algorithm to obtain the answer to the latter question does not seem to be described in public literature.

In this paper, we describe an algorithm that extends the standard X.509 algorithm in order to allow validation of a certificate at a time in the past. Our primary objectives were to fall-back on the standard algorithm when current time validation is possible and to present the algorithm in the simplest possible fashion. To that end, we define a number of very elementary notions that we combine together to obtain derivation rules and show the correctness of our algorithm. We also adapt this algorithm to validate digital signatures in the past, and finally we show how they can be applied to validate common formats of digital signatures, when naive approaches can present a risk.

The rest of this paper is organized as follows: section 2 discusses related work. Section 3 describes our security model. Section 4 presents our new algorithm together with more standard approaches. Section 5 defines a number of elementary notions and inference rules to show the correctness of these algorithms. Section 6 shows the application of our algorithm for signature validation. Finally, Section 7 concludes the paper.

2   Related Work

In general, certificate validation depends on the security model and the PKI architecture [3]. The most commonly used architectures are based on the X.509 standard [1]. Internet X.509 PKI [2] profiles this standard for use in the Internet. It describes a certificate path validation algorithm which is widely implemented in systems where certificate validation is needed (e.g. a system which verifies a signature generated by a remote entity). However, it is well known that this algorithm only suits authentication services (the algorithm takes as input the current time).

Several authors revisited the basic notions of public key authenticity and non-repudiation with models that allow to validate (or evaluate) a public key certificate [4, 5]. An interesting approach is presented by Maurer in [6] and extended by other authors in [7, 8]. The model defines a set of statements including Certificate (the fact that the relying party holds a public key certificate), Authenticity (the fact that a public key belongs to its legal owner), Trust (the fact that an entity is trustworthy for issuing certificates). The certificate validation algorithm boils down to deriving the authenticity of the public key in the certificate to validate from a set of axioms (initial trust and authenticity belief) using a predefined set of derivation rules. However, the scope of this model is limited to authentication services where verifiers need to ascertain the authenticity at the current time.

Other models discussed the issue of validating a certificate in the past. In [9], the author extended Maurer's model to support long-term validation by modeling additional features (such as revocation, expiration and time-stamping) and new derivation rules to allow the derivation of certificate validity at a time in the past. However, the definitions proposed in the paper are fairly complex and the paper does not propose a practical validation algorithm.

In [10], the authors surveyed three validity models for certificate validation. Namely, the shell model (which is merely the algorithm described in [2]), the modified shell model and the chain model. The latter models take into account the time at which the signing of a certificate occurred. The authors showed that while the shell model is only suitable for authentication services, the modified shell and the chain model allow long-term validation and therefore are also suitable for non-repudiation services. However again, the authors did not propose any practical certificate validation algorithm.

3   Security Model and Notation

For our purposes, we consider a PKI environment composed of a set of certificates and other validation data (e.g., CRLs, time-stamps, . . .). This section presents our model and the notations used.

Certificates. A certificate is a message signed by a Certification Authority (CA) and associates an identity (the Subject) with a private-public key pair. In addition to the issuer (the CA) and the subject, the certificate binds other information (e.g., validity interval, serial number, allowed usages, various extensions, . . .) to the public key. In our model, we will focus on the core and will use the simple notation $Cert_{X \to Y}$ for a certificate where X is indicated as the issuer and Y as the subject. Y may be an end entity or another certification authority.

Note that the notation $Cert_{X \to Y}$ does not mean that the certificate was actually issued by X to Y. Rather it means that X is marked as being the issuer of the certificate and Y is marked as the subject. The whole point of certificate validation is precisely to ascertain that a certificate was signed by the correct signer and that this signer is known and "trusted" to provide a correct identity for Y. Also note that a certificate commonly has an issuance date and an expiration date. These dates typically impact the result of certificate validation. For instance, an expired certificate should usually not be relied upon anymore. However, for the sake of readability, we will omit the dates of the certificate and assume a certain level of relevance in the certificate dates.

Revocation. A certificate is usually valid only within a period of time indicated in the certificate. Various circumstances (e.g., the private key is compromised or lost, the identity of the certificate owner has changed, . . .) may cause a certificate to become invalid prior to its expiration date. Under such circumstances, the issuing CA needs to revoke the certificate by issuing a signed revocation object.

In the general case, the revocation object may be issued by the same issuer of the certificate or by a third party authorized by the certificate issuer. We will only consider the first setting, but our algorithm can be simply extended to the second one. A typical method to publish revocation is using Certificate Revocation List (CRL [2]) which consists in a black list of revoked certificates. The CRL has an issuance date and a prospective date for the next update of the list. An honest CA must continue to issue revocation information for each issued certificate until at least the expiration date of the certificate.

Before using a revocation object to check the revocation status of a certificate, it is necessary to check that the revocation object is in scope for the certificate. This notably includes checking that the revocation issuer is authorized to issue revocation information for this certificate and that the issuance date of the revocation object is within the validity interval of the certificate. A revocation object issued at a time t by a certification authority X will be denoted $Rev_{X,t}$. We will focus on the core and to abstract the complexity of checking a certificate against a revocation object, we will assume that we have a function checkRev() to query a revocation object about the revocation status of a given certificate. This function returns one of the following values:

- *unknown*, in the case the revocation object is not in scope for the certificate.
- The revocation time r, in the case the revocation object is in scope for the certificate and the certificate is marked as revoked at r.
- The symbolic time ∞, in the case the revocation object is in scope for the certificate and the certificate is not marked as revoked.

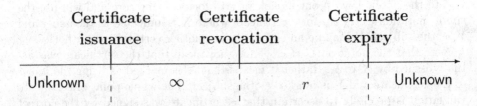

Fig. 1. Possible outputs of checkRev() for a certificate $Cert_{X \to Y}$

Fig. 1 shows a very typically setting for revocation. Revocation information issued prior to the existence of a certificate will usually not provide any information on the said certificate. Revocation information produced before the revocation of the certificate will flag it as unrevoked. Revocation information produced after will provide the exact revocation time. A revocation information produced after its expiration are often again not in scope to avoid storing such information eternally.

PKI Assumptions

A traditional assumption in a PKI context is that all participants (and most notably the trust anchors and the certification authorities) behave honestly. This means they only issue certificates to correct and honest entities and that every participant has sole control of its private keys under normal circumstances. A side effect of this assumption is that honesty is somehow "propagated" from honest participants to others through certificates.

To balance this assumption, we will assume that any participant can be compromised. Such a compromise means that the private key of a participant can be used by an attacker. In the case of such a compromise, we assume that the certificate of the corresponding participant is revoked immediately. In other words, this means the exact time of the compromise will be made available, that no object may have been signed by the attacker before this time, and that the attacker may produce any kind of signed object with the private key after this time. Note that we consider compromise of trust anchors. In such a case, we assume the revocation date is immediately made available to all parties through out-of-band channels.

We will not consider certificate "suspension" into details. Indeed, some PKI suspend certificates in case of a suspected compromise, and either revoke it (at the time of the actual compromise) or remove the suspension later. To handle this case, we simply consider that a revocation object stating that a certificate is suspended is not in scope for this certificate.

Cryptographic Verification. All validation objects (certificates, revocation objects, ...) used in the model are signed objects. In the general case, we will denote $Cert_{X \to Y} : S$ if the signed object S verifies with the public key in $Cert_{X \to Y}$. This notation does not imply that X is the actual issuer of S but only the fact that the certificate embeds the verification key for S. However, whether the corresponding private key is owned by X (and under the sole control of X) is an assertion left to certificate validation.

Trust Anchor and Certificate Chain. A trust anchor is an entity used as a common source of trust by relying parties in a PKI environment. A trust anchor is generally speaking a binding between an identity and a key which is known by out-of-band methods. A common way to model a trust anchor X is through a self signed certificate $Cert_{X \to X}$. We will use this notation throughout this article.

The most widely used PKI trust model is a hierarchy of CAs [3]. In this model, the validation of an end-entity certificate consists in constructing and validating a certificate chain from a trust anchor to the certificate. Each certificate in the chain before the trust anchor, is signed by the public key of the next certificate. A certificate chain will be denoted $\{ Cert_{X_1 \to X_0}, \ldots, Cert_{X_n \to X_{n-1}}, Cert_{X_n \to X_n} \}$ where X_n is a trust anchor and $Cert_{X_1 \to X_0}$ is an end-entity certificate.

4   Certificate Validation Algorithms

In our model, a verifier wants to validate a certificate $Cert_{X \to Y}$. The semantics of certificate validation depends on the application and the security properties that are associated with the certificate [4, 5]. In this paper, we are interested in two typical contexts where certificates are used with different validation models. Namely, authentication model and non-repudiation model. A preliminary step to certificate validation is building a certificate chain from the certificate to validate to a trust anchor. All the algorithms below take as input a certificate chain and output a validation boolean. *true* means that the certificate is "valid". What "valid" exactly means will be more explicit with the terminology that will be presented in the next section. To simplify the presentation of the algorithms, we group together the information that a certificate is not "valid" and the absence of such information with the output *false*. Real implementations should however differentiate between the two.

This section presents three certificate validation algorithms. The algorithms and their correctness will be analyzed in the next section.

4.1   Certificate Validation Algorithm in the Authentication Model

The objective of certificate validation in an authentication service is to take a decision about the validity of a certificate at the current time. PKIX standard [2] defines such an algorithm. A simplified form of this algorithm is depicted in Algorithm 1. Our description of the algorithm assumes that the current time is within the validity interval of each certificate in the chain, and that they cryptographically chain correctly. The algorithm boils down to the following: for each certificate in the chain, obtain a revocation object recently issued by the issuer of the certificate. If all certificates are not revoked, then the certificate is accepted as valid; invalid otherwise.

---

input : The certificate chain $\{ Cert_{X_1 \to X_0}, \ldots, Cert_{X_n \to X_{n-1}}, Cert_{X_n \to X_n} \}$ such that $Cert_{X_1 \to X_0}$ is the certificate to validate and X_n is a trust anchor
output: Validation boolean.
begin validateSimple
    for $i \leftarrow n$ **to** 1 **do**
        Find a revocation object $Rev_{X_i, \text{now}}$ in scope for $Cert_{X_i \to X_{i-1}}$, or **return** *false*;
        if checkRev$(Rev_{X_i, \text{now}}, Cert_{X_i \to X_{i-1}}) \neq \infty$ **then**
            return *false*;
    return *true*;

Algorithm 1. Standard Certificate Validation Algorithm

Obtaining a revocation object issued at the current time may be (almost) possible with some revocation schemes that allow to check the revocation status of a certificate in real time (e.g., Online Certificate Status Protocol [11]).

However, in practice, we use a revocation object $Rev_{X_i,\text{now}-\epsilon}$ issued shortly before the current time, and make the approximation that it is in fact issued at now. This approximation will be necessarily later to show the correctness of the algorithm. Indeed, without this approximation, a certificate may have been revoked between now $- \epsilon$ and now. This is a well known theoretical issue which has moderate practical consequence, and which we will not discuss further [12].

4.2   Certificate Validation Algorithm in the Non-repudiation Model

Non-repudiation relies on the authenticity of the signer's public key that can be derived from the certificate. A critical objective in a non-repudiation service is to be able to demonstrate former validity of a signature. This requires to be able to validate the signer's certificate even after it is revoked, provided the revocation is posterior to the signature creation. It is straightforward to see that the simple certificate validation algorithm (Algorithm 1) does not fit these requirements. Indeed, this algorithm requires to have a revocation object which indicates that each certificate in the chain is not revoked at the current time. The objective is to extend the standard certificate validation to use a time in the past. We propose two extensions. The first one implements a "naive" approach (it is called naive because it is not correct as we will show later). The second algorithm depicts our validation approach.

Naive Past Validation Algorithm. Algorithm 2 depicts a naive approach to validate a certificate at some time in the past. The idea behind this algorithm is the following: perform a validation at current time using the standard algorithm, store all the information for later and simply "replay" the standard algorithm by adjusting the dates. Hence, the algorithm takes as input revocation informations in addition to the certificate chain. We will show later that this naive approach does not work (see section 6.2). The intuition is that the revocation objects may have been forged in the meantime.

---

input :
- The certificate chain $\{Cert_{X_1 \to X_0}, \ldots, Cert_{X_n \to X_{n-1}}, Cert_{X_n \to X_n}\}$ such that $Cert_{X_1 \to X_0}$ is the certificate to validate and X_n is a trust anchor.
- Revocation objects Rev_{X_i,t_i} in scope for $Cert_{X_i \to X_{i-1}}$

output: Validation boolean
begin validateNaive
   for $i \leftarrow n$ **to** 1 **do**
      if checkRev$(Rev_{X_i,t_i}, Cert_{X_i \to X_{i-1}}) \neq \infty$ **then**
         return *false*;
   return *true*;

Algorithm 2. Naive Past Validation Algorithm

Our Past Validation Algorithm. The next algorithm (Algorithm 3) is our proposed past validation algorithm. It takes as input the certification chain and obtains revocation information in the past. Note that we could also take some information as input without loss of generality. The main difference with the naive algorithm is that we require the existence of some objects to be ascertained at a moving time. The intuition behind these extra steps is to enable a safe "replay" of the standard algorithm by ensuring that the objects we use have not been forged in the "future".

---

input : The certificate chain $\{Cert_{X_1 \to X_0}, \ldots, Cert_{X_n \to X_{n-1}}, Cert_{X_n \to X_n}\}$ such that $Cert_{X_1 \to X_0}$ is the certificate to validate and X_n is a trust anchor

output: a validation boolean and an upper validation date

begin validateLongTerm

  $u_n \leftarrow$ now[1];

  for $i \leftarrow n$ **to** 1 **do**

    Find a revocation object Rev_{X_i, t_i} in scope for $Cert_{X_i \to X_{i-1}}$, or **return** *false*;

    Ascertain the existence of Rev_{X_i, t_i} and $Cert_{X_i \to X_{i-1}}$ at u_i, or **return** *false*;

    $u_{i-1} \leftarrow min(t_i, \text{checkRev}(Rev_{X_i, t_i}, Cert_{X_i \to X_{i-1}}));$

  return $(true, u_0)$;

Algorithm 3. Our Past Certificate Validation Algorithm

5   Analysis and Algorithms Correctness

We will first introduce some simple notions which will help us analyze the standard X.509 algorithm and its extension to the past.

5.1   Definitions

The first notion we define is *honesty*. We need a way to link participants to an initial source of trust.

Definition 1 (Honesty). *A participant is said to be honest if it is a trust anchor, or if it owns a certificate issued by an honest participant.*[2]

The second notion expresses the fact that a signed object has indeed been signed by an entity claiming to have done so. Technically, this notion encompasses two

---

[1] Alternatively, if the trust anchor is revoked, set u_n to the revocation date. Note that this is an interesting and surprising feature of our algorithm: it can handle old trust anchors which have been compromised or brute-forced.

[2] Note that we say that the certificate must be issued by an honest participant, not by the key belonging to an honest participant, so a certificate issued by the compromised key of an honest participant does not infer honesty.

things: first, the existence of a link between the cryptographic key allowing to verify the signature on the signed object and the claiming entity, and second the insurance that the signing key has not been used by a different entity to sign the object.

Definition 2 (Genuineness). *A signed object S is said to be X-genuine (denoted X-$\mathcal{G}(S)$, or simply $\mathcal{G}(S)$ when the claimed signer is obvious) if and only if it was signed by X.*

The third notion is related to the previous one and expresses the fact that at some date t, a private key (corresponding to a public key identified in a certificate) is under the sole control of the legitimate owner of the certificate.

Definition 3 (Control). *A certificate $Cert_{X \to Y}$ is said to be t-controlled (denoted $\mathcal{C}(Cert_{X \to Y}, t)$) if and only if the corresponding private key is under the sole control of Y before time t.*

The intuitive objective of certificate validation is to prove the honesty of a participant and the t-control of its certificate. When a t-controlled certificate belongs to an honest participant, we will say that it is t-trusted.

Definition 4 (Trust). *A certificate $Cert_{X \to Y}$ is said to be t-trusted (denoted $\mathcal{T}(Cert_{X \to Y}, t)$) if and only if Y is honest and $Cert_{X \to Y}$ is t-controlled.*

The last notion is what we call Proof of Existence (POE). If we have an object available now, this gives a "proof" that this object exists now. This notion can be extended to any time in the past. We will denote $\mathcal{P}(O, t)$ a proof that an object O existed at time t. A typical mean to derive a proof of existence at a time in the past is using time-stamping services [13, 14]. A time-stamp is a digital attestation signed by a trusted third party, called Time-Stamping Authority (TSA), that a submitted digital document has been presented to the TSA at a certain time. Other sources to derive proofs of existences include the issuance date of an object (e.g., the issuance date of a certificate) provided the issuer is trusted to use reliable source of time and is not compromised. Other services can provide proofs of existence by various means (electronic notaries, archival services, etc)...

5.2   Derivation Rules

We now define a number of derivation rules based on the previously introduced notions.

Proposition 1 (Derivation of Honesty). *Given a participant X and a certificate $Cert_{X \to Y}$, if*

1. *X is honest;*
2. *the certificate $Cert_{X \to Y}$ is genuine;*

then Y is honest.

This can be written with the following derivation rule:

$$\frac{\mathcal{H}(X) \qquad \mathcal{G}(Cert_{X \to Y})}{\mathcal{H}(Y)} \tag{1}$$

This is essentially a simple rewriting of the definitions: since $Cert_{X \to Y}$ is genuine it means it has indeed been issued by X. Since X is honest, so is Y.

Proposition 2 (Derivation of Genuineness). *Given a certificate $Cert_{X \to Y}$ and a signed object S, if*

1. *the certificate $Cert_{X \to Y}$ is t-controlled;*
2. *S verifies with the public key in $Cert_{X \to Y}$;*
3. *there exists a proof of existence of S at t;*

then the signed object S is Y-genuine.

This can be written with the following derivation rule:

$$\frac{\mathcal{C}(Cert_{X \to Y}, t) \qquad Cert_{X \to Y} : S \qquad \mathcal{P}(S, t)}{Y\text{-}\mathcal{G}(S)} \tag{2}$$

The proposition above is again a fairly direct application of the definitions: since the certificate is t-controlled, it means its private key is under the sole control of Y before t, furthermore S has been signed by this very key before t (since S is proven to exist before t), hence S has been signed by Y.[3]

Proposition 3 (Derivation of Control). *Given a certificate $Cert_{X \to Y}$ and a revocation object $Rev_{X,d}$ in scope for $Cert_{X \to Y}$, if*

1. *X is honest;*
2. *the certificate $Cert_{X \to Y}$ is genuine;*
3. *the revocation object $Rev_{X,d}$ is genuine;*

then

- *if checkRev($Rev_{X,d}$, $Cert_{X \to Y}$) = ∞, the certificate $Cert_{X \to Y}$ is d-controlled.*
- *if checkRev($Rev_{X,d}$, $Cert_{X \to Y}$) = r, the certificate $Cert_{X \to Y}$ is r-controlled.*

This can be written with the following derivation rule:

$$\frac{\mathcal{H}(X) \qquad \mathcal{G}(Cert_{X \to Y}) \qquad \mathcal{G}(Rev_{X,d})}{\mathcal{C}(Cert_{X \to Y}, min(d, \text{checkRev}(Rev_{X,d}, Cert_{X \to Y})))} \tag{3}$$

Since X is honest, and $Cert_{X \to Y}$ is genuine (hence issued by X), $Cert_{X \to Y}$ actually belongs to Y. $Rev_{X,d}$ is also genuine (hence issued by X) and is in scope for $Cert_{X \to Y}$. Since X is honest, $Rev_{X,d}$ provides truthful information on the certificate. If $Rev_{X,d}$ indicates the certificate is unrevoked, we can conclude it is controlled at the time on issuance of the revocation information. If it provides a revocation date r, we know it is r-controlled.

---

[3] Note that when t=now, this rule simply says that an object signed by the certificate of an uncompromised participant is genuine.

Proposition 4 (Derivation of Trust). *Given a certificate $Cert_{X \to Y}$, a certificate $Cert_{Y \to Z}$ and a revocation object $Rev_{Y,d}$ in scope for $Cert_{Y \to Z}$, if*

1. *the certificate $Cert_{X \to Y}$ is t-trusted;*
2. *the certificate $Cert_{Y \to Z}$ and the revocation object $Rev_{Y,d}$ verify with the certificate $Cert_{X \to Y}$;*
3. *there exists a proof of existence of $Rev_{Y,d}$ at t.*
4. *there exists a proof of existence of $Cert_{Y \to Z}$ at t.*

then the certificate $Cert_{Y \to Z}$ is $min(d, \mathsf{checkRev}(Rev_{Y,d}, Cert_{Y \to Z}))$-trusted.

This can be written in the following derivation rule (the fact that $Cert_{Y \to Z}$ and $Rev_{Y,d}$ verify with the public key in $Cert_{X \to Y}$ will be omitted from the rules for readability):

$$\frac{\mathcal{T}(Cert_{X \to Y}, t) \qquad \mathcal{P}(Rev_{Y,d}, t) \qquad \mathcal{P}(Cert_{Y \to Z}, t)}{\mathcal{T}(Cert_{Y \to Z}, min(d, \mathsf{checkRev}(Rev_{Y,d}, Cert_{Y \to Z})))} \tag{4}$$

This is derived by the application of the previous rules:
t-trust is honesty and t-control, so we can apply rule (2):

$$\frac{\mathcal{H}(Y) \qquad \mathcal{C}(Cert_{X \to Y}, t) \qquad \mathcal{P}(Rev_{Y,d}, t) \qquad \mathcal{P}(Cert_{Y \to Z}, t)}{\mathcal{H}(Y) \qquad \mathcal{G}(Rev_{Y,d}) \qquad \mathcal{G}(Cert_{Y \to Z})}$$

From there, we apply rule (3):

$$\frac{\mathcal{H}(Y) \qquad \mathcal{G}(Rev_{Y,d}) \qquad \mathcal{G}(Cert_{Y \to Z})}{\mathcal{H}(Y) \qquad \mathcal{G}(Cert_{Y \to Z}) \qquad \mathcal{C}(Cert_{Y \to Z}, min(d, \mathsf{checkRev}(Rev_{Y,d}, Cert_{Y \to Z})))}$$

And finally we apply rule (1):

$$\frac{\mathcal{H}(Y) \qquad \mathcal{G}(Cert_{Y \to Z}) \qquad \mathcal{C}(Cert_{Y \to Z}, min(d, \mathsf{checkRev}(Rev_{X,d}, Cert_{X \to Y})))}{\mathcal{H}(Z) \qquad \mathcal{C}(Cert_{Y \to Z}, min(d, \mathsf{checkRev}(Rev_{Y,d}, Cert_{Y \to Z})))}$$

5.3   Correctness of the Certificate Validation Algorithms

Proposition 5 (Correctness of Algorithm 1). *If* $\mathsf{validateSimple}(\{Cert_{X_1 \to X_0}, \ldots, Cert_{X_n \to X_n}\}) = true$, *then* $Cert_{X_1 \to X_0}$ *is* now*-trusted.*

By nature, the trust anchor is now-trusted.
Let us rewrite rule (4) in the scope of this algorithm:

$$\frac{\mathcal{T}(Cert_{X_n \to X_n}, \mathsf{now}) \qquad \mathcal{P}(Rev_{X_n, \mathsf{now}}, \mathsf{now}) \qquad \mathcal{P}(Cert_{X_n \to X_{n-1}}, \mathsf{now})}{\mathcal{T}(Cert_{X_n \to X_{n-1}}, min(\mathsf{now}, \mathsf{checkRev}(Rev_{X_n, \mathsf{now}}, Cert_{X_n \to X_{n-1}})))}$$

The certificate chaining is directly implied by the definition of the certificate chain and is ignored in the notation. Since a revocation object in scope has been found (else the algorithm would return false), we have the POE at current time on the revocation object. The POE on the certificate is obvious: the certificate belongs to the inputs. Finally, the checkRev() returns ∞ (else the algorithm would again return false); so we can rewrite the rule as:

$$\frac{T(Cert_{X_n \to X_n}, \text{now})}{T(Cert_{X_n \to X_{n-1}}, \text{now})}$$

A simple recursion eventually leads us to $T(Cert_{X_1 \to X_0}, \text{now})$.

Proposition 6 (Correctness of Algorithm 3)
If validateLongTerm($\{Cert_{X_1 \to X_0}, \ldots, Cert_{X_n \to X_n}\}$) $= (true, u)$, *then the certificate* $Cert_{X_1 \to X_0}$ *is u-trusted.*

By nature, the trust anchor is now-trusted (or α-trusted for some α). Using the same notation as in the algorithm (and since u_n is set to now (or α)), we can rewrite rule (4) as:

$$\frac{T(Cert_{X_n \to X_n}, u_n) \qquad P(Rev_{X_n, t_n}, u_n) \qquad P(Cert_{X_n \to X_{n-1}}, u_n)}{T(Cert_{X_n \to X_{n-1}}, min(t_n, \text{checkRev}(Rev_{X_n, t_n}, Cert_{X_n \to X_{n-1}})))}$$

which can be rewritten:

$$\frac{T(Cert_{X_n \to X_n}, u_n) \qquad P(Rev_{X_n, t_n}, u_n) \qquad P(Cert_{X_n \to X_{n-1}}, u_n)}{T(Cert_{X_n \to X_{n-1}}, u_{n-1})}$$

The algorithm assumes the existence of a revocation object in scope for the certificate and proofs of existence of both objects, which allows us to apply the derivation rule bringing us from $T(Cert_{X_n \to X_n}, u_n)$ to $T(Cert_{X_n \to X_{n-1}}, u_{n-1})$. A simple recursion leads to $T(Cert_{X_1 \to X_0}, u_0)$.

Note that this proof highlights the generalization performed on the algorithm for "authentication". One can consider that we have added a time dimension to the notion of trust of a certificate. A certificate is only trusted up to a certain point in time, and we need to ensure that the object we consider were produced before that time. Provided this, we can infer a new trusted time, which "slides", for the next object. If no certificate is revoked (or expired) and all revocation information is current, we stay in one dimension: the time of trust never slides, and we fall back to the standard authentication algorithm.

6   Application to Long-Term Signature Validation

Digital signatures are the main tool to provide non-repudiation services. The goal in long-term conservation of digital signatures is to be able to demonstrate former validity of a signature (commonly called long-term validation). This requirement becomes more critical when the signatures are intended to be used as valid non-repudiation evidences in the settlement of possible disputes which may occur long after the signature creation.

In this section, we extend our past validation algorithm to signed document validation. As will be shown below, this extension is very straightforward. Indeed, we only need to show that the signed document is *genuine* and signed by an honest signer.

Intuitively, we have shown in previous sections that an object signed by a t-trusted certificate is genuine provided there exists a proof of existence of this object before time t. We have also shown that our extended validation algorithm precisely assesses the t-trust (for some time t) of the end-user certificate. If we view the signed document as simply an extra layer in the chain, the only remaining operation to prove the genuineness of the signed document is therefore to show a proof of existence of that document at t.

The signature validation algorithm is described in Algorithm 4. It takes as input a signature S such that $Cert_{X_1 \rightarrow X_0} : S$ and a certificate chain for $Cert_{X_1 \rightarrow X_0}$.

---

input :
 – The signature S such that $Cert_{X_1 \rightarrow X_0} : S$
 – The certificate chain $\{Cert_{X_1 \rightarrow X_0}, \ldots, Cert_{X_n \rightarrow X_{n-1}}, Cert_{X_n \rightarrow X_n}\}$

output: Validation boolean
begin validateSignature
    $(status, u) \leftarrow$ validateLongTerm($\{Cert_{X_1 \rightarrow X_0}, \ldots, Cert_{X_n \rightarrow X_n}\}$);
    if $status = false$ then
        | return *false*;
    else
        if *there exists a proof of existence of S at u* then
            | return *true*;
        else
            | return *false*;

Algorithm 4. Signature Validation Algorithm

The correctness of the algorithm is straightforward and simply an application of the same reasoning as before.

6.1   Advanced Electronic Signatures

For the above algorithm to work, involved certificates and revocation objects need to be stored "indefinitely" (or at least during the desired archiving period) together with the time-stamps. Moreover, time-stamps are usually also electronic signatures that must be validated in order to derive the proofs of existence. Hence, the validation data used to validate the time-stamps must also be stored leading to recursive time-stamping. Several standards defined ways to optimize the storage and renewal of the initial validation data. These standards include Evidence Record Syntax [15] and Advanced Electronic Signature (AdES) [16–18].

AdES are a special type of signatures to which an European directive attaches a particular legal value [19]. A major concern while developing AdES has been the ability to validate signatures many years after the signing took place. This relies on extending a basic signature to an advanced signature form with long-term validation data. These extensions are performed through the addition of timestamps of various items (the signed document itself, certificates, CRLs, OCSP, previous timestamps, etc). In the terminology we use in this article, these timestamps provide us with the proof of existence needed to actually perform our past validation algorithm.

We will now discuss of one of the most commonly used forms, the so-called "-T" form. This form includes a regular signature on the hash of the document to be signed as well as on some signature attributes. It also includes a timestamp on the value of the signature (the output of the cryptographic signature algorithm). Note that, among the signature attributes, there is necessarily the hash of the signer certificate, which implies a proof of existence of that certificate at the time of the timestamp.

6.2   Analysis of an Example

Let us consider the following simple setting (Fig. 2):

- X_2 is an (uncompromised) trust anchor, X_1 is a certification authority, and X_0 is the signer.
- A certificate chain to validate the signer certificate is $\{ Cert_{X_1 \to X_0}, Cert_{X_2 \to X_1}, Cert_{X_2 \to X_2} \}$.
- S_X is an object correctly signed by certificate $Cert_{X_1 \to X_0}$
- We have $Rev_{X_2,\alpha}$ such that $\mathsf{checkRev}(Rev_{X_2,\alpha}, Cert_{X_2 \to X_1}) = \infty$
- We have $Rev_{X_1,\beta}$ such that $\mathsf{checkRev}(Rev_{X_1,\beta}, Cert_{X_1 \to X_0}) = \infty$
- The signature has been timestamped at some time t
- We will finally assume that $t <= \beta <= \alpha$. This is the most "favorable" situation. We will see later that in other cases, we can infer even less information than in this one.

Let us now analyze what we can infer. We know that:

- The trust anchor $Cert_{X_2 \to X_2}$ is by nature now-trusted
- The timestamp gives us a proof of existence of $Cert_{X_1 \to X_0}$ at t
- The timestamp gives us a proof of existence of S at t

We can infer that $Cert_{X_2 \to X_1}$ and $Rev_{X_2,\alpha}$ are genuine and therefore that $Cert_{X_2 \to X_1}$ is α-controlled (and actually α-trusted since X_2 is honest). Now, since $t <= \alpha$, this means $Cert_{X_1 \to X_0}$ is genuine. And because X_1 is honest, so is X_0. These results are described on Fig. 3.

Now, the only remaining thing would be to shown that $Cert_{X_1 \to X_0}$ is t-controlled (which would show that S_X is genuine thanks to the proof of existence on S_X at t before β). To do so, however, we need a proof of existence of $Rev_{X_0,\beta}$ at α. And this is where there is a gap for attacks. Specifically, suppose that the

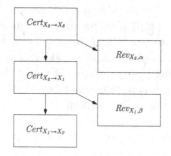

Fig. 2. Simple PKI setting

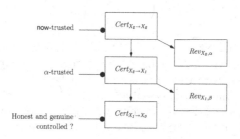

Fig. 3. Analysis of trust

certification authority X_1 (which is α-controlled) has in fact been compromised after α. Then, the revocation object $Rev_{X_0,\beta}$ may have been forged, and may indicate the opposite result as the original one regarding the revocation status of $Cert_{X_1 \rightarrow X_0}$, yielding an incorrect genuineness result on the signed document.

Note that in the naive approach $t = \beta = \alpha$, and such a proof of existence is not performed. The naive approach is therefore prone to the attack above.

This all means we really need the aforementioned proof of existence. In practice, there are two obvious way to obtain it. The first one is to obtain a timestamped copy of $Rev_{X_0,\beta}$ at α (or anytime between β and α). The second one is to use $\alpha = $ now. Indeed in this case, $Cert_{X_2 \rightarrow X_1}$ is now-controlled, and we can infer an implicit proof of existence on $Rev_{X_1,\beta}$ at β, since X_1 is honest.

Our algorithm encompasses both approaches: one can use an "old" revocation object for the CA if a proof of existence on the "old" revocation object for the signer certificate is available, or one can validate the CA at current time and use an "old" revocation object for the signer certificate.

Note that the naive algorithm actually works (in this scenario) if the PKI hierarchy has two levels instead of three, which is a somewhat common case. Indeed, if the signer certificate is directly issued by the trust anchor, then a past revocation information regarding this signer will always be genuine, so long as the trust anchor is now-controlled.

For this reason many implementations make the conscious (or not) assumption that certification authorities are never compromised, or that such compromise will be known and flagged by out-of-band mechanisms. This assumption more or less amounts to considering that all CAs are trust anchors and therefore that a hierarchy is always of depth two. While this argument holds to a certain extent, we nevertheless encourage implementors to take into account the difficulties we underlined when performing past validation. Even if the risk of actual attack is weak today, it will certainly raise when old 1024 bit RSA CA keys are brute-forced. This will happen eventually, normally long after the life span of the CA, but will affect old signatures anyway. It is therefore important to underline that our algorithm may provide a way to ascertain the genuineness of a legitimate signature even after some extreme events such as CA or trust anchor compromise or cryptanalytic breakthroughs.[4]

7   Conclusion

We have proposed an extension to the standard X.509 algorithm for certificate validation which can validate certificates in the past, and works even when some certification authorities (or even trust anchors) have been compromised. This extension is rather simple as it essentially consists in adding a sliding time window based on proofs of existence of some objects. It is very well suited for being added to existing implementations, since it falls back on the standard algorithm in an authentication setting. We have also defined a number of elementary notions to present the correctness of the algorithm in an hopefully simple way. And we have finally shown that for the most widely used signature formats, using a naive approach to past validation opens the gap to attacks. We hope that the light we put on past certificate validation will help with the analysis and implementation of long term signature validation algorithms, which are today becoming more and more widespread, notably within the European Union.

Acknowledgements. The authors would like to thank the anonymous referees for their valuable comments.

References

1. ITU/ISO, X.509 information technology open systems interconnection-the directory: Authentication frameworks, Tech. Rep. (2000)
2. Cooper, D., Santesson, S., Farrell, S., Boeyen, S., Housley, R., Polk, W.: Internet X.509 public key infrastructure: Certificate and CRL profile. IETF, Tech. Rep. RFC 5280 (2008)
3. Agarwal, G., Singh, S.: A comparison between public key authority and certification authority for distribution of public key. International Journal of Computer Science and Information Technologies 1(5), 332–336 (2010)

---

[4] Note that the consequences of such an event are plentiful and that we do not claim to provide a magic solution for all cases. Nevertheless, the concept of t-control may be reused in some other contexts to analyze the exact scope of the damages and possibly mitigate them.

4. Huang, J., Nicol, D.: A calculus of trust and its application to pki and identity management. In: IDtrust 2009: Proceedings of the 8th Symposium on Identity and Trust on the Internet, pp. 23–37. ACM, New York (2009)
5. Kohlas, R.: Decentralized trust evaluation and public-key authentication. Ph.D. dissertation, University of Bern (2007)
6. Maurer, U.M.: Modelling a Public-Key Infrastructure. In: Martella, G., Kurth, H., Montolivo, E., Hwang, J. (eds.) ESORICS 1996. LNCS, vol. 1146, pp. 325–350. Springer, Heidelberg (1996)
7. Marchesini, J.C., Smith, S.: Modeling Public Key Infrastructures in the Real World. In: Chadwick, D., Zhao, G. (eds.) EuroPKI 2005. LNCS, vol. 3545, pp. 118–134. Springer, Heidelberg (2005)
8. Bicakci, K., Crispo, B., Tanenbaum, A.S.: How to incorporate revocation status information into the trust metrics for public-key certification. In: ACM Symposium on Applied Computing, pp. 1594–1598. ACM (2005)
9. Ben MBarka, M., Krief, F., Ly, O.: Modeling Long-Term Signature Validation for Resolution of Dispute. In: Proceedings of the Theory of Security and Applications, TOSCA 2011, ETAPS 2011, Saarbrücken - Germany. Springer, Heidelberg (2011)
10. Baier, H., Karatsiolis, V.: Validity Models of Electronic Signatures and Their Enforcement in Practice. In: Martinelli, F., Preneel, B. (eds.) EuroPKI 2009. LNCS, vol. 6391, pp. 255–270. Springer, Heidelberg (2010)
11. Myers, M., Ankney, R., Malpani, A., Galperin, C.A.S.: Online Certificate Status Protocol - OCSP. IETF, Tech. Rep. RFC 2560 (1999)
12. Solworth, J.A.: Instant Revocation. In: Mjølsnes, S.F., Mauw, S., Katsikas, S.K. (eds.) EuroPKI 2008. LNCS, vol. 5057, pp. 31–48. Springer, Heidelberg (2008)
13. Haber, S., Stornetta, W.S.: How to Time-Stamp a Digital Document. In: Menezes, A., Vanstone, S.A. (eds.) CRYPTO 1990. LNCS, vol. 537, pp. 437–455. Springer, Heidelberg (1991)
14. Marinescu, C.: Design requirements for a secure time-stamping scheme. In: EuroIMSA 2008: Proceedings of the IASTED International Conference on Internet and Multimedia Systems and Applications, pp. 94–99. ACTA Press, Anaheim (2008)
15. Gondrom, T., Brandner, R., Pordesch, U.: Evidence Record Syntax (ERS). Tech. Rep. RFC 4998 (2007)
16. ETSI, CMS Advanced Electronic Signatures (CAdES), Tech. Rep. ETSI TS 101 733 V1.7.4 (2008)
17. ETSI, XML Advanced Electronic Signatures (XAdES), Tech. Rep. ETSI TS 101 903 V1.3.2 (2006)
18. ETSI, PDF Advanced Electronic Signature Profiles;part 1: PAdES overview - a framework document for PAdES, Tech. Rep. ETSI TS 102 778-1 V1.1.1 (2009)
19. European Union, Directive 1999/93/ec of the european parliament and of the concil of 13 december 1999 on a community framework for electronic signatures

A Hijacker's Guide to the LPC Bus

Johannes Winter and Kurt Dietrich

Institute for Applied Information Processing and Communications,
Graz University of Technology,
Inffeldgasse 16a, 8020 Graz, Austria
{johannes.winter,kurt.dietrich}@iaik.tugraz.at

Abstract. In this paper, we analyze the communication mechanism of trusted platform modules via the low-pin-count bus. While the trusted platform module is considered to be tamper resistant, the communication channel between this module and the rest of the trusted platform turns out to be comparatively insecure. It has been shown that passive attacks can be mounted on the TPM and its bus communication with fairly inexpensive equipment, however, similar active attacks have not been reported, yet. We tackle this problem and show how the communication on the LPC bus can be actively manipulated with simple and inexpensive equipment. Moreover, we show how our manipulation can be used to circumvent the chain of trust provided by trusted platforms.

1   Introduction

In this paper, we present a simple hardware attack based on modification of bus signals found on typical trusted PC platforms. Our intention is to show how a motivated adversary with limited resources can break the integrity of the transitive chain of trust constructed either by static or dynamic roots-of-trust for measurement (RTMs). The attack discussed in this paper directly affects the trust properties and assumptions of software systems like [14], [11], [10], [3] and [15] which rely on dynamic roots of trust as an esstential trust establishing platform building block.

We assume that the reader of this paper is familiar with basic trusted computing concepts like platform configuration registers, local and remote attestation as well as static and dynamic roots of trust. Section 1.1 gives a high-level overview of Trusted Computing concepts used and addressed in this paper.

It is out of scope of section 1.1 to give an in-depth discussion of the relevant Trusted Computing concepts. We refer to secondary literature like [5], [6] [20] and [21] for a complete and detailed introduction into the relevant topics.

1.1   A Very Short Introduction to Trusted Computing

From the perspective of this paper, it is sufficient to view the Trusted Platform Module (TPM) as a platform building block which is capable of recording and reporting the current software configuration of the platform in a trustworthy

S. Petkova-Kikova, A. Pashalidis, G. Pernul (Eds.): EuroPKI 2011, LNCS 7163, pp. 176–193, 2012.

way. To record the platform software configuration, the TPM uses a fixed set of platform configuration registers (PCRs). In general, these PCRs are neither resettable nor directly assignable. The only mechanism to "extend" PCRs is a special TPM primitive which chains the old value of a PCR to a new measurement value by applying a cryptographic hash function.

Remote attestation is a mechanism to prove the current platform software configuration state to a remote verifier by means of a digitally signed receipt of the PCR values held by the TPM. Sealing or local attestation is another TPM primitive which allows binding of sensitive data blobs to a particular platform in a particular software configuration state. Due to the construction of the sealing primitive it is only possible to decrypt the protected data blob on the correct platform which additionally must be in the correct state.

Roots-of-trust for measurement (RTMs) provide the root anchors for building transitive chains of trust based on the extend primitive provided by PCRs. Typical trusted PC platforms have a single static RTM (S-RTM) originating in the platform BIOS which is responsible for building an initial chain of measurements, starting at platform boot.

Advanced trusted PC platforms additionally provide dynamic RTMs (D-RTMs) based on special "late-launch" processor and platform extensions. The idea behind D-RTMs is to enable transitions from arbitrary, probably untrusted, platform states with long (static) measurement chains into trusted platform states which start with short (dynamic) measurement chains. To accomplish the transition from potentially untrusted into trusted states, platforms with D-RTMs perform special hardware assisted "late-launch" sequences similar to a platform reset.

1.2   Structure of the Paper

This paper is structured into 6 major sections. The first section describes our motivation for the attack discussed in this paper and very briefly introduces the relevant Trusted Computing concepts. Pointers to related work are in section 1.3, followed by a brief discussion of low-level aspects of PC platforms with TPMs in section 2. In section 3 we discuss details of the LPC bus and its relationship to the TPM. Based on the foundations of section 3, we introduce a bus modification attack targeting the LPC bus in section 4.

Experimental results with our bus modification attack are given in section 5. At the beginning of section 5 we describe an experimental hardware setup used to simulate a trusted PC platform with a TPM and D-RTM capabilities. Based on this simulated platform and the results from section 4 we continue to investigate the D-RTM startup mechanism in section 5.1 with the ultimate goal of spoofing a legitimate D-RTM startup sequence.

Later in section 5.2, we verify the results obtained so far on an actual D-RTM enabled desktop PC platforms. We finish the discussion of experimental results in section 5.3 with an alternate type of LPC cycles suitable for applying the attack discussed in 4. Finally, section 6 concludes the paper.

Additional information on the bus modification technique introduced in section 4, including the complete VHDL implementation of the attacker device discussed in section 5, can be found in appendix A.

1.3   Related Work

One particularly simple hardware attack against trusted desktop platforms which is commonly known as "TPM Reset Attack" has been described independently by Kauer [10] and Sparks et al. [18]. Essentially the reset attack relies on a peculiarity of the mechanism used to signal platform resets on the LPC bus which connects a TPM to the remaining platform. The reset signal of the LPC bus is implemented as active-low signal, enabling an attacker to assert an LPC bus reset by simply forcing the LPC reset line to a logic low level using a plain piece of wire or a small resistor connected to ground.

The authors of [10] and [18] observed that forced assertion of the LPC bus reset signal only impacts devices, like the TPM, which are immediately connected to the LPC bus without affecting other parts of the PC platform. Being able to independently reset the TPM and the main processor, however, breaks any trust assumptions on the static RTM and allows an attacker to construct arbitrary spoofed PCR measurements.

Another approach to attack the LPC bus as the weakest link between the TPM and the remaining platform has been shown by Schellekens et al. in [16]. The authors of [16] passively analyzed the communication of version 1.1 TPMs with the remaining platform and observed that certain operations like unsealing used to transmit TPM protected secrets in plain over the LPC bus.

We recently demonstrated a version of the LPC bus sniffing attack based on the ideas found in [16] at the 4th European Trusted Infrastructure Summer School (ETISS). Our demonstration focused on a simple low-budget LPC bus sniffing device which can be constructed by virtually anybody with basic knowledge of digital circuits and FPGAs. All material related to our bus sniffing demonstration can be found at [22].

An alternative approach to extract secrets from trusted platforms which does not directly target the TPM is the "cold-boot attack" discussed in [7]. The cold-boot attack exploits remanence effects of dynamic RAMs at low temperature. According to Halderman et al. [7] the content of dynamic RAM memories can survive loss of power for extended periods of time, when the memory bars are cooled down. Exploiting these memory remanence effects allows an adversary to physically remove RAM memories from a trusted platform without destroying memory content like cryptographic key material.

The idea of using LPC bus modification attacks with special LPC devices which generate bus cycles has been discussed at least since 2007 in the blog posting found at [12]. A security assessment of TPMs which is not only focussed on a hardware centric view can be found at [17]. Finally, Tarnovsky [19] demonstrated publicly that secrets held inside a TPM can be extracted by means of invasive chip-level attacks if sufficient resources are available.

2 Anatomy of a "Trusted" PC Platform

Logically a trusted PC platform is structured into different hardware and software components with varying levels of trust and with varying responsibilities. Localities are the mechanism provided by the TPM to enable this kind of distinction between static roots of trust, normal operating systems, trusted applications and dynamic roots of trust.

Each command block submitted to the TPM has an associated locality which is determined by the TPM register address to which the block had been submitted. The mapping between TPM localities and register addresses shown in figure 1 is defined in the TPM TIS [21] standard. Depending on the active locality of a TPM command various restrictions can be in effect.

Address	Locality
0x0000-0x0FFF	0 - Static RTM
0x1000-0x1FFF	1 - Trusted OS
0x2000-0x2FFF	2 - Trusted OS
0x3000-0x3FFF	3 - Auxiliary
0x4000-0x4FFF	4 - Trusted Hardware (D-RTM)

Fig. 1. TPM I/O address to locality mapping

The TPM I/O address space spans a logically and physically distinct 16-bit address space on the LPC bus, which is broken up into partitions corresponding to the localities supported by the TPM. Neglecting support for legacy applications, the locality of TPM cycles can be determined directly by looking at the four most significant bits of the target address of TPM I/O cycles as shown in figure 1.

On the PC platform, locality 4 has special importance in context of dynamic roots-of-trust for measurement (D-RTMs). The intended purpose of D-RTMs is to allow the platform to switch from a previously untrusted state into a trusted state. Conceptually a D-RTM late-launch is comparable to a special kind of system reset which directly jumps to a piece of trusted software instead of the platform BIOS entry point.

To establish an initial good measurement of the trusted software invoked by the D-RTM launch sequence, special hardware and microcode support is integrated into the main CPU. D-RTM capable systems like Intel's TXT [4] heavily rely on the inability of an attacker to fake or reproduce the measurements done by the hardware upon invocation of the D-RTM launch sequence.

In essence, these assumptions boil down to the attacker's inability to extend Platform Configuration Registers (PCRs) in range 17 to 22 with arbitrary values of his choice. On the TPM side, integrity of PCRs 17 to 22 is guaranteed by restricting any extend operations to these PCRs to locality 4. On platforms with a D-RTM normal software including the operating system is not able to access the TPM I/O addresses in the locality 4 address range. Any attempts to initiate read or write operations to these address ranges are filtered by the I/O controller hub (Southbridge) of the platform. In case of Intel's TXT technology, a special processor instruction (called "SINIT") is used to load and launch an authenticated code module (ACM) provided by Intel itself. This code module[1] is the only entity being able to communicate with the TPM using the locality 4 address range. Integrity of the ACM is validated by the CPU itself using an public key signature. The public key used for signature verification is authenticated by a through a hash value stored in the Southbridge of the platform chip-set.

Likewise AMD's SVM[1] provides a similar SKINIT processor instruction which can be used to invoke a D-RTM launch sequence. In contrast to Intel's SINIT instruction, no digital signature verification is performed by the CPU when the "Secure Loader" code block is launched with AMD's SKINIT instruction. In this sense AMD's implementation of the D-RTM is more "open" by not forcing the platform user into trusting binary code blobs signed by the chip-set vendor. Apart from this obvious difference in the trust model, SVM and TXT can be considered as equivalent from the point of view of this paper.

3   The Low Pin Count Bus

The Low Pin Count (LPC) [8] bus was introduced to replace older legacy bus standards on PCI-bus based PC platforms. One of the main objectives for the design of the LPC bus was to retain functionality inherited from older bus standards like the ISA bus while minimizing the number of required bus wires.

The LPC bus achieves this design goal quite effectively through a simple bidirectional architecture with multiplexed address/data lines. In its minimal configuration the LPC bus only requires four bi-directional address/data lines, a single start of frame signal, a reset signal and a clock signal. Optional support for interrupts and DMA operation can be added at the cost of a few extra bus-lines.

In current desktop PC mainboards, the LPC bus is primarily used to interface the platform's Southbridge controller to firmware flash chips, Super-I/O controllers and other peripheral devices with low data-transfer bandwidth demands. From the perspective of this paper, the most interesting LPC bus user is the Trusted Platform Module which, being itself neither a bandwidth nor a latency critical device, perfectly fits on the LPC bus.

3.1   I/O Address Spaces

The LPC bus inherits some of the concepts found in the ISA bus architecture, including a dedicated I/O address space, memory mapped I/O and optional direct memory access (DMA) functionality. Additionally, the LPC bus provides support for a simple bus-mastering protocol, which is intended to replace ISA-style direct memory access (DMA) in certain situations. For the purpose of analyzing and tampering with TPM communication it is sufficient to focus on a small subset of the LPC bus functionality. DMA and bus-mastering capabilities can be completely omitted in this discussion.

---

[1] More precisely the CPU microcode invokeing this module.

The LPC bus provides two distinct, non-overlapping memory address spaces for communicating with peripheral devices. The I/O address space comprises a range of 64k locations and can be accessed using dedicated input and output instructions. Access to the I/O address space is performed on a single-byte basis. Larger write or read operations are broken down into a sequence of individual single byte operations. In addition to the I/O address space, the x86 architecture supports memory mapped I/O (MMIO) using the regular flat 32-bit address space. Memory mapped I/O is performed using the normal load and store instructions supported by the x86 instruction set. On a PC platform the Southbridge decodes certain MMIO address ranges, optionally translates memory accesses into I/O or TPM cycles and forwards them to the LPC bus.

3.2   Structure of LPC Target Cycles

All LPC target cycles follow a simple common structure depicted in figure 2. Each new LPC target cycle begins in the START phase, when the host asserts the frame signal for one or more consecutive clock cycles. During the START phase the host indicates the major type of the following bus cycle on the multiplexed address/data lines.

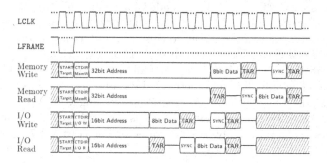

Fig. 2. LPC I/O and memory cycles

During the following clock cycles, the host drives the minor target cycle type, the target address and data to be written (in case of a write cycle) on the LPC bus data lines. Then the bus ownership is transferred from the host to the device during two turn-around (TAR) phases.

It is now the responsibility of the device to acknowledge the LPC bus cycle during the SYNC phase. When needed, a peripheral device can insert additional wait-states by driving the address/data lines to special "wait short" or "wait long" values until the bus transaction can proceed.

During the next phase the peripheral signals its ready or error status response on the address/data lines. Irrespective of the response status the following two clock phases are used for data transfer from the device to the host (in case of a read cycle). At the very end of the bus cycle two turn-around phases are used to return bus ownership from the device to the host.

As visible in figure 2, the only format difference between target I/O and target memory cycles is the different length of the address phase. I/O cycles are used for implementation of the 16-bit wide x86 I/O address space and require four clock cycles to transfer the target address. Memory cycles are used for memory mapped I/O within a 32-bit address space and need eight clock cycles for transmission of the target address.

3.3   Usage by the TPM

Prior to version 1.2 of the TPM specification, there was no common standard for the software-visible register interface of the TPM. Consequently, each of the vendors of version 1.1(b) TPMs had to develop its own more or less similar yet incompatible interface. In particular, there was no standardised way to indicate the locality of software talking to the TPM.

As part of version 1.2 of the TPM specification, the Trusted Computing Group released a common interface standard [21] for the PC client platform. This interface standard defines a common software-visible hardware interface for the TPM. The "TPM Interface Standard" (TIS) eliminates the need for vendor specific device drivers in favor of a single generic TPM TIS driver.

In addition to a standard register interface definition, the TIS specification clearly defines the LPC bus cycles intended for communication with the TPM. The TIS specification allows LPC I/O and memory cycles to be used for legacy applications only. The standard way to communicate with version 1.2 TPM are special LPC TPM cycles introduced in the TIS specification.

The format of these TPM cycles is virtually identical to I/O LPC cycles discussed earlier. The only difference between TPM and I/O cycles is the value sent during the START phase of LPC transactions. Existing I/O cycles are "target" cycles in LPC bus terminology and use 0x0 as their 4-bit START value. The new TPM cycles use the previously reserved value 0x5 as start value.

4   Active LPC Frame Hijacking

Trusted PC platforms, in particular those intended to support a dynamic RTM, enforce restrictions on software access to the individual locality levels in hardware, typically using a filtering mechanism implemented in the Southbridge. Unauthorized or spurious write attempts to inappropriate TPM localities are dropped, read attempts are ignored and return 0xFF for each byte.

On platforms with a dynamic RTM the most interesting locality, from the viewpoint of an adversary, is locality 4 due to its special role in the D-RTM launch sequence. Communicating with the TPM at locality 4 poses a significant challenge to any adversary who is restricted to software-only attacks.

Any attempts to generate locality 4 bus cycles from within normal application or operating system software are filtered by the Southbridge of the platform and never reach the TPM. Here the hardware based locality filtering mechanism implemented on trusted PC platforms provides a strong barrier against adversaries which are restricted to software-only attacks.

At its downside this mechanism provides little to no protection against adversaries with physical hardware access to the platform. In the remainder of this section we focus on relatively simple hardware attack based on manipulation of the signals found on the LPC bus connection between the TPM and the Southbridge.

4.1 Hijacking LPC Bus Cycles

As explained earlier, there is just a tiny difference between the LPC I/O cycles visible in 2 and the LPC cycles used for TPM communication. Closer consideration of the LPC cycles given in figure 2 unreveals that the only noticeable difference between memory and I/O (or TPM) cycles is the length of the target address phase.

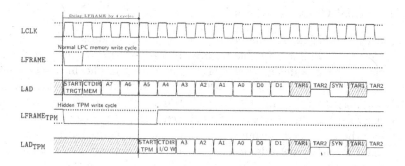

Fig. 3. Hijacking an LPC memory write cycle (principle)

When started at the same time, a memory cycle requires four additional clock cycles in comparison to an I/O cycle due to the longer address phase. The address and data parts of an I/O write cycle take six clock cycles while the equivalent parts of a memory write cycle take ten clock cycles.

Now we can conduct a thought experiment and shift the start of the I/O cycles in figure 2 by four clocks cycles to the right while leaving the start of the memory cycles at their original position. The result of this shift is that the trailing parts of the memory and I/O cycles are now perfectly aligned starting at the data-phase, in case of the write cycles or the host to peripheral turn-around phase in case of the read cycles. We now observe that the address phases of the memory read and write cycles entirely overlap the shifted I/O cycles.

Figure 3 depicts the same result obtained by performing the shift experiment with a memory write and a TPM write cycle. Based on this observation it is now possible to construct a simple hardware device, which is capable of hijacking an ordinary memory cycle and promoting it to a TPM cycle. Our frame hijacker device has to detect the start of an appropriate memory cycle by watching the

LPC frame and data signals. When triggered. the device should intercept the LPC frame signal to the TPM and delay its de-assertion by four clock cycles. From the TPM's point of view the LPC cycle shown in figure 3 starts after the A5 phase of the original memory cycle with de-assertion of the intercepted frame signal.

At this point we refer to the LPC bus specification [8] which explicitly allows the frame signal to be active for more than one consecutive clock cycle. According to the LPC bus specification a device *must* consider the last value observed on the address/data lines, while the frame signal was active, as START value. Coincidentally, this is just the behavior we need for the frame hijacker attack.

Instead of having to circumvent the locality filtering mechanism of the platform's Southbridge, we just need to attach a simple hardware device to the platform and to generate LPC memory cycles with specially crafted addresses.

4.2   Practical Considerations

The basic cycle hijacking technique outlined in figure 3 is immediately applicable if the adversary is willing and able to directly force a logic low level on the LPC frame line. Using a sufficiently strong output driver in the hijacker device it should be possible to override the LPC frame signal from the Southbridge by directly forcing it to a logic low level. Such a brute force approach has three major drawbacks: While we have experimental evidence that a typical PC Southbridge withstands the increased output current on the output pin driving the LPC frame signal for short periods of time, permanent damage to the Southbrigde I/O pads is likely to be caused by excessive current flows on the long run.

Furthermore, the brute-force approach kills any other non-TPM LPC cycles as long as the hijacker is active since we have to intercept any LPC target cycles during their start phase. Finally, the brute-force approach could be easily detected by the Southbridge, just by comparing the expected frame output signal with the actual logic level observed at the LFRAME pad.

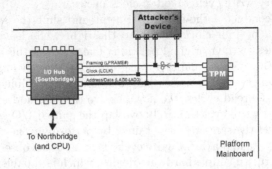

Fig. 4. Hardware setup (principle) for the LPC frame hijacking attack

These threes issues can be solved at once, if we allow the LPC frame line to be physically cut along its path to the TPM. Figure 4 shows a revised hardware setup for the frame hijacking attack. With the new hardware setup it is possible to *selectively* trigger the frame hijacking device on memory cycles targeted to certain memory addresses without interfering with any other LPC bus users. To do so, we monitor the START, CTDIR, A7 and optionally A6 phases visible in figure 3. Instead of asserting the LPC frame signal right from the beginning of the hijacked memory cycle's START phase we only generate a single framing pulse during the memory cycle's A5 phase.

5   Experimental Results

The experimental hardware setup shown in figure 5 has been used to verify the LPC frame hijacker attack discussed in the preceding section. Our setup consists of two FPGA boards and a TPM daughterboard mounted on a breadboard socket adapter.

Fig. 5. Experimental setup for the LPC frame hijacker

The upper (green) FPGA board shown in figure 5 is a Xilinx Spartan-3A DSP 1800 Starter Kit simulating the I/O controller hub (Southbridge) of a PC platform. The Spartan-3A FPGA contains a Xilinx MicroBlaze soft-core processor with 16K of on-chip RAM clocked at 66 MHz and a custom LPC bus master interface clocked at 33 MHz. The LPC bus master core used in this setup supports LPC I/O, memory and TPM target cycles as well as single-byte firmware read and write cycles. Our LPC bus master core is a deliberately simple design, written in approximately 490 lines of VHDL source code. The interface wrapper for the PLB bus supported by the MicroBlaze processor takes approximately 850 lines of VHDL code, which was mostly auto-generated.

In the center of figure 5, the breadboard socket adapter used to connect to the TPM daughter-board is visible. Our adapter board consists of a 2x10 pin header for the TPM daughter-board connection, several smaller pin headers for connecting to the FPGA boards and pull-up resistors for currently unused or unimplemented LPC signals. The TPM daughter-board used in the experiment hosts a version 1.2 TPM from a major vendor. It is available as add-on module for various PC motherboards with optional TPM support (e.g. manufactured by ASUS or by GIGABYTE). In principle our attack should work with *any* version 1.2 TPMs implementing an LPC bus interface conforming to the TPM Interface Standard (TIS) independent of the actual TPM vendor.

The actual LPC cycle hijacker is implemented in the red FPGA board visible at the bottom of figure 5. This board is an old Xilinx Spartan-3E100 evaluation kit [13] containing a Spartan-3E FPGA together with a Cypress-FX2 micro-controller. The setup discussed in this paper does not use the Cypress-FX2 micro-controller, the USB connector of the board is solely used for power supply purposes. Inbound LPC clock, frame and data signals are routed using the two groups of small wires connecting the breadboard adapter with the red FPGA board. The large red wire visible on the left of figure 5 carries the hijacked TPM frame signal generated by the red FPGA board to the TPM. The white wire provides the common ground connection for the TPM board and the red FPGA board.

The full VHDL source code for the LPC frame hijacker core used on the lower FPGA board can be found in appendix A. By default, our frame hijacker core requires all four address/data lines of the LPC bus to be probed by the attacker. This does not pose a problem with the experimental setup shown in figure 5 or on PC motherboards which use TPM daughter-boards.

On motherboards with soldered on TPMs it can be an advantage for the attacker to reduce the number of signals to be probed. Under certain assumptions, the LPC frame hijacker device introduced in this paper can work reliably with only two address/data line probes (see appendix A for more details).

5.1 Performing a D-RTM Startup Sequence (From the TPM's Point of View)

Upon start-up of a dynamic RTM, an initial measurement of the D-RTM code is performed by the platform hardware itself. On currently available D-RTM enabled PC systems this initial measurement is done by the main processor as part of executing a special D-RTM launch instruction. On the TPM side a special-purpose register interface is exposed, which allows the main processor to perform this initial measurements and the associated PCR reset operations in a simple manner.

The TPM exposes three registers shown in figure 6 in the locality 4 address range, which are used during D-RTM start-up. Initially, the processor is expected to perform a dummy write to the TPM_HASH_START register to indicate that a D-RTM startup sequence is about to begin. During the next phase the data to be extended during D-RTM start-up is sent byte-wise to the TPM_HASH_DATA

Address	Register
0x4020	TPM_HASH_END
0x4024	TPM_HASH_DATA
0x4028	TPM_HASH_START

Fig. 6. TPM 1.2 TIS registers used during D-RTM startup

register. The end of the D-RTM start-up code measurement is indicated by a dummy write to the TPM_HASH_END register.

Upon completion of the D-RTM start-up sequence, PCR 17 contains the value obtained by extending zero with the hash of the data stream sent to the TPM_HASH_DATA register. The PCRs in range 18 to 22 are cleared to all zero values and a TPM internal flag to indicate the presence of a "Trusted Operating System" is set. In order to simulate the same sequence on a manipulated platform with a LPC frame hijacker device, we simply have to generate a sequeence of proper LPC memory write cycles.

Finding the physical memory addresses. For now, we assume that the attacker has reprogrammed the Southbridge to generate LPC memory cycles when reading or writing to memory locations in the 0xA0000000-0xA0FFFFFF physical address range. In order to generate the proper TPM write cycles, we have to reconsider the overlap between the memory write and TPM write cycles shown earlier in figure 3.

We already noted that the A5 address phase of the hijacked memory cycle corresponds to the start phase of the TPM write cycle. Moreover, we know that the A4 address phase of the memory cycle corresponds to the type/direction field of the piggy-backed TPM write cycle. The trailing four address cycles A3-A0 directly correspond to the 4-bit locality and 12-bit register address of the TPM cycle being generated.

Based on this knowledge, we can derive the physical memory addresses required to generate piggy-backed TPM write cycles for the fake D-RTM startup sequence as follows: With the information about TPM cycle start and type/direction values given in the TIS specification we fix the values for A5 to 0x5 and A4 to 0x2. The values for A7 and A6 are already given as 0xA and 0x0 by the choice of the "trigger" address range for the frame hijacker device. We now obtain the final physical memory addresses for hijacked TPM writes to register 0x0000 as 0xA0520000. To access the other TPM registers used during the D-RTM startup sequence we simply have to add the appropriate offsets found in figure 6 to this base address.

Figure 7 shows the proof-of-concept D-RTM startup simulator implementation used in our experiments to trigger the frame hijacker logic. The base address for the memory mapping was determined by adding the locality 4 base address 0x4000 to the trigger base address of the hijacker device. The 0x20, 0x24 and 0x28 offsets were obtained directly from the table in figure 6 by subtracting the locality 4 base address.

```
#include <sys/mman.h>
#include <fcntl.h>
#include <unistd.h>

#define LOC4_WR_BASE 0xA0524000
static char pcr17_data[] = { ... };

int main(int argc, char **argv) {
    int fd = open("/dev/mem", O_RDWR);
    char *tpm = mmap(0, 4096, PROT_READ|PROT_WRITE,
             MAP_SHARED, fd, LOC4_WR_BASE);
    char *src = pcr17_data;
    unsigned size = sizeof(pcr17_data);

    tpm[0x28] = 0x00; // TPM_HASH_START
    while (size--) {
      tpm[0x24] = *src++;  // TPM_HASH_DATA
    }
    tpm[0x20] = 0x00; // TPM_HASH_END
    return 0;
}
```

Fig. 7. Proof-of-concept D-RTM startup simulator

5.2   Verification on a D-RTM Capable PC Platform

The initial verification of our LPC frame hijacking attack, including the simulated D-RTM start-up sequence was done with the Southbridge simulator and experimental hardware setup discussed earlier. To verify our attack on a real PC platform we decided to attach the hijacker device in passive "sniff-only" mode to an Intel TXT capable HP Compaq DC7900 computer with an Intel ICH10 Southbridge. However for warranty reasons we refrained from cutting any motherboard PCB traces - thus we only tested the hijacker device's ability to generate properly manipulated LPC frames in this setup.

After installing appropriate probe wires, the only remaining obstacle was to find a method to reprogram the Southbridge controller of the victim platform to generate suitable memory write cycles. By coincidence the ICH10 Southbridge installed in the target PC supports a programmable decode area for LPC memory cycles, which is *not* locked down by the BIOS after platform startup. The corresponding Southbridge configuration register is called LGMR [9, Ch. 13.1.27] and can be found in PCI device 31, function 0 at register offset 0x98–0x9B. To reprogram this register with the values calculated in section 5.1, an adversary can use the setpci program which is part of the Linux pciutils package as follows:

```
# setpci -s 00:1f.0 0x98.L=0xA0520001
```

Afterwards, the D-RTM simulator program from listing 7 can be used to generate the appropriate TPM cycles from hijacked LPC memory cycles. To verify correct functionality of the hijacker device on the PC platform we integrated a Xilinx ChipScope Integrated Logic Analyzer (ILA) IP-core into the hijacker device and compared the observed signals with the known good results results from using the Southbridge simulator. If the adversary intends to generate TPM read instead of write cycles, he has to reprogram the LGMR register to a slightly different value:

```
# setpci -s 00:1f.0 0x98.L=0xA0500001
```

5.3   Using LPC Firmware Cycles Instead of Memory Cycles

The success of the frame hijacking attack crucially depends on an adversary's ability to generate long LPC bus cycles which can be used to piggyback the faked TPM cycles. On the Intel ICH10 based mainboard we used to verify our attack, it is particularly easy to generate suitable LPC memory cycles due to the freely accessible, programmable memory decode window of the LPC host controller. On other motherboards or chip-sets without an equivalent feature we have to resort to alternative means of generating the required cycles.

One alternative solution to hijacking LPC memory cycles is to use LPC firmware cycles. Firmware cycles are intended to access LPC flash chips containing the BIOS or option ROMs during platform boot. This type of bus cycles slightly differs from memory cycles in their addressing scheme and the support for different data transfer sizes.

There are two primary issues with using firmware cycles. The first difficulty we observed are the small firmware decode window sizes supported by common Southbridges. Out of the eight address fields of an LPC firmware cycle only five were usable on most mainboards tested by us.

The address phase of a typical LPC firmware cycle is followed by an extra field indicating the size of the read or write transfer. For one byte firmware cycles the size field is fixed to the value 0x0. Combined with the small number of freely usable address fields these limitations restricts our ability to generate hijacked TPM cycles from single-byte firmware cycles to TPM registers addresses which are evenly divisible by 16 only.

Another severe difficulty with firmware cycles is that Southbridges usually block firmware write cycles in order to prevent unauthorized re-flashing operations of the platform BIOS. To generate usable firmware write cycles, an adversary first has to circumvent to BIOS re-flash protection mechanism.

The LPC bus specification defines firmware read and write cycles with different sizes ranging from single byte access up to 128-byte blocks. Apart from mandatory support for single byte cycles all other sizes are optional. We want to point out that firmware write cycles with data sizes larger than one byte can be hijacked as TPM cycles without suffering the modulo 16 TPM address constraint discussed above.

We have successfully verified the use of hijacked LPC firmware cycles instead of memory cycles on our Southbridge simulator. Best results, in terms of reachable TPM TIS registers were obtained with 2- and 16-byte firmware write cycles. Actually the case of a hijacked 16-byte firmware write cycle was our initial idea and implementation of the frame hijacking technique before we even considered the LPC memory cycle based method outlined in this paper.

6   Conclusion

Our attack does *not* allow direct retrieval of TPM protected data, like private parts of non-migratable keys. To extract this kind of information it is still necessary to resort to invasive high-effort methods like [19] which directly target the TPM chip. However, the attack discussed in this paper closes the gap between the TPM reset attack [18][10] and the mechanisms used by current D-RTM implementations to counteract the reset attack.

We point out that the attack discussed in this paper is within the bounds set by David Grawrock [5, Ch. 10, p. 132] for simple hardware attacks against trusted PC platforms with D-RTM support. Hardware equipment required for setting up the active LPC bus attack discussed in this paper is accessible to anybody with sufficient interest, motivation and knowledge of basic electronics. We demonstrated the feasibility of emulating the TPM interactions with a D-RTM implementation like Intel's TXT or AMD's SVM architecture. By combining the attack discussed in this paper with the classic TPM reset attack it becomes possible to fake arbitrary platform configurations in terms of TPM PCR values. Effectively, this ability largely voids the trust assumptions put into remote and local attestation. With crafted PCR values in place, the only remaining barriers preventing an attacker from triggering TPM operations are usage secrets placed on TPM keys and blobs. In case of low-entropy usage secrets, this protection margin will be quite small if the attacker manages to secretly install a passive LPC bus sniffing device usable to bootstrap off-line attacks like [2]. Based on the results of this paper and earlier results from [16], [22], [18] and [10] we finally conclude that remote *and* local attestation largely fail to meet their trust promises on current PC platforms when using the LPC bus for communication with TPMs, if the attacker model includes even simple forms of hardware attacks.

Acknowledgements. We thank the anonymous reviewers for their helpful comments. This work has been supported in part by the European Commission through the FP7 programme under contract 257433 SEPIA.

References

1. AMD: Amd64 architecture programmer's manual. System programming, vol. 2 (2007), http://www.amd.com/us-en/assets/content_type/ white_papers_and_tech_docs/24593.pdf, publication No. 24593; Revision 3.14
2. Chen, L., Ryan, M.: Attack, Solution and Verification for Shared Authorisation Data in TCG TPM. In: Degano, P., Guttman, J.D. (eds.) FAST 2009. LNCS, vol. 5983, pp. 201–216. Springer, Heidelberg (2010)
3. Cihula, J., Wei, J., Wang, S.: Trusted Boot (2007), http://tboot.sourceforge.net/
4. Corp., I.: Intel trusted execution technology. software development guide (2008), http://download.intel.com/technology/security/downloads/315168.pdf, document Number: 315168-005

5. Grawrock, D.: Dynamics of a Trusted Platform: A Building Block Approach. Intel Press (2009)
6. TCG Group, TPM Working Group: TPM Main Part 1 Design Principles (July 9, 2007), Specification available online at:
   http://www.trustedcomputinggroup.org/files/resource_files/ACD19914-1D09-3519-ADA64741A1A15795/mainP1DPrev103.zip, specification version 1.2 Level 2 Revision 103
7. Halderman, J.A., Schoen, S.D., Heninger, N., Clarkson, W., Paul, W., Calandrino, J.A., Feldman, A.J., Appelbaum, J., Felten, E.W.: Lest we remember: cold-boot attacks on encryption keys. Commun. ACM 52(5), 91–98 (2009)
8. Intel: Intel Low Pin Count (LPC) Interface Specification, revision 1.1 (August 2002), http://www.intel.com/design/chipsets/industry/25128901.pdf
9. Intel: Intel i/o controller hub 10 (ich10) family datasheet (October 2008)
10. Kauer, B.: OSLO: improving the security of trusted computing. In: Proceedings of 16th USENIX Security Symposium on USENIX Security Symposium, pp. 16:1–16:9. USENIX Association, Berkeley (2007), http://portal.acm.org/citation.cfm?id=1362903.1362919
11. Krautheim, F., Phatak, D., Sherman, A.: Introducing the Trusted Virtual Environment Module: A New Mechanism for Rooting Trust in Cloud Computing. In: Acquisti, A., Smith, S.W., Sadeghi, A.-R. (eds.) TRUST 2010. LNCS, vol. 6101, pp. 211–227. Springer, Heidelberg (2010), http://dx.doi.org/10.1007/978-3-642-13869-0_14, doi:10.1007/978-3-642-13869-0_14
12. Lawson, N.: TPM hardware attacks (part 2), Blog posting archived at: http://rdist.root.org/2007/07/17/tpm-hardware-attacks-part-2/
13. Avnet electronics marketing: Spartan-3e evaluation kit from avnet, Product folder available online at: http://www.xilinx.com/publications/xcellonline/xcell_53/xc_pdf/xc_avnet53.pdf, product annoncement of ADS-XLX-SP3E-EVL100 board in Xilinx Xcell Journal Issue #53
14. McCune, J.M., Parno, B.J., Perrig, A., Reiter, M.K., Isozaki, H.: Flicker: an execution infrastructure for tcb minimization. In: Proceedings of the 3rd ACM SIGOPS/EuroSys European Conference on Computer Systems, Eurosys 2008, pp. 315–328. ACM, New York (2008), http://doi.acm.org/10.1145/1352592.1352625
15. Pirker, M., Toegl, R., Gissing, M.: Dynamic Enforcement of Platform Integrity. In: Acquisti, A., Smith, S.W., Sadeghi, A.-R. (eds.) TRUST 2010. LNCS, vol. 6101, pp. 265–272. Springer, Heidelberg (2010), http://dx.doi.org/10.1007/978-3-642-13869-0_18, doi:10.1007/978-3-642-13869-0_18
16. Schellekens, D., Preneel, B., Kursawe, K.: Analyzing trusted platform communication, https://www.cosic.esat.kuleuven.be/publications/article-591.pdf
17. Sparks, E.R.: A Security Assessment of Trusted Platform Modules. Tech. rep., Department of Computer Science, Dartmouth College, Hanover, NH 03755, USA (June 28, 2007)
18. Sparks, E.R., et al.: TPM Reset Attack, http://www.cs.dartmouth.edu/~pkilab/sparks/
19. Tarnovsky, C.: Hacking the Smartcard Chip, presentation archived at: http://www.blackhat.com/html/bh-dc-10/bh-dc-10-archives.html#Tarnovsky
20. Trusted Compuring Group: TCG Specification Architecture Overview, revision 1.4 (August 2, 2007), http://www.trustedcomputinggroup.org/

21. Trusted Computing Group: TCG PC Client Specific TPM Interface Specification (TIS), version 1.2 FINAL. For TPM Family 1.2; Level 2 (July 11, 2005), http://www.trustedcomputinggroup.org/

22. Winter, J.: Eavesdropping Trusted Platform Module Communication (July 2009), presented at 4th European Trusted Infrastructure Summerschool (ETISS) (2009), Slides and report are available online at: http://embedded.iaik.tugraz.at/

A   VHDL Implementation of the Frame Hijacker Device

This appendix gives the complete VHDL source code of the LPC frame hijacker device introduced in section 4. The four top-most bits of the memory cycle trigger address can be configured with the C_A7_ADDR parameter. The default parametrization shown below uses the read and write addresses discussed in section 5.1.

```
library ieee;
use ieee.std_logic_1164.all;
use ieee.numeric_std.all;
entity sp3e_tpm_hijacker is
  generic (C_A7_ADDR : std_logic_vector(3 downto 0) := x"A");
  port (lclk        : in   std_logic;
        lreset      : in   std_logic;
        lframe_in   : in   std_logic;
        lframe_out  : out  std_logic;
        lad         : in   std_logic_vector(3 downto 0);
        enable      : in   std_logic);
end entity sp3e_tpm_hijacker;

architecture rtl of sp3e_tpm_hijacker is
  constant START_TGT : std_logic_vector(3 downto 0) := "0000";
  constant CT_MEM_RD : std_logic_vector(3 downto 0) := "0100";
  constant CT_MEM_WR : std_logic_vector(3 downto 0) := "0110";
  type lad_array_t is array(2 downto 0) of std_logic_vector(3 downto 0);
  signal q_lad         : lad_array_t;
  signal q_lframe      : std_logic_vector(2 downto 0);
  signal force_frame   : std_logic;
  signal is_tgt_cycle  : std_logic;
  signal is_mem_cycle  : std_logic;
  signal is_valid_frame : std_logic;
  signal is_valid_a7   : std_logic;
  signal is_triggered  : std_logic;
begin   -- architecture rtl
  -- LAD and LFRAME input shift registers
  lad_shift_reg : process (lclk, lreset) is
  begin
    if lreset = '0' then
      q_lframe <= (others => '1');
      q_lad    <= (others => (others => '-'));
    elsif lclk'event and lclk = '1' then
      q_lframe <= (2 => lframe_in, 1 => q_lframe(2), 0 => q_lframe(1));
      q_lad    <= (2 => lad, 1 => q_lad(2), 0 => q_lad(1));
    end if;
  end process lad_shift_reg;

  -- Trigger logic
  is_tgt_cycle  <= '1' when q_lad(0) = START_TGT else '0';
  is_mem_cycle  <= '1' when (q_lad(1) = CT_MEM_RD) or
                           (q_lad(1) = CT_MEM_WR) else '0';
  is_valid_a7   <= '1' when q_lad(2) = C_A7_ADDR else '0';
  is_valid_frame <= q_lframe(2) and q_lframe(1)
                           and not q_lframe(0);
  is_triggered  <= enable and is_valid_frame and is_tgt_cycle
```

```
                    and is_mem_cycle and is_valid_a7;
  -- Force FRAME output register
  delayed_frame_gen : process (lclk, lreset) is
  begin
    if lreset = '0' then
      force_frame <= '1';
    elsif lclk 'event and lclk = '1' then
      force_frame <= not is_triggered;
    end if;
  end process delayed_frame_gen;

  -- Output frame multiplexer
  lframe_out <= force_frame when enable = '1' else lframe_in;
end architecture rtl;
```

Our prototype implementation includes an additional **enable** input which can be used to control the hijacker core. When disabled, the hijacker core does not interfere with the LPC frame signal and directly forwards lframe_in to lframe_out allowing normal operation of the bus.

A.1   Reducing the Number of LPC Address/Data Lines to Probe

The cycle hijacker device usually evaluates all four LPC lad input signals to distinguish LPC memory cycles from other cycle types. Reconsidering the LPC bus start fields and type/direction values defined in [8, Ch. 4.2.1, p.15] reveals that probing only lad[3] and lad[2] is sufficient for reliable operation:

Currently the only defined LPC START values with lad[3:2]=2b00 are used for bus master and for target cycles. In case of target cycles the type and direction is indicated by the LPC CTDIR field. Coincidentally LPC memory read and write cycles can be distinguished from all other LPC target cycles by the lad[3:2]=2b01 value in their CTDIR field. We can now tie the lad[1] and lad[0] inputs to a constant logic zero value and operate the LPC hijacker device with only the lad[3] and lad[2] inputs connected to actual bus probes. The disadvantages of this reduced setup are that we loose the two least-significant bits of the trigger address given in C_A7_ADDR and that we must ensure that no bus master grant cycles occur while the hijacker device is active.

Secure Event Logging in Sensor Networks

An Braeken[1], Antonio De La Piedro[1], and Karel Wouters[2]

[1] Erasmushogeschool Brussel, IWT,
Nijverheidskaai 170, 1070 Brussel, Belgium
[2] K.U. Leuven ESAT/SCD-COSIC and IBBT,
Kasteelpark Arenberg 10, B-3001 Leuven-Heverlee, Belgium

Abstract. This paper proposes protocols for secure logging of events in sensor networks by gathering in a secure and reliable way all information at one central point. Not only the chronological order of logged events sent by the different sensors is guaranteed. Also modification, deletion, and addition of other data is made impossible. As proof of concept, we have designed a prototype of the gateway sensor on an FPGA platform.

Keywords: Sensor Network, Secure logging, Linked time-stamping protocol, FPGA implementation.

1 Introduction

Wireless sensor networks are gaining popularity. They are used in consumer and industrial applications, including home automation, healthcare applications, industrial process monitoring and control, environment and habitat monitoring, and traffic control. The sensor nodes in a network can capture sensitive and valuable information. This information is collected in a central server for further analysis. The transmission of these data needs to be secured and therefore, the research community is focusing on the security protocols to achieve this, and on the underlying threat model.

In this paper we focus on the secure logging of the information gathering from the different nodes. The goal is to prove the chronological order, in a reliable way, of the observations and events in nodes. It can be useful to prove that a certain event at node x occurred before another event at node y. For instance, consider the setting of a wireless body area sensor network (WBAN) in a hospital. A secure logging of the outputs of sensors from different patients enables the study of the flow and effects from the hospital bacteria. Another example is the study of the original source in a large forest fire, containing a network of sensors with fire detection features. Our approach leaves no possibility to re-order events afterwards, if this is in the interest of a certain involved party.

The proposal in this paper is based on the notion of linked time-stamps, in which a message digest chain is formed through events to be logged. The linking takes place at so-called gateway nodes, acting as communication hubs, and at the central server node. Consequently, the gateway node becomes responsible for ordering the information from the sensors of its network, while the central

S. Petkova-Kikova, A. Pashalidis, G. Pernul (Eds.): EuroPKI 2011, LNCS 7163, pp. 194–208, 2012.

server orders the information of the different gateway nodes. For structuring this information, we introduce the concept of layered threaded authentication trees, in which the leaf nodes are threaded authentication trees themselves.

In the context of WBAN, a gateway node is often a PDA or a cell phone [12]. In this paper, we design a dedicated piece of hardware as prototype for the gateway node. The reason for this approach is that it becomes increasingly difficult to implement a fully secure mobile phone application. Moreover, a dedicated device gives more control over various parameters that influence the user's experience: battery power, several models for mobile phones/PDA, cost, etc.

The paper is organised as follows. Section 2 describes previous work on the related notion of time-stamping protocols. In Section 3 the setting, security requirements and assumptions are discussed. Section 4 explains the linking and communication protocols. In Section 5, an implementation on FPGA is proposed. We end in Section 6 with some conclusions and future work.

2   Related Work

A time-stamp delivers a proof for the existence of a certain piece of information, prior to the time, indicated by the time-stamp. Following [2], there are three types of time-stamping protocols: simple, linked, and distributed schemes. In a distributed scheme multiple issuers cooperatively generate a time-stamp, which is outside the context of this paper. In a simple scheme, a third party (also called the time-stamp authority, TSA) generates a time-stamp by means of a signature on the hash of the document and the actual time. This is an easy and compact algorithm. However the main weakness of the system is that once the private key of the TSA expires or gets compromised, all time-stamps become useless and, in case of a compromise, back-dated time stamps can be generated. Moreover, any signature implementation consumes a relatively high amount of energy and time, which can be a problem in a sensor network. The linked time-stamp scheme makes the time-stamp dependent of the previously issued time-stamps in a one-way fashion, by means of a hash function. If such a time-stamp gets published in a widely witnessed medium, it becomes computationally hard to delete, alter or add time-stamps situated before the published one, even by the TSA himself. Several approaches have been proposed to implement linked time-stamps: linear linking schemes [9], binary linking schemes [5], and threaded authentication tree schemes [4] are well-known examples.

In our proof of concept we implemented a algorithm based on threaded authentication trees. This scheme provides hash chains of optimal length through two time-stamps, from one published value to another. We include the concept of time-stamping on the level of sensor networks, meaning that a node (the gateway node) in the network is actually generating the linking information, to be included in a linking scheme at a higher level. In previous work, Cotroneo et al.[6], implemented a linear linking protocol for mobile applications. Using threaded authentication trees allows for faster verification of the (shorter) hash chains.

Note that the concept of data aggregation is slightly different with our goal of secure logging. In data aggregation, data coming from different sensors, is combined and redundancy is removed. Very often these algorithms are also tree-based protocols. However, for secure logging, a linked tree is required since the chronological order of the messages is of importance.

3   Setting, Security Requirements and Assumptions

3.1   Setting

We consider a set of sensor networks, each communicating to a central server by means of its own gateway node. This node is uniquely linked to the sensors of its network. Figure 1 depicts a schematic overview of such a network.

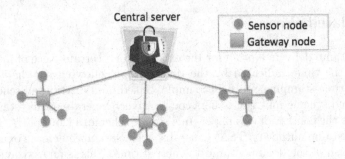

Fig. 1. Setting of sensor network

The sensor nodes submit their inherent information at irregular times or in emergency cases to the gateway. The gateway collects the information of each sensor node and computes a time-stamp on it. If storing capacity might be an issue, one can agree on computing time-stamps on the emergency situations only. By the end of a certain time frame, for instance a day, the gateway node sends the information to the central server, which collects the inputs of all the different gateway nodes. We explain in Section 4.2 the communication protocols more into detail.

3.2   Security Requirements

A basic requirement in sensor networks is the authentication of data and entities. Depending on the application, also confidentiality and privacy can play an important role. For instance, communicating healthcare information is more sensitive than communicating information on environmental parameters.

In this paper, we add the property of secure logging of the transmitted data. Secure logging refers to the capability of delivering entry integrity, meaning that log trails (and hence also the order of the logged events) cannot be changed once recorded. Changing includes modification, as well as deletion and adding. Instead of absolute time binding (issuing time-stamps that contain a time indication), we restrict ourselves to the relative case of linked time-stamping, which focuses on relative position in time. This still enables us to verify which of two events happened earlier. An indication of time can be extracted from the publication times, and it can be embedded into the time-stamp itself as metadata. Note that we do not need any clock synchronisation among all sensors in the network [11]. Finally, the scheme should be resistant to situations where one or more sensor nodes or even the gateway node accidentally lose their key.

3.3 Security Assumptions

In order to offer authentication of data and entity (and eventually confidentiality), cryptographic keys are deployed in the sensor network. It is clear that a first basic assumption is that the key material in the sensor nodes, the gateway node, and the central server are stored in the tamper resistant part of the hardware.

A second assumption is that the gateway node also stores, in a tamper resistant part of the hardware, a list of active sensor IDs. Moreover, for each sensor ID, also a list of their counter values, and their corresponding message events, and information related to compute the time-stamps is saved.

Finally, as the gateway node and the central server are both trusted to generate linking information similar to time-stamps, they should satisfy several security-related requirements. The Internet X.509 Public Key Infrastructure Time-Stamp Protocol [2] enumerates eleven recommendations. Among them, most important is that a time-stamp is taken upon receiving a valid request from the requester. Note that thanks to the use of a structure similar to linked time-stamping protocols, the trust in the entities that generate the linking information can be greatly reduced, as mentioned in the previous section.

4 Protocol

We start by describing the core of the system, namely the linking protocol. Afterwards, we shortly explain the cryptographic techniques used for the communications from sensor node to gateway node and from gateway node to central server.

4.1 Linking Protocol Based on Threaded Authentication Trees

We first explain the general concept of threaded authentication trees. Then, we show how these trees can be applied in the context of secure logging for sensor networks. We here distinguish between gateway nodes and central server.

Threaded authentication trees

An example of the linking structure that fixes the order of the logged events in our scheme, is depicted in Figure 2. These structures, called threaded authentication trees, are described in [4]. The vertices (nodes) in this graph represent hash values, computed using the concatenation (denoted by ||) of all their ancestor nodes, indicated by the edges in the graph. A threaded authentication tree is built, starting from a simple binary tree. First, a source vertex is added (labelled 1 in Figure 2), with edges to each of the leaf vertices (2 to 9). Then, for each path from the root 1, through a leaf vertex (e.g. 9) to the sink vertex (16 in the example), edges from each left child of the vertices in the path are added, ending in the leaf vertex. In case of the path 1-9-13-15-16 through 9, this results in adding edges 8-9, 12-9 and 14-9: Edge 8 is the left child of edge 13, 12 is the left child of 15 and 14 is the left child of 16. Finally, one unlabelled vertex is added for each leaf vertex, and an edge from the unlabelled vertex to the leaf vertex is added. The depth of the tree equals to the logarithm of the number of nodes, minus 1.

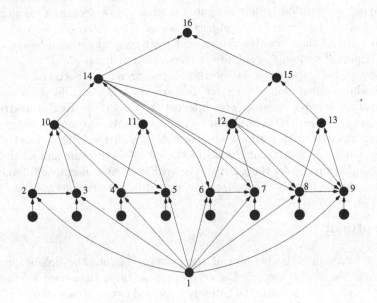

Fig. 2. Threaded tree of depth 3

For example, Figure 2 consists of 16 nodes and thus represents a threaded tree of depth 3. The vertex node 8 is computed as

$$H_8 = H(X||H_1||H_{12}||H_{14}),$$

in which X is the hash value of the unlabelled node, attached to node 8. The unlabelled nodes in the graph represent the hash values of log information of the events in the sensors. In this example, node 1 can be a previously published value, while leaf node 2-9 will have a hash value of information to be logged, attached to it. The linking information related to a specific log entry will consist of those nodes that are necessary to compute from bottom (H_1) to top (H_{16}). This information corresponds to the time-stamp. For vertex node 8 in the example, the time-stamp t_8 equals to

$$t_8 = (X, H_1, H_{12}, H_{14}, H_9).$$

This information allows for the computation of a hash chain going through the source and the sink of the directed graph: $1 \rightarrow 8 \rightarrow 13 \rightarrow 15 \rightarrow 16$. The union of the linking information of two log entries will hold enough information to compute a hash chain, starting from node 1, ending in node 16, going through both involved leaf nodes. This establishes the temporal relation between the logged events. In the example, with the time-stamps for vertex 4 and 8, the following path can be computed.

$$1 \rightarrow 4 \rightarrow 11 \rightarrow 14 \rightarrow 8 \rightarrow 13 \rightarrow 15 \rightarrow 16$$

The number of edges in such a path is always less than $2d + 2$.

In general, a threaded authentication tree of depth d can cover 2^d log entries (leaves) and has size $k(2^{d+1})$, where k is the size of the used hash function. The maximum linking information or in fact the time-stamp, related to a specific log entry, is proved to be optimal and equals to $k(d + 3)$.

Layered threaded authentication trees

In our context, the gateway nodes are building threaded authentication trees for log entries, relating to events in the sensor nodes that they serve. This establishes a temporal relationship between all the logged events within the nodes depending on a single gateway node. When the tree is completed, or after a certain time interval, the gateway node transfers the top value to the central server, followed by all hash values of the log entries. The central server verifies the threaded authentication tree, and links the top values of all the gateway sensors in the network into a new threaded authentication tree. When the new tree is completed, the resulting top value is used as a new bottom node for the fresh threaded tree in the gateway nodes. Consequently, at a fixed point of time, the resulting threaded authentication tree generated by the central server consists of nodes from which almost half of them represent again a threaded authentication tree (generated by one of the gateway nodes). We call this structure a layered threaded authentication tree.

In an ideal situation, this would look like Figure 3. In this case, four gateway nodes collected 8 events each, and have sent these to the central server. The server then links the top of each of the four trees together, in a new threaded authentication tree. As can be seen in the picture, two events of different gateway nodes, within the same threaded server tree, cannot be compared. In all other cases, a hash chain can be computed through any two logged events. In conventional linked time-stamping, intermediate hash values get published in a

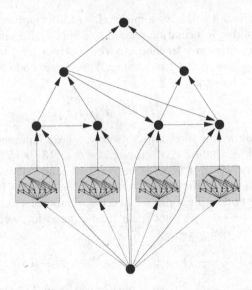

Fig. 3. Logging structure at a fixed point in time for 4 gateway nodes with 8 logging events each

widely witnessed medium, to permanently fix all previously issued time-stamps. In our setting, a similar approach should be taken by the central server. Periodically, it will publish the top of its threaded tree. Once this is done, all events logged by the nodes in its network are fixed and should be reproduced when the system is audited. This requires a storage of the logged events together with the tree structure.

In practise, gateway nodes log their events in an unsynchronised way. To solve this, the gateway node will have to keep a temporary buffer of events to be logged, and wait until the server provides a value to start a new threaded tree. If certain gateway nodes do not generate enough logged events, the server might also ask them to fill up the rest of their threaded tree with null values to force their completion. In case a gateway node fails to respond, the server can send a new root value such that the gateway node can recompute a threaded tree for the next round. Its value in the current server's tree will then be null, or taken by another gateway node. Gateway nodes can adjust the size of their threaded tree dynamically, each time doubling the current capacity.

Chaining trees in the central server

When a central server has completed a tree such as depicted in Figure 3, a new tree for the next time-slot is started with the initial value set to the top of the previously generated tree, such that hash chains can be computed across different time-slots. Figure 4 represents a ideal situation across 3 time-slots.

Denote by n_g the number of gateway nodes in the network and by n_s the number of events logged by the sensor nodes for each gateway node. For simplicity, we here consider n_s to be equal for all gateway nodes, and that publication

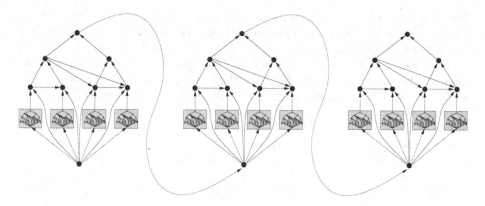

Fig. 4. Central server hash chain structure for 3 time-slots

happens after each time-slot. A possible use of the log structure is to verify the authenticity of one logged event of a certain gateway node. This requires a computation of a hash chain between two published values, so the hash chain length will be $\log n_g + \log n_s$, to traverse the central server and gateway node trees.

Another use is to explicitly check the time relation between two logged events As stated before, 2 events in the same time-slot but measured by 2 different gateway nodes can not be compared. In the other case, the length of a hash chain from one published value to another , passing through an event in time-slot i and time-slot $i+j$ is $2 \log n_s + (j+1) \log n_g$. Comparing events in the same time-slot and in the same gateway requires a hash chain length of $\log n_g + \log n_s$.

This scales relatively well; if we assume the setting of a WBAN with $n_g = 1024$ patients, with $n_s = 4096$ observations to be logged per day (time-slot) per patient, followed for a year, the maximum chain length equals to 3684 for comparing events (of day 1 and day 365). Note that in practise, it is more likely that the events will be verified between their two published values, which can also be compared because they occured in a widely witness medium. Checking one event in this setting involves a hash chain of length 22.

4.2 Communication Protocols

The communication from sensor node to gateway node is based on symmetric key cryptography because of the limited sources in the sensor nodes. Communication from gateway node to central server can pass by means of asymmetric key based cryptography.

The main disadvantage of symmetric key cryptography is the key agreement. One elegant way to solve this problem is by means of a pre-installation of the key $K_{GSi} = S_K(ID_{Si})$ at each sensor Si in the gateway's node. Here K_{GSi} represents the signature S of the unique ID_{Si} of sensor Si under the secret key K of the gateway node. Note that instead of the signature algorithm, also a message authentication code can be used. Another remark is that in general there is a belief that higher security can be reached when the key for encryption differs from the key for authentication purposes. For simplicity in notation, we here restrict to one key.

Consequently, if the sensor Si sends its ID_{Si} number, the gateway node can compute the shared secret key K_{GSi} on the spot. Note that the gateway node needs to store the list of IDs of the active sensor nodes in order to avoid that an older (eventually compromised) sensor can still participate in the communication. Together with the ID of the sensor, also a list containing the different values of the counter, logged events and the corresponding hash value is stored. Usage of a counter is advised in order to avoid replay attacks.

In [2], a formal description is given on the format of a request and of the response from the time-stamping system. In the response, the time-stamp information is encapsulated. However, a security context between the gateway node and its depending nodes already exists, and the time-stamp information will be sent to the central server by the gateway node. Therefore, the data, collected by the depending nodes is sent over to the gateway node as is, using the established symmetric keys to ensure confidentiality and authenticity.

Consequently, the above discussion leads to the following communication protocols.

Sensor node to gateway node. The sensor node Si sends at either irregular times or emergency cases a message m to be recorded and timestamped by the gateway node G. The counter c has as major goal the protection against replay attacks.

$$E_{K_{GSi}}(m||c) \, || \, MAC_{K_{GSi}}(m||c)$$

Here E_K represents a symmetric encryption algorithm like AES and MAC_K a message authentication code like for instance HMAC, both by means of a secret key K. Note that the encryption mode AES-CCM combines both functionalities. We prefer to hide the identity of the sensor node in the communication because of privacy reasons. Since the gateway node contains a limited list of keys, it just needs to check the different options.

Gateway node to sensor node. The gateway node responds with the a simple confirmation message, based on the original request and a nonce, denoted by c'.

$$E_{K_{GSi}}(c') \, || \, MAC_{K_{GSi}}(m||c||c')$$

Gateway node to central server. Since there is no real restriction in computing resources at both sides, communication can be realised by means of symmetric or asymmetric key cryptography. As explained before, the hash value of the top of the gateway node's authentication tree, together with the hash values of the leaf nodes are enough for reconstruction of the entire tree at the side of the central server.

5   Proof of Concept

As a case study, we implemented a prototype for the gateway node on FPGA. The FPGA contains an Ethernet port for connection to the central server through a router. For the communication between sensor nodes and gateway node, a Zigbee 802.15.4 wireless radio is added. Also the linked time-stamping protocol, AES-CCM, and SHA-256 are implemented on the FPGA. Figure 5 gives a schematic overview of the communication media in our setting. We first describe an overview of the system architecture, followed by a more in depth explanation of the software implementation of the linked time-stamping protocol.

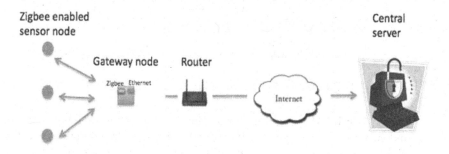

Fig. 5. Communication media in our setting

5.1   System Architecture

The platform consists of a HW/SW co-design on a Xilinx Spartan-6 XC6SLX45T FPGA. It is based on $45nm$ technology and provides an optimal balance between power consumption and high performance. The FPGA consists of 43.661 logic cells and 2.088 Kbytes of block RAM. The Spartan-6 supports the Processor Local Bus (PLB) and the new AXI bus. Despite the latter offers a better performance, it is still in preproduction phase at the time of writing. Consequently, our final architecture is based on the former.

The design contains a MicroBlaze soft processor with a 32-bit Harvard RISC architecture, optimised for Xilinx FPGAs. It has been connected to a Processor Local Bus (PLB). The PLB is a full synchronous bus that offers a width of 32 bits and is the backbone of the whole design. It also connects all the other hardware blocks of the platform: external DDR RAM memory, cache memory, Block RAM, the interrupt controller, communication logic to AES-CCM and SHA-256, the Ethernet controller, and the IEEE 802.15.4 (Zigbee) stack. Figure 6 represents the architecture of the SLS.

The software of the time-stamping protocol is stored in external memory of 256MB. This external memory is cached in Block RAM of 64 Kbytes. The size of the cache is configurable and the Block RAM has been split into a data cache and an instruction cache. Both caches use 32 Kbytes of memory. This memory is directly connected to the MicroBlaze.

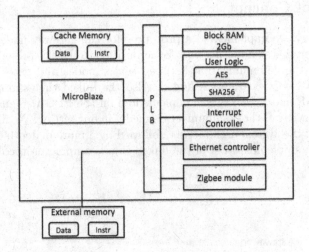

Fig. 6. General overview of architecture for SLS

The extra Block RAM is required for storing the list of sensor IDs, counters, events, and corresponding hash values. These hash values are computed in each round of the time-stamping algorithm. The memory has a size of 2 GByte. Suppose the sensor ID consists of 8 bytes (64 bits), the counter of 4 bytes (32 bits), the event information of 32 bytes (256 bits), and the hash value of SHA-256 of 32 bytes (256 bits). Then 27% of the 2 GByte can be devoted to the storage of hash values. This corresponds to approximately 17.045 hash values. A tree of depth d is able to log 2^d events and consists of 2^{d+1} nodes. Since the hash value at each node in the tree is stored, 8.192 events can be logged with this size of memory. It is also possible to save the hash values in non volatile Flash, having the advantage that the values are not lost when the design is powerless.

The interface with the sensor nodes is performed by a 2.4 GHz link based on a reduced version of the IEEE 802.15.4 standard. The stack is implemented in the FPGA following a HW/SW division approach which has been suggested by [3] and [8]. Several medium access control (MAC) layer functions, such as the frame check sequence (FCS) computation and the AES encryption algorithm have been implemented in dedicated units in hardware and they have been optimised in area to reduce the processor load. In addition, two reception and transmission FIFOs of reduced size have been implemented in the FPGA logic to store the payload until the processor is interrupted. The physical layer is connected to an external RF front-end. The software part contains the stack initialisation code and implements a small set of the 802.15.4 MAC layer primitives. They have been implemented in software to avoid large finite state machines (FSM) in the FPGA. The software part performs the Carrier Sense Multiple Access with Collision Avoidance (CSMA-CA) algorithm and provides the association/disassociation, channel scanning, send and receive primitives. Hence, the external memory of the

MicroBlaze shares the time-stamping protocol with the medium access control (MAC) layer of the 802.15.4.

Many commercial and academic IP cores can be found for implementations of AES and SHA-256, but they are not always optimised in area which is important in a design based on FPGA on which new modules can be updated and added. Our AES based implementation, which is shared between the 802.15.4 stack and the authentication protocol, has been optimised in terms of area instead of throughput. The implementation follows the approach based on the iterative-folded architecture of [10]. Also the hashing algorithm, SHA-256, is implemented following an iterative approach to reduce area on the FPGA.

Since we are not aware of any implementation in literature of the time-stamping protocol based on threaded authentication trees, we now explain some implementation details of this algorithm.

5.2   Implementation of the Threaded Authentication Tree Structure

The threaded authentication tree structure is implemented in software because of the variable depth of the tree, causing a dynamic memory usage. Moreover, this approach makes our implementation easily modifiable to any linking scheme, based on acyclic directed graphs. In essence, a node (vertex) in a threaded tree is a structure that contains the location (label) of the node, a integer containing an address of the associated hash value, and a pointer to a linked list, with the nodes that contain the data necessary to compute this node's associated hash value, i.e. all nodes that have a directed edge towards this node.

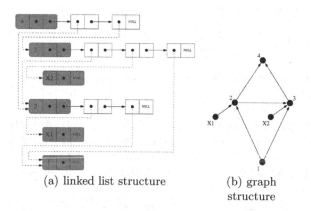

(a) linked list structure   (b) graph structure

Fig. 7. Implementation of a threaded tree with depth 1

Opting for a network of pointers that mimics the edges in the tree allows for a small memory footprint, alternative linking structures, and fast look-up of the nodes, necessary to compute the hash value associated to a certain node.

Figure 7 illustrates a linked list that consists of a tree of depth 1. Every node contains the address value that points to the hash value it represents.

5.3   Implementation of the Logging Component

The MicroBlaze runs the software with the threaded tree structure. First a tree is generated, meaning that the linked list has been completely built with the values of the address initialised to zero. For the first tree, an initial value needs to be submitted. Then the program waits for logged events.

Each time when an event has been submitted by one of the depending nodes, the padding is computed and then the data is sent to the interface registers of the hash function. When all the registers are filled, the MicroBlaze sends out an instruction to start the hash function. After the computation of the hash value, the interrupt controller will interrupt the MicroBlaze such that it jumps to the interrupt handler. The next steps are saving the hash value in memory of the Block RAM and storing the addresses in the tree at the correct node. Because a hash value has 256 bits, it needs eight addresses of the memory. Only the first one is stored in the tree.

In the last step, the tree is checked for nodes that can be completed. In case a node can be completed, the program sends the concatenation of the hash values in all parent nodes to the hash function and saves the result in the correct node. When the tree is completed, it is sent to the central server. The MicroBlaze then creates a new tree and waits for a new initial value to be sent by the central server. While waiting, new event to be logged can already be added to the tree.

Setting up the simple tree of Figure 7 takes 99.743 clock cycles. Each time a logged event occurs, the MicroBlaze needs 235 cycles to hash and to store the logged event. This number has been computed for the first logged event (X1). The computations of the nodes in higher levels request more time because they are linked to multiple nodes.

6   Conclusion and Future Work

We have described the concept of secure logging of information in the context of sensor networks. This enables a secure and reliable way for gathering information at a central point. For this, we have introduced the concept of layered threaded authentication tree, which represents a threaded authentication tree from which almost half of its nodes represent again a threaded authentication tree. As a proof of concept, we implemented a structure, similar to linked time-stamping on an FPGA platform for simulating the role of the gateway node.

Note that such a system can also be used as a kind of personal embedded logger, serving e.g., a laptop. This could be in particular useful for log-generating hosts that cannot participate in the log infrastructure, like for instance a computer not connected to the home organisation's network. Such an embedded device would have to be handed in regularly to the IT department, to extract its logged events, and to merge them with the central log server. It becomes even more interesting if the personal embedded logger is combined with the idea of a software protection dongle. If the dongle is not authenticated and connected, the depending software will not run or only in restricted mode. This principle is often used by proprietary vendors as a form of copy protection or digital rights management. In such context, the personal embedded logger will in addition also check if the user is not blocking the software to log events to the dongle. If so, the corresponding program stops working immediately. Consequently, the user cannot simply unplug the personal embedded logger and execute authorised but policy-infringing actions, nor can he/she simply delete its action from the log without cracking or destroying the dongle. When the dongle is synchronised with the central log facility, any unauthorised action will be detectable.

An example of such a context is the following. Suppose an employee of a television station is working in a video-editing program and is finishing the last seconds of a popular television series. Just before finishing, the employee saves the whole result to its hard drive. While this might be a completely authorised action for this employee, it might be interesting to have such an event logged when the content shows up unexpectedly on the Internet. To summarise, for delicate company software, our solution can be used to ensure that every important action is logged securely.

References

1. RFC 3161, Internet X.509 Public Key Infrastructure Time-Stamp Protocol (TSP) RFC Time Stamping (2001),
   http://www.ietf.org/rfc/rfc3161.txt?number=3161
2. International Organization for Standardization and International Electrotechnical Commission, ISO/IEC Standard 18014: Information Technology - Security Techniques - Time stamping services (2002)
3. Bernier, C., Hameau, F., Billiot, G., de Foucauld, E., Robinet, S., Lattard, D., Durupt, J., Dehmas, F., Ouvry, L., Vincent, P.: An Ultra Low Power SoC for 2.4ghz IEEE 802.15.4 Wireless Communications. In: Proceedings of Solid-State Circuits Conference (ESSCIRC), pp. 426–429 (2008)
4. Buldas, A., Lipmaa, H., Schoenmakers, B.: Optimally Efficient Accountable Time-Stamping. In: Imai, H., Zheng, Y. (eds.) PKC 2000. LNCS, vol. 1751, pp. 293–305. Springer, Heidelberg (2000)
5. Buldas, A., Laud, P., Lipmaa, H., Villemson, J.: Time-Stamping with Binary Linking Schemes. In: Krawczyk, H. (ed.) CRYPTO 1998. LNCS, vol. 1462, pp. 486–501. Springer, Heidelberg (1998)
6. Cotroneo, D., di Flora, C., Mazzeo, A., Romano, L., Russo, S., Saggese, G.P.: Providing Digital Time Stamping Services to Mobile Devices. In: Proceedings of Ninth IEEE International Workshop on Object-Oriented Real-Time Dependable Systems, p. 94 (2003)
7. Kumar, M., Sharma, T.P.: Secure Data Aggregation in Wireless Sensor Network: A Survey. International Journal of Engineering Science and Technology (IJEST) 3(3) (2011)
8. de la Piedra, A., Touhafi, A., Cornetta, G.: An IEEE 802.15.4 Baseband SoC for Tracking Applications in the Medical Environment Based on Actel cortex-m1 Soft-core. In: Proceedings of IEEE Symposium on Communications and Vehicular Technology in the Benelux (SCVT) 2010, pp. 1–5. Springer, Heidelberg (2010)
9. Haver, S., Stornetta, W.: How to Time-Stamp a Digital Document. Journal of Cryptology 3(2), 99–111 (1991)

10. Chodowiec, P., Gaj, K.: Very Compact FPGA Implementation of the AES Algorithm. In: Walter, C.D., Koç, Ç.K., Paar, C. (eds.) CHES 2003. LNCS, vol. 2779, pp. 319–333. Springer, Heidelberg (2003)
11. Sundararaman, B., Buy, U., Kshemkalyani, A.D.: Clock Synchronization for Wireless Sensor Networks: a Survey. Ad Hoc Networks 3(3), 281–323 (2005)
12. Zhong, L., Sinclair, M., Bittner, R.: A Phone-centered Body Sensor Network Platform: Cost, Energy Efficiency and User Interface. In: Proceedings of the International Workshop on Wearable and Implantable Body Sensor Networks, pp. 179–182 (2006)

Author Index